AQUINAS' SUMMA

An Introduction and Interpretation

With Gratitude

— to the Rev. Charles H. Hollencamp, Ph.D., and the Rev. John J. Jennings, S.T.D., lifelong students of St. Thomas, for reading portions of the manuscript and offering many helpful suggestions for improving it.

— to the Institute for Ecumenical and Cultural Research, Collegeville, Minnesota, which provided a stimulating atmosphere and a beautiful setting for writing a large part of this book.

AQUINAS' SUMMA

An Introduction and Interpretation

by

Edward J. Gratsch

ALBA · HOUSE  NEW · YORK

SOCIETY OF ST. PAUL, 2187 VICTORY BLVD., STATEN ISLAND, NEW YORK 10314

Library of Congress Cataloging in Publication Data

Gratsch, Edward J.
Aquinas' Summa.

1. Thomas Aquinas, Saint, 1225?-1274. Summa theologica. 2. Catholic Church—Doctrines—Early works to 1800. 3. Theology, Doctrinal—Early works to 1800. I. Title.
BX1749.T6G73 1985 230'.2 85-15842
ISBN 0-8189-0485-2

Nihil Obstat:
Rev. John J. Jennings, S.T.D.

Imprimatur:
Most Rev. James H. Garland
Auxiliary Bishop of Cincinnati

Designed, printed and bound in the United States of America by the Fathers and Brothers of the Society of St. Paul, 2187 Victory Boulevard, Staten Island, New York 10314, as part of their communications apostolate.

3 4 5 6 7 8 9 (Current Printing: first digit)

CONTENTS

Introduction

The First Part

The First Part of the Second Part

The Second Part of the Second Part

The Third Part

INTRODUCTION

This book is an introduction to the *Summa Theologiae* of St. Thomas Aquinas (1225-74). The Latin title, *Summa Theologiae*, means a *Synthesis of Theology* or *Summation of Theology*. The *Summa* is Thomas' main work, and it was written for students of theology. It is the most successful and influential synthesis of Catholic theology ever composed. More than any other theological work, it enjoys the approbation of the teaching authority of the Church. The *Summa* is remarkable for its doctrinal soundness, completeness, lucidity, and depth. For the *Summa* Thomas drew on the teaching of the Scriptures and the Fathers of the Church, while at the same time he utilized the greatest purely philosophical system of the ancient world, that of Aristotle (384-322 B.C.). The *Summa* is the object of profound study by the theologians of the Church. Apart from the Bible and collections of official Church teachings, there is no book of comparable theological significance. In a burst of enthusiasm, the Jesuit Philip Labbe (1607-1667) said: *Neque aliud superest nisi lumen gloriae post Summam Thomae* ("After the *Summa* of Thomas there remains only the light of glory.")

The *Summa* is an example of Scholastic (or speculative) theology. Scholastic theology is to be distinguished from positive theology. Both types of theology rely upon revelation and reason to probe the mystery of God; but positive theology examines the deposit of revelation, that is, Scripture and tradition, in order to find out what God has actually disclosed about himself. Scholastic theology examines the truths of revelation in order to explain, develop, and systematize them. For example, Scripture teaches that God can be known from the visible world (Ws 13:1; Rm 1:20). By his famous five "ways" of demonstrating the existence of God, Thomas shows how God can be known from the visible world. Again, the prologue of John's Gospel speaks of Jesus Christ, the Son of God, as the Word of God. Thomas illustrates the point by comparing the generation of the Son by the Father to the generation of an idea or mental word by the human mind. Or—to give a third example—the Bible takes for granted the responsibility of human beings for their actions. Thomas examines the conditions for human responsibility and the factors which can diminish it.

Scholastic theology not only explains and develops the truths of revelation as the preceding examples suggest, but it also systematizes them by presenting them in an orderly fashion, as the study of the *Summa* will make abundantly clear. Thus, in the third part of the *Summa* Thomas treats first the Savior and his work, then the sacraments which derive their efficacy from his life, death, and resurrection, and finally the goal of eternal life to which the sacraments bring us through the power of Christ. The *Summa*, therefore, is a synthesis of Catholic theology. Thomas shows how the truths of Catholic theology are related in a logically consistent way. He lifts the particular theological truth out of isolation and studies it in conjunction with others. One thinks of a weaver who takes threads of many colors and weaves them into a beautiful tapestry. One thinks too of a gardener who carefully arranges the flowers in his garden so as to display their harmony and beauty.

The Life of St. Thomas

St. Thomas Aquinas was born at Roccasecca, midway between Rome and Naples, Italy, about 1225. He was the youngest son of the Count of Aquino. His father belonged to the Lombard nobility; his paternal grandmother, Francesca di Suabia, was a sister of Frederick Barbarossa (1123?-90), emperor of the Holy Roman

Empire; and his mother was descended from Norman nobility. At the age of five, Thomas was entrusted to the Benedictine monks of Monte Cassino, a few miles from his birthplace. Here he made his first studies and remained from 1230 to 1239. In the latter year, at the age of fourteen, Thomas entered the University of Naples, the first state university in the western world. At Naples, Thomas was introduced to the works of Aristotle. Five years later, in 1244, he joined the Dominican order at the age of nineteen. He was attracted to the Dominicans by their ideal of evangelical poverty, study, and service to the Church without ecclesiastical preferments. Setting out for Paris, Thomas was kidnapped by his brothers, who were soldiers; and for a year he was held prisoner in one of his father's castles. His family was angry with Thomas' decision to become a friar. The famous incident of Thomas' temptation took place during his confinement. To dissuade him from following the religious life, his family introduced a young woman into his room while he was sleeping. Upon awakening, Thomas leapt up, grabbed a flaming firebrand from the fireplace, and chased her from the house. It was said that Thomas never experienced the temptations of the flesh thereafter. Subsequently, in 1245, Thomas was released and made his way to Paris.

At Paris Thomas entered the greatest university of the western world. There he came under the influence of St. Albert the Great (1206-80), a Dominican too. Three years later, in 1248, Thomas accompanied Albert to the newly established Dominican house of studies at Cologne, Germany, and remained there until 1252. At Cologne, Thomas completed his studies and was ordained to the priesthood. As a student, Thomas was sometimes called "the dumb ox" by his fellow students; they mistook his reserved and self-effacing manner for stupidity. Albert defended Thomas by saying, "You call this man a dumb ox, but I tell you that the time will come when the bellowing of his doctrine will be heard to the ends of the earth."

At the age of twenty-seven, Thomas was recalled to Paris, to the Dominican convent of St. Jacques, to lecture on the Scriptures and the *Sentences* of Peter Lombard (c. 1100-64?). Here he was drawn into the disputes between the secular and mendicant masters of the university. The secular masters resented the growing influence of the mendicants. Subsequently, Thomas became professor of theology at the University of Paris.

From 1259 to 1269 Thomas was engaged in writing, lecturing, preaching, and academic administration at various cities in Italy—Anagni, Orvieto, Rome, and Viterbo. He worked incessantly, and witnesses report that he dictated to three and even four secretaries at a time on different subjects. In 1269, after a sojourn of ten years in Italy, Thomas was sent back to the University of Paris. There he was involved in controversy with the Averroists, who misinterpreted Aristotle, and with some secular masters who renewed the attack on the religious orders. Thomas continued to write at a furious pace. After three years, in 1272, Thomas was called back to Naples to erect a Dominican house of studies and to teach. He died March 7, 1274, at the Cistercian monastery of Fossanuova between Naples and Rome on his way to the Second Council of Lyons (1274) in southern France. He had devoted the far greater number of his forty-nine years to study, writing, and teaching.

Thomas was canonized by Pope John XXII in 1323, less than fifty years after his death. The many witnesses at the canonization proceedings had little to say about extraordinary acts of penance and miraculous deeds in the life of Thomas; but they testified unanimously to his humility, simplicity, love of peace, prayerfulness, moderation, and love of poverty. In 1567, Thomas was declared a Doctor of the Church. He is known as *Doctor Angelicus*, the "Angelic Doctor."

The Writings of St. Thomas

Thomas' literary production was immense. Much of it was the product of his lectures in the classrooms; some of it, however, was never delivered in the classroom, though generally Thomas wrote for the advancement of his students. He authored three theological syntheses: a commentary on the *Sentences* of Peter Lombard, the *Summa contra Gentiles*, and the *Summa Theologiae*. The *Sentences* of Peter Lombard was the theological textbook of Thomas' day, and Thomas wrote his commentary on it around 1256 when he assumed his teaching duties in Paris for the first time. The *Summa contra Gentiles (Summa against the Infidels)* dates from the early part of Thomas' teaching activity in Italy between 1261 and 1263. It was intended for Dominican missionaries laboring among the Moors and pagans in Spain and elsewhere. The *Summa Theologiae* was written between 1265 and 1273 in Paris and Italy and left unfinished at Thomas' death. It was completed by Reginald of Piperno, Thomas' friend and secretary, mainly from book four of Thomas' commentary on the *Sentences*.

But Thomas wrote much more. His *Quaestiones Disputatae (Controverted Questions)* and *Quaestiones Quodlibetales (Random Questions)* were the fruit of academic disputations or discussions held by Thomas throughout his academic career. These *Questions* are concerned with such matters as truth, the power of God, the soul, the union of the incarnate Word, evil, virtue, the structure of the universe, and the extent to which one must obey an erring conscience. There is even a question, probably posed by students out of sheer high spirits, namely, "Which is stronger: wine, the king, women, or truth?"

Thomas wrote commentaries on the books of Sacred Scripture including Job, the Psalms, the Song of Songs, Isaiah, Jeremiah, the Gospels, and the Epistles of Paul. Thomas produced commentaries on the works of Aristotle (384-322 B.C.), Boethius (480?-524?), a Roman philosopher, and Pseudo-Dionysius (5th-6th cent. of the Christian era). He composed polemical writings against the secular masters and Averroists at Paris. Finally, he wrote works of a special nature including his *De Ente et Essentia (On Being and Essence)*, the *Compendium Theologiae (Compendium of Theol-*

ogy), and liturgical pieces and sermons such as the Office for the feast of Corpus Christi.

Cultural Factors

Several cultural factors influenced the composition of Thomas' works. In the twelfth century western Europe came at last into contact with Aristotelian thought. The works of Aristotle were translated into Latin—sometimes from the original Greek, but more often from Arabic into which his works had been translated by Arabian scholars. After the Crusades and especially in Spain there was great intellectual contact between Arabian and western culture. The *Logic* of Aristotle had been studied in western schools since the time of Boethius; but now the main body of Aristotelian thought dealing with natural philosophy, metaphysics, ethics and psychology challenged the West. A vast literature translated from Greek and Arabic came to the attention of western philosophers and theologians. From Aristotle and the Greeks the Scholastics acquired a knowledge of strict scientific method and an interest in ultimate metaphysical problems. Aristotle offered a world-system, an explanation of the whole of reality. One of the great tasks of thirteenth century Scholasticism was to examine critically the whole new body of knowledge, rejecting what was false and enlisting what was true in the service of the Christian faith.

Among the Scholastics, Albert the Great, the teacher and mentor of St. Thomas, was one of the first to employ Aristotelian thought in the elaboration of Christian theology. He wrote paraphrases of Aristotelian works on logic, metaphysics, physics and ethics; and he incorporated Aristotelian elements into his own philosophical and theological system. At the same time, however, he sympathized strongly with the Neo-Platonist and Augustinian traditions.

St. Thomas carried to completion the process well advanced by

Albert. Thomas wrote commentaries on Aristotle's works, using William of Moerbeke's direct translations from the Greek. There was a close affinity between Aristotle and Thomas. Brentano, using a felicitous word, spoke of a congeniality between them. Thomas' philosophy was shaped by the philosophy of Aristotle; and Thomas employed Aristotelian thought widely in his theological writings. For Thomas there was no need to reject or despise whatever pagan reason had discovered of the truth.

Truth is an expression of reality. Truth can be discovered in two ways: either God can instruct human beings through revelation or else human beings can investigate reality through the faculty of reason. Both revelation and reason are sources of truth. Individual truths, whether revealed or discovered by reason, express different aspects of total reality. One truth throws light on another. Truth, like reality, is interconnected. In a sense, its method of discovery is irrelevant. What is more, there are some truths about God which exceed the capacity of human reason, while there are others which are accessible to human reason. Both come under theology since God has seen fit to reveal both and propose them to the human race for belief. Both kinds of truth have been incorporated into the *Summa Theologiae*. Nevertheless, despite his use of Aristotelian thought, Thomas continued to hold certain fundamental, Platonist doctrines which had come down through Augustine (354-430) and Pseudo-Dionysius.

The influx of literature from Greek and Arabic sources could not have made its great impact upon Scholasticism without the establishment of the universities. The University of Paris was founded in 1215, receiving its charter from the Pope. It became the intellectual capital of Christendom in the thirteenth century, and it was the scene of the triumph of Aristotelianism. Universities were also founded at Oxford, Cambridge, Toulouse, Bologna, Salerno and elsewhere. They received their charters from the Pope or emperor. They conferred degrees which empowered the student to teach. Generally, there were four faculties: theology, medicine, law, and the arts. The faculty of arts quickly developed into a school of philosophy. In the faculty of theology the student listened to lectures on the Bible and the *Sentences* of Peter Lombard. An important part of the curriculum was the disputation or formal discussion of a theological topic undertaken by the students under the direction of the professor. It involved arguments, objections, replies, and a summation. The final result, arranged by the professor, was published as a *Quodlibet (Random Question)*.

Two mendicant religious orders, the Dominicans and Franciscans, were founded in 1216 and 1223 respectively. Both orders embraced the evangelical ideal of poverty and made the Bible the guide to Christian doctrine and life. Thomas entered the Dominican order because, as the witness at his canonization proceedings put it, he was "an especial lover of poverty." Moreover, Thomas' profuse use of the Bible in his theological writings is explained at least partially by his adherence to the voluntary poverty movement. The Dominicans and the Franciscans as well as the Augustinians and Carmelites obtained chairs of theology at Paris and other universities. The orders encountered considerable opposition from the secular clergy who were inspired in part by jealousy. In addition to their Biblical orientation, the religious orders represented other currents of thought too. The Franciscans, for example, favored Augustinianism, while the Dominicans favored Aristotelianism.

Thomas' Philosophy

In many ways, Thomas' philosophical stance is similar to that of Aristotle. This similarity extends to the areas of logic, the general lines of their physics and metaphysics, and the outline of their psychology and ethics. Thomas adopted Aristotelian philosophy—with some reservations—because he thought it was true, because, in other words, it was a reflection of reality. Still,

Thomas made use of the thought of other thinkers too, such as Augustine, Pseudo-Dionysius, Moses Maimonides (1135-1204), a Jewish philosopher and rabbi, and Arabian philosophers. The philosophy of Aquinas is substantially the doctrine of Aristotle; but it is the doctrine of Aristotle rethought by a powerful mind in the service of Christian theology, a theology which is based on articles of faith completely alien to the Hellenic mind.

For St. Thomas, philosophy seeks the ultimate explanation of reality by relying simply and solely on the natural light of human reason. Philosophy arises out of wonder at the unknown. The human mind seeks to know the causes of things. Only the knowledge of God, the ultimate cause, can really satisfy the human mind. The various branches of philosophy are distinguished according to the object with which they are concerned. Logic is the art which enables a person to proceed in an orderly manner, easily, and without error in the process of reasoning. Natural philosophy is the science of ''mobile'' being; that is to say, it is concerned with beings subject to motion and change. Natural philosophy includes general natural philosophy, cosmology and psychology. Metaphysics is concerned with beings precisely as beings and culminates in the knowledge of God. Metaphysics includes epistemology, ontology, and natural theology. Finally, moral philosophy or ethics is concerned with human conduct and includes individual ethics, economics and politics.

Natural Philosophy. The natural starting point of Thomas' philosophy is corporeal substances. For Thomas, there is no innate knowledge. All knowledge begins with the activity of the senses whose proper object is the sense qualities inherent in corporeal mobile beings. Reflection discovers a distinction between the substantial nature of these bodies and their accidental modifications. Following Aristotle, Thomas distinguishes substance and nine categories of accidents. One can distinguish even more profoundly in material substances an underlying substratum of change (called prime matter) and an element which characterizes and determines it (called substantial form). Thus, the food we human beings eat is assimilated by our bodies. In the course of this substantial change, one element, prime matter remains and is common to the food and the human body; but the element which determines matter, the form, is changed, the form of food giving way to the form of the body. This is the doctrine of hylomorphism originally taught by Aristotle. Each physical body is rendered numerically individual solely by matter signed by quantity. In every mobile being except man, the form is educed out of the potentiality of the matter. Thomas affirmed the unicity of the substantial form in each substance.

Metaphysics. The distinction between matter and form applies only to corporeal beings; and it is an example of a more profound distinction which applies to all finite beings including incorporeal creatures (angels). This is the distinction between potency and act. Potency is the capacity for actuality; act is the realization of that capacity. Every finite being offers many examples of potency and act. The child, for example, has some measure of actuality; but it also has the capacity or potentiality to become an adult. Another example of the distinction between potency and act is the distinction between essence and existence. For example, the essence of a corporeal being is the substance composed of matter and form; but that by which the essence is actualized is existence (or *esse*). The existence of a finite being is something distinct from its essence or substance. Essence is to existence as potency to act.

The knowledge of corporeal substances leads to the knowledge of God. Thomas held that the existence of God can be proved by human reason *a posteriori*, that is to say, through an examination of God's effects. Thomas developed five ways of proving the existence of God—from motion, efficient causality, contingency, the degrees of perfection in the things of this world, and teleology or finality. These five ways demonstrate the existence of an unmoved mover, a first cause, a necessary being, a supreme being, and an architect and governor of the universe whom we are wont to call God. These five ways support the words of the book of Wisdom (13:1-9) and of St. Paul in Romans (1:20) that God can be known from his works, as transcending his works.

Analyzing the concepts of an unmoved mover, a first cause, a necessary being, and so on, we can come to know God better in our limited way by recognizing what he is not and what he is. For this analysis, Thomas employs the famous *via negativa* or way of negation and the *via affirmativa* or way of affirmation. Negatively, Thomas denies to God all those predicates of creatures which are incompatible with the concepts of an unmoved mover, a first cause, and a necessary being. For example, Thomas denies that God is many, mutable, or finite. Positively, Thomas affirms of God in a preeminent manner all those predicates of creatures which are demanded by the concept of the divine nature as disclosed by the five proofs. For example, Thomas affirms that God is living, wise, and good. God is "pure act," having no potentiality whatsoever; and in him every possible perfection is wholly realized. In this way, Thomas arrives at the theistic conception of God.

The words that we apply to God, such as wise, living, and good, have been derived originally from creatures. They are applied to God neither univocally nor equivocally, but analogously. This means that they are predicated of God because there are resemblances along with profound differences between God and his creatures.

The teaching about God leads naturally to the teaching about creation. The first cause and supreme being is necessarily one. All else is contingent and depends upon God for its existence. Did God produce the world out of himself or out of some pre-existent material? God did not produce the world out of himself, since he is not subject to division or alteration. Nor did God produce the world out of some pre-existent material independent of God, since there can be only one necessary being. Hence, God must have *created* all else, that is, produced it out of nothing. Not that nothing is a kind of material out of which God produced the world, but simply that there was nothing and then there was something. God is the efficient cause of creation; there was no material cause. Only God can create; this power cannot be shared by a creature. God created the world freely in order to communicate his goodness to beings outside himself. Since God is eternal, he might have created the world from eternity; but faith teaches that the world was created in time.

While God created the world, he did not will the evil to be found in it per se, that is, for its own sake. God is essential goodness, and he created the world to communicate his goodness to creatures. He cannot will what is opposed to his goodness; he cannot will evil. God willed the universe and permits the evil associated with it for the sake of a higher good. The teaching of faith about the fall of mankind and its redemption by Jesus Christ sheds more light on the problem of evil.

Psychology. The crown of visible creation is man and woman. They are a composite of body and soul. The soul is the unique substantial form of the human composite. By informing prime matter directly, the soul confers upon man and woman their unique characteristics as human beings: their bodiliness, their vegetative, sensitive and spiritual faculties. There is a real distinction between the soul and its faculties and between the faculties themselves. The vegetative faculties are those of nutrition, growth and reproduction. The sensitive faculties include the five exterior senses, four interior senses and the sensitive appetite. The soul has three spiritual faculties: the passive intellect, the active intellect, and the will. The nature of the operations of these spiritual faculties demonstrates the spirituality and immortality of the soul. The two intellectual faculties have being in general as their object. The will has the good in general as its object. The will necessarily desires happiness, a necessity springing from the nature of the will itself; but it is free to choose the means of achieving happiness. Actually, perfect happiness is to be found only in the possession of God, the infinite good; but human beings are not always aware of this fact.

How do we come to know the world around us? For Thomas, there are no innate ideas. He believed that all knowledge begins in the senses. The senses apprehend particular objects such as animals and houses. Phantasms or images of the particular objects arise in the imagination. The active intellect illumines the phantasm and abstracts from it the "intelligible species." The intelligible species reveals the universal element contained implicitly in the phantasm. The active intellect impresses the intelligible species upon the passive intellect; and an "impressed species" is produced in the passive intellect. Then the passive intellect modified by the impressed species produces an "expressed species" or idea. The idea is the general concept latent in a particular object and refers to all the objects of that group without, however, their particular determinations. Thus, the idea or concept of an animal refers to all animals but abstracts from particular considerations such as the number of legs, actual color, size, and so on. The concept is the means by which the mind knows extramental reality. For St. Thomas, the universal, as expressed by the concept, is rooted in the particular, but it is only in the mind that the universal exists apart from its particular modifications. Hence, St. Thomas held what is called moderate realism.

Ethics. What is the goal of human life and how is it to be achieved? The ethics or moral theory of St. Thomas responds to this question. Human beings seek happiness. Perfect happiness is not to be found in any created good such as riches, sensible pleasure, power, or the knowledge of created things. All these are disappointing in some respect. Rather, perfect happiness is to be found only in the possession of God, the supreme good, by way of knowledge and love. Human beings achieve their goal by acting in a truly human way, that is, with knowledge and freedom. Human acts are good or bad insofar as they do or do not bring us to perfect happiness in the end. Those human acts which are in harmony with the order established by God bring us to perfect happiness, the possession of God, in the end. Those human acts which are not in harmony with the order established by God do not bring us to perfect happiness. The order established by God is discovered by reason as it reflects upon the nature of God, man, and creation. Such reflection reveals both the eternal law of God which is God's law for the universe, and the natural law which is God's eternal law impressed on human reason. Every human act is either good or bad. An indeliberate act, such as coughing or yawning, may be indifferent; but no human, deliberate act can be indifferent, that is, neither good nor bad.

Thomas followed Aristotle's teaching about the virtues. The faculties or powers of human beings are modified by intrinsic principles called habits. Habits are characterized by a certain measure of permanence. When habits are directed toward the morally good, they are called virtues; and when they are directed toward the morally evil, they are called vices. Aristotle defined a virtue as that which makes a person and his actions good. Virtues are acquired by practice, by repeated actions; and they facilitate the performance of subsequent acts for the same end. For example, a person acquires and intensifies the virtue of truthfulness by telling the truth repeatedly, and the virtue of truthfulness makes it easier for him or her to tell the truth in the future. Virtue consists in a mean; that is to say, a virtuous action measures up to the norm prescribed by reason, and it does not violate the norm either by excess or defect. Thus, the temperate person eats what is necessary to sustain life, while the intemperate person eats too little or too much. In this sense, virtue consists in a mean. By living virtuously, a person attains his or her final end.

Thomas also followed Aristotle's political theory. Human beings are social or political beings, born to live in a community with other human beings. Only in a community can they fulfill all their needs. If the community or state is to function properly, there must be a civil authority or government to direct the activities of individuals with a view to the common good. The common good consists in civil peace, the cooperation of citizens to fulfill their mutual needs, and protection against enemies and criminals. The role of the legislator is to make and enforce laws for the common good. The state is a perfect (self-sufficient) society; it has at its disposal all the means necessary for the attainment of its end. Although the state is autonomous in its own sphere, its end, being this-worldly, is inferior to that of the Church which is supernatural and eternal. The authority of the state is ultimately from God, but the state abuses its authority if it requires what is opposed to the common good. St. Thomas recognized three legitimate forms of government: democracy, aristocracy and monarchy.

How Thomas employed this philosophy in the elaboration of his theology will be explained later when the contents of the *Summa Theologiae* are discussed in some detail.

Thomas' Theology

For Thomas, theology employs both reason and revelation to study God and his creatures, while philosophy employs only reason to that end. As a Scholastic theologian, Thomas examined the deposit of revelation in Scripture and ecclesiastical tradition in order to explain, develop and systematize it. Theology is concerned with certain fundamental Christian verities such as the Trinity and Incarnation which can be known only because God has revealed them. But theology is also concerned with revealed truths which can be known by reason too. The latter are also contained in the Scriptures and the tradition of the Church for the instruction of mankind. There can be no real contradiction between theological and philosophical truths. Both are reflections of reality. If an apparent contradiction arises, either the theologian or the philosopher has argued erroneously.

The role assigned by Thomas to reason in "doing" theology is an important one. The function of reason is, first of all, to establish by a rigorous philosophical demonstration the preambles of faith.

The preambles of faith are those rational truths which are established in philosophy and are presupposed by the act of faith. The preambles of faith include such a basic truth as the existence and unity of God. Secondly, reason has to defend the articles of faith, not by proving the truth of these articles—for this is impossible—but by showing that they are truly a part of divine revelation and by refuting the objections raised against them. For Thomas, the refutation of heresy was a very important duty of the theologian. Thirdly, the role of reason in theology is to deduce new truths from those which have been revealed and to show how one revealed truth explains another. Thus, Thomas explains the fact of Christ's perfections and weaknesses by his mission as redeemer. Finally, the role of reason is to try to understand and explain revealed truths insofar as this is possible. This is done mainly by offering analogies and congruent reasons. For example, Thomas develops the parallel between the natural and supernatural life of human beings in order to explain the existence of the seven sacraments.

For Thomas, God's revelation is to be found in the Scriptures as a privileged source. The authority of the Scriptures is absolute; it is sufficient to settle questions of faith. Yet, Thomas was aware that it is not always easy to get at the true sense of the Scriptures, and so one must interpret them according to the doctrine of the Church which correctly understands them. The doctrine of the Church is proclaimed by the councils and especially by the Pope. It is the responsibility of the Pope to determine what matters are of faith. A person is guilty of heresy when he rejects a doctrine taught by ecclesiastical authority, an authority which resides principally in the Roman Pontiff. The Church of Peter has always been firm in the faith.

Thomas also drew upon the Fathers of the Church to explain or substantiate his position. The Fathers are the ancient writers who are witnesses to, and teachers of, the faith of the early Church. For example, Thomas cites the Fathers of the Alexandrian school in Egypt many times in the *Summa*. Of all the Fathers, however,

Augustine, the bishop of Hippo in Africa, exercised the greatest influence upon Thomas; he is cited more than two hundred and fifty times in the *Summa*. From Augustine, Thomas drew many ideas about the Blessed Trinity, the person of Christ, Our Lady's place in the plan of salvation, and grace. Thomas made frequent use of the writings of Pseudo-Dionysius, especially when he spoke about divine providence and angels. Finally, Thomas showed his respect for St. John Damascene (c.675-c.749), the "Doctor of the Incarnation," by citing his writings repeatedly in the Christological sections of the *Summa*.

Thomas' theology does not differ from other Catholic theologies in its adherence to the truths of divine faith and in its appeal to the Scriptures and Fathers of the Church. Rather, it is characterized by its use of Aristotelian philosophy, its special attention to certain subjects such as angels, the Incarnation, and the sacraments, and its particular stance on certain controverted questions such as the motive of the Incarnation. Thomas' theology is also characterized by its completeness, lucidity and depth. The bulk of the following pages will be devoted to a summary of Thomas' theology.

Ecclesiastical Approval

The theology of Aquinas enjoys a favored position in the Catholic Church. It has been endowed by many councils and Popes. The Council of Vienna (1311-12), the Council of Florence (1439-45), the Council of Trent (1545-63), and the First Vatican Council (1869-70) clearly employed Thomas' writings in the formation of their statements and decrees. In 1567 Pope Pius V declared Thomas to be a Doctor of the Church. In more recent times Pope Leo XIII wrote that "reason, borne on the wings of Thomas to its human height, can scarcely rise higher, while faith can scarcely expect more or stronger helps from reason than those which she has already obtained through Thomas.''[1] The Code of Canon Law promulgated in 1917 decreed that professors in seminaries should present the studies of philosophy and theology to their students according to the method, doctrine and principles of the Angelic Doctor.[2] Pope Pius XI wrote that ''Thomas should be called not only the Angelic, but also the Common or Universal Doctor of the Church.''[3] The influence of Thomas is quite evident in the encyclical, *Humani Generis* (1950) of Pius XII.

In its decree on priestly training, the Second Vatican Council decreed: ''In order to clarify the mysteries of salvation as completely as possible, students should learn to penetrate them more deeply with the help of speculative reason exercised under the guidance of St. Thomas.''[4] In its document on Christian education, the same council noted that the Church seeks to show how faith and reason give harmonious witness to the unity of all truth. The Church pursues such a goal after the manner of her most illustrious teachers, especially St. Thomas Aquinas.[5] Subsequently, Pope John Paul II enjoined the observation of recent papal documents regarding the teaching of Aquinas.[6]

In an address to the Eighth International Thomistic Congress (1980), the same Pope, John Paul II, praised St. Thomas as a model for today's Catholic philosophers and theologians. Thomas was remarkable for his fidelity to the truth. As a philosopher, Thomas was faithful to the truth manifested by the voice of created reality. Indeed, in this respect, he can be considered as an authentic pioneer of modern scientific realism. As a theologian, Thomas was faithful to the truth as it was manifested by the voice of the Church. Thomas was convinced that there could be no discord between faith and reason, for God was the author of both. Pope John Paul II noted that Pope Paul VI had called Thomistic philosophy ''the natural philosophy of the human mind.'' For Thomas, almost the whole of philosophy was directed to the knowledge of God. One thing that makes Thomas particularly relevant for today was his lively sense of the dignity of man, that noble creature, the image of God, who unites within himself heaven and earth, time and eternity. The Pope concluded by saying that Thomas had begun an enterprise that can and must be carried on without betraying the spirit and principles of its beginning.[7]

Finally, the Code of Canon Law, promulgated in 1983, calls for seminarians to learn to probe the mysteries of salvation more deeply, especially under the guidance of St. Thomas.[8]

Thomas' philosophy and theology enjoy a favored position in the Catholic Church for several reasons: Thomas' thought is basically true; it clarifies revealed doctrine in a remarkable manner; it resumes so much Biblical and patristic teaching; and Thomas' synthesis is characterized by depth, lucidity and completeness.

The Genesis of Aquinas' Summa

In medieval Scholasticism, whose founder was St. Anselm of Canterbury (1033-1109), a synthesis of the whole of theology was called *Sententiae (Sentences)* or *Summa*. The *Sentences* appeared before the *Summa* and were collections of material taken from the Fathers, theologians, and canon law, and arranged in an orderly fashion. The first medieval *Sentences* of note were compiled and arranged by Anselm of Laon (d. 1117) and William of Champeaux (d. 1121). The collection of *Sentences* most widely used in the schools was the *Libri Quattuor Sententiarum* or *Four Books of Sentences* composed by Peter Lombard. This work served as a handbook of theology in theological schools and formed the subject of innumerable commentaries, including one by St. Thomas. In his work, Peter Lombard treated God in his unity and trinity, creation including man and original sin, the Incarnation, the sacraments, and the glorification which awaits the just. In 1215 the Fourth Lateran Council approved Peter's teaching and confirmed his position in the schools.

The *Summa* was a more original work representing a systematic exposition of speculative theology composed by a master theologian. It was characterized by its freedom from dependence on the Lombard's text and its individual approach to the whole of theology. The first theological *Summae*, such as those of Martin of Cremona, Peter of Capua, Simon of Tournai, and Praepositinus of Cremona, appeared at the beginning of the thirteenth century; and the genre was largely confined to that century. Many other theologians, such as Alexander of Hales (d. 1245), Albert the Great, and Henry of Ghent (d. 1293), composed *Summae*. St. Thomas wrote his *Summa* between 1265 and 1273 in Paris and Italy. While he never expounded it in school, he wrote it nonetheless for students of theology.

The History of Aquinas' Summa

At the outset, the teachings of Thomas encountered considerable opposition. In 1277 Bishops Tempier of Paris and Kilwardby of Oxford condemned certain propositions drawn from Thomas' works. Franciscan theologians also attacked certain teachings of Thomas, especially his teaching regarding the unity of the substantial form in man. But the reputation of Thomas was too great to suffer eclipse. The University of Paris regarded him as one of its greatest sons. The Dominican order did everything possible to promote the study and defense of Thomas' teachings among its members. The Italian poet, Dante Alighieri (1265-1321), enshrined Thomas' thought in verse. The canonization of Thomas by Pope John XXII in 1323 officially vindicated the orthodoxy of Thomas' writings.

Thereafter, the establishment of new universities in Italy, Spain, Portugal, Germany, Bohemia, Vienna, Cracow and Louvain, together with the multiplication of manuscripts of Thomas' works, contributed to the diffusion of his thought. In the fourteenth century, the *Summa Theologiae* was translated into Armenian, Greek and Middle High German. The invention of printing in the fifteenth century helped to spread not only the text of Thomas' major works, but also numerous commentaries, expositions, manuals and defenses.

In the sixteenth century, the Protestant Reformation offered a vigorous challenge to the Catholic Church. Unfortunately, Martin Luther (1483-1546) and nearly all his contemporaries knew very little about Thomistic thought and the Scholasticism of the Middle Ages; Luther himself had been educated in the Nominalist school. The Council of Trent was convoked to deal with the issues raised by the Reformers; and it was guided by the teaching of St. Thomas, especially in its decrees on justification and the sacraments. In 1567 Pope Pius V declared Thomas to be a Doctor of the Church and ordered his complete works to be collected and published. The establishment of seminaries and universities after Trent created a renewed demand for Thomistic teachers and textbooks.

The period that followed the Council of Trent has been called the silver age of Scholasticism. The use of the *Summa Theologiae* at the council confirmed the unique position it already occupied. The great commentaries on the *Summa* were written for the most part in the sixteenth and seventeenth centuries when the *Summa* replaced the *Sentences* of Peter Lombard as the theological textbook in Catholic institutions of higher learning. The commentary of John Capreolus (d. 1444) was composed in the fifteenth century. At the beginning of the sixteenth century, commentaries were prepared by three Dominicans, Thomas de Vio Cajetanus (d. 1534) in Italy, Conrad Köllin (d. 1536) in Germany, and Peter Crockaert (d. 1514) in Paris. Cajetanus or Cajetan remains one of the wisest companions in the study of the *Summa*. Crockaert lectured on the *Summa* at Paris; and his illustrious pupil, the Dominican Francis de Vitoria (d. 1546), introduced the practice into Spain where he adopted the *Summa* as a classroom text and the basis of his lectures at the University of Salamanca. Francis was the founder of a Thomistic school which achieved a felicitous union of positive and speculative theology. Among the members of the school were

Melchior Cano (d. 1560), Peter de Soto (d. 1561), Batholomew Medina (d. 1580), and Dominic Bañez (d. 1604), all of whom were Dominicans and all of whom wrote commentaries on parts of the *Summa*. Dominican theologians continued to write distinguished commentaries on the *Summa* well into the seventeenth century. Among the commentators were John of St. Thomas (d. 1644) who ranks with Cajetan, Dominic de Marinis (d. 1677), and Charles Billuart (d. 1757). The *Cursus theologicus Salmanticensis* (seventeenth century) was produced by the Discalced Carmelites in the tradition of the Dominican commentaries.

The Jesuit Fathers too commented upon the *Summa*. They departed from the Dominican interpretation to some degree and created an independent tradition. Among the most notable commentators were Francis Toletus (d. 1596), Francis Suarez (d. 1617), Gabriel Vasquez (d. 1604), Ruiz de Montoya (d. 1623), and Silvester Maurus (d. 1687). Suarez developed a system based on principles similar to those of St. Thomas and almost rivaling it in the favor of Catholic philosophers and theologians.

Interest in Thomistic studies flagged in the eighteenth century because of Wolffian and Cartesian influences within the Scholastic tradition and because of excessive conservatism on the part of Thomistic scholars in the face of new scientific discoveries. But there was a revival of interest in the nineteenth century. This revival was initiated by Catholic scholars confronted by contemporary problems and was supported by historical and doctrinal studies of medieval thinkers. The *Summa* of Thomas was published in Naples, Parma, Bologna and Paris. It became the textbook of theological studies at the Dominican College of St. Thomas (Minerva) in Rome and in the seminaries of Spain. The reestablishment of the Dominican order in France in 1850 by J. Lacordaire, O.P., renewed interest in Thomas' thought in that country. The outstanding German Thomist of the period was a Jesuit, J. Kleutgen (1811-83), whom some called *Thomas redivivus* or "Thomas resurrected."

At the end of the nineteenth century, Pope Leo XIII lent papal authority to the revival of Thomistic studies. His encyclical, *Aeterni Patris* (1879), called for the restoration of Thomas' philosophy and theology to a position of preeminence in the Catholic Church. Leo founded the Roman Academy of St. Thomas in the same year in which he published the encyclical. A year later (in 1880) he ordered the establishment of the Institut Supérior de Philosophie in Louvain, Belgium, as a "center of studies for promulgating the doctrines of St. Thomas." At the instigation of the Pope the Dominican order undertook a new edition of the works of the saint. The Catholic University of Fribough, Switzerland, was founded in 1890; and the theological faculty was entrusted to the Dominicans. Several journals dealing with Thomistic thought began publication, among them *Divus Thomas* and the *Revue Thomiste* which appeared in 1880 and 1893 respectively. The successors of Leo XIII in the papacy continued to affirm their vigorous support of Thomistic theology and philosophy. By 1930 there were strong centers of Thomistic studies in almost every country of Europe and North America.

The tradition of commenting upon the *Summa* of St. Thomas was maintained. In the nineteenth and twentieth centuries commentaries on parts of the *Summa* were prepared in the Latin language by F. Satolli; L. Billot, S.J.; M. Lepicier, O. Serv. B.V.M.; L. Janssens, O.S.B.; L. Paquet; R. Tabarelli; H. Buonpensiere, O.P.; N. del Prado, O.P.; and others. A huge commentary on the *Summa* was published in the French language by T. Pègues with the title *Commentaire français littéral de la Somme théologique de Saint Thomas d'Aquin*; it was begun in 1906.

The *Summa* was translated into English by the Dominicans of the English province in 1911. A revised edition was published in London in 1920. This edition was reissued by Benziger Brothers in 1948 and included an extensive commentary. The Benziger edition was reprinted in 1981 by Christian Classics of Westminster, Maryland. A new translation of the *Summa* together with a commentary in the English language has been published by the English Dominicans in sixty volumes. Begun in 1964, the massive work is now complete. A shorter commentary on the *Summa* in English is that by Walter Farrell, O.P., *A Companion to the Summa*.[9]

It is impossible to mention the names of all the contemporary scholars who have produced a flood of studies, expositions, manuals, and articles in the Thomistic vein. Since 1924, the bibliographic organ of Thomism, the *Bulletin Thomiste*, has given notices and reviews of hundreds of works each year. There are more than twenty specialist Thomistic journals, including the *Thomist* which is published in the United States. Actually, no other philosophical and theological group seems to have so many thinkers in its ranks and so many centers of study at its disposal.

The Spirit, Form and Division of the Summa

In the prologue to the *Summa*, St. Thomas explains his purpose in writing: "Because the master of Catholic truth must teach not only advanced students, but also beginners . . . , we intend to treat in this book whatever pertains to the Christian religion in such a way as to be helpful to beginners." In the past, Thomas goes on to say, beginners have run into a number of difficulties in certain theological works, namely, the multiplication of useless questions and arguments, the lack of systematic arrangement and sequence, and the frequent and futile repetition of the same topics. Thomas hopes to avoid these difficulties and discuss sacred doctrine clearly and briefly to the degree the matter permits.

Thomas divided the *Summa* into three main parts. He explains the reason for this division: "Sacred doctrine aims principally to teach the knowledge of God, not only as he is in himself, but also as he is the beginning and end of all things, especially of rational creatures. Therefore, in our effort to explain this science, we shall treat first of God [in part 1], secondly of the way in which rational creatures return to God [in part 2], and thirdly of Christ who, as man, is our way to God [in part 3]" (1a.2.*init.*). John of St. Thomas commented upon this division as follows: "St. Thomas divided the whole doctrine of the *Summa Theologica* according to this threefold consideration of God as cause, namely, as the efficient principle, as the final beatitude, as the savior and redeemer. And thus from God in himself and in his being, through God as the efficient, final, and saving cause, the return is made to God as the object of happiness in the ultimate glory of the resurrection—such is the truly golden circle of theology described in the sacred *Summa* of St. Thomas."[10]

Each of the three main parts of the *Summa* is subdivided into what are called questions. The first part of the *Summa* is divided in 119 questions. The second part of the *Summa* is divided into two lesser parts called the first part of the second part and the second part of the second part. The first part of the second part is divided into 114 questions; the second part of the second part, into 189 questions. Finally, the third part of the *Summa* is divided into 90 questions. Since Thomas died before he was able to complete the *Summa*, his secretary, Reginald of Piperno, completed it by adding a *Supplement* which is divided into 101 questions. Thus there are 613 questions in all. The questions, of course, deal with more specific topics. For example, questions 2-26 of the first part (which is concerned with the general topic of God) deal with the divine essence; questions 27-43, with the trinity of divine persons; and questions 44-119, with God as creator.

Finally, each question of the *Summa* is further divided into articles, 3125 in all. The title of the article is expressed as a question and is introduced by the Latin word *Ultrum?* which means "Whether?" The title of the article gives a precise formulation of the point of issue. Thereupon, St. Thomas gives a number of arguments or objections directed against the position that he himself will take. As a rule, the objections are not numerous. Then, with the stereotyped formula, *Sed contra*, which means "On the contrary," there follows a counter argument which announces the answer St. Thomas gives to the point at issue. Generally, there is only one counter argument in the *Sed contra* which, with few exceptions, indicates the solution given in the body of the article which follows immediately.

The *corpus articuli* or body of the article is the most important and decisive portion of the article. It prepares, states, and establishes the solution to the question under discussion. The solution is introduced with the phrase *Respondeo dicendum* or "I answer by saying that. . . ." On the basis of the solution given in the body of the article, and of the proofs advanced in its support, the last part of the article answers the objections or arguments brought forth in the beginning. There are about 10,000 answers to objections in all.

The structure of the article can be illustrated by the very first article of the *Summa*. It may be translated in this way:

> Whether any other knowledge, besides philosophy, is necessary?
>
> We proceed thus to the first article. It seems that no other knowledge, besides philosophy, is necessary.
>
> Objection 1. For man should not seek to know those things which are above reason, according to the passage of Scripture which says, "Do no meddle in those things which are beyond human understanding" (Si 3:22). But those things which are not beyond human understanding are sufficiently treated in philosophy. So, any knowledge, besides philosophy, seems superfluous.
>
> Objection 2. What is more, knowledge can be concerned only with being; for nothing is known save what is true, and all that is, is true. But philosophy treats of all beings and even of God, so that there is a part of philosophy which is called theology or divine science, as Aristotle has said. Therefore, no other knowledge, except philosophy, is necessary.
>
> On the contrary, it is written: "All Scripture is divinely

inspired and is useful for teaching, reproof, correction, and instruction in holiness'' (2 Tm 3:16). But divinely inspired Scripture has nothing to do with philosophy which relies only on human reason. Therefore, it is useful that there should be some other divinely inspired knowledge besides philosophy.

I answer by saying that it is necessary for human salvation that there be some knowledge revealed by God over and above philosophy which relies only on human reason. First, indeed, because man is ordained to God, as to an end which exceeds the comprehension of reason, according to the words of Isaiah, ''The eye does not see without you, O God, what you have prepared for those who love you'' (64:4). However, if men are to direct their thoughts and actions to that end, that end must first be known to them. Therefore, it was necessary for human salvation that man should learn through divine revelation certain things which surpass human reason.

With respect to those things which can be known about God by human reason, it was necessary that man be instructed by divine revelation. The reason is that the truth about God as discovered by human reason would be known only by a few and only after a long time and with many errors, whereas the whole salvation of man, which is in God, depends upon the knowledge of this truth. Consequently, it was necessary for man to be instructed about the things of God through divine revelation in order to provide more suitably and surely for his salvation. It was necessary, therefore, that over and above philosophy which relies on human reason there should be a sacred science learned through revelation.

Reply to Objection 1. Although those things which surpass human reason are not to be sought through reason, nevertheless, once God has revealed them, they are to be accepted by faith. Hence, the Scripture adds, ''Many things above the understanding of man have been shown to you'' (Si 3:25). And in this sacred doctrine consists.

> Reply to Objection 2. Sciences are distinguished according to the different ways by which they obtain their knowledge. Thus, the astronomer and the physicist may both come to the same conclusion, for example, that the earth is round. However, to prove this conclusion, the astronomer uses mathematics which abstracts from matter, while the physicist uses matter itself. Hence, there is no reason why those things which are treated by philosophy insofar as they are known by the natural light of reason should not be treated by still another science insofar as they are known by the light of divine revelation. Hence, the theology which pertains to sacred doctrine is essentially different from that theology which is a part of philosophy.

The symbols for the parts of the *Summa* are these:
The first part, *Pars Prima*, 1a.
The first part of the second part, *Prima Secundae*, 1a2ae.
The second part of the second part, *Secunda Secundae*, 2a2ae.
The third part, *Pars Tertia*, 3a.
The Supplement, *Supplementum*, Suppl. or 3a.Suppl.

A reference to the *Summa* is made in this way: 1a.16.7. This citation refers to the first part, question 16, article 7. A second example: 2a2ae.162.8. This citation refers to the second part of the second part, question 162, article 8.

Interpreting the Summa

To interpret the *Summa*, to get at the meaning St. Thomas intended, one can do several things:

(1) One should consider the title of the individual article carefully for a formulation of the issue to be discussed. Then, after reading the text of the article, one must bear in mind its place in the general plan of the *Summa*. Often the body of the article presup-

poses what has been discussed previously. One should note also that the objections are usually formulated and answered in syllogistic fashion.

(2) To get at the meaning of the *Summa*, it is helpful to consult parallel passages in other works of St. Thomas. Frequently editions of the *Summa* will note the parallel passages. Thomas is the best interpreter of his own thought. Then, after consulting the other works of St. Thomas, one may go to the commentators for an explanation.

(3) It is useful to investigate the sources employed by Thomas in composing the *Summa*, that is, the Scriptures, the writings of the Fathers, the decrees of the councils, canon law, and the writings of Aristotle, non-Christian thinkers and Christian contemporaries. The investigation of the sources employed by Thomas becomes more difficult, the nearer we come to his own time. In speaking of those near his own time, Thomas as a rule employs the anonymous Latin word, *quidam*, which means "a certain person."

(4) Finally, one can gain a better understanding of the *Summa* as well as the other writings of St. Thomas by studying the criticisms directed against him by his contemporaries, and the defenses written by his earliest followers.

The Contents of the Summa

The *Summa Theologiae* is divided into three main parts. The first part treats of God; the second part, of the rational creature's advance towards God; and the third part, of Christ, who, as man, is our way to God.

The First Part of the Summa. Thomas begins with an introductory question which shows the need of revelation and theology over and beyond philosophy (q.1). Then Thomas takes up the existence of God and the divine essence, what God is and what he is not, and the operations which are proper to God (qq. 2-26). Next

Thomas considers the trinity of persons in the one God. Here he speaks of the origin of the persons, the relations which ground the distinction between them, and the persons themselves considered both absolutely and relatively (qq.27-43). The first part of the *Summa* concludes with the treatise on God the creator. This treatise discusses the production of creatures, the various categories of creatures (angels, corporeal creatures, and man), and the conservation and government of creatures by God (qq.44-119).

The Second Part of the Summa. In the second part of the *Summa*, St. Thomas is concerned with the advance of the rational creature towards God. Men and women are free moral agents. They have it in their power to tend towards God by their actions or to turn away from him as their ultimate end. The first part of the second part of the *Summa* treats of God as the ultimate end of human activity (qq.1-5) and, in a general way, of human acts by which men and women tend towards, or deviate from, this end. This general consideration of human acts is divided into two main sections: the treatise on human acts in themselves (qq.6-48) and that on the principles of these acts, including habits, law and grace (qq.49-114).

While St. Thomas is concerned with the general principles of morality in the first part of the second part of the *Summa*, he deals with the morality of particular actions in the second part of the second part. The latter is largely a treatise on the virtues. The virtues are reducible to seven: the three theological virtues of faith, hope and charity, which are considered first (qq.1-46), and the four cardinal virtues of prudence, justice, fortitude and temperance, under which all the moral virtues may be ranged (qq.47-170). Whereas Thomas' teaching on the virtues holds good for all men and women and all states of life, he concludes the second part of the second part with a consideration and appraisal of particular states and kinds of life, such as the active and contemplative lives, the episcopacy, and the religious state (qq. 171-189).

The division of the second part of the *Summa* into two parts appears in the manuscripts of the thirteenth century and is explained by Ptolemy of Lucca: "Thomas divided the *Summa* into three parts: the *Summa naturalis*, because he there treats of the nature of things, first of the nature of God and then of created things. The second part he called the *Summa moralis*, which he divided into two volumes. The first volume deals with the general subjects of morality and is termed the *Prima Secundae*. The second volume contains an exposition of the particular virtues and vices; it is founded on, and enriched with, the sayings and reasons of philosophers and the authorities of sacred doctrine. This volume we call the *Secunda Secundae*. The third part of the *Summa*, which forms the fourth volume of the work, is called the *Summa sacramentalis*, because it treats of the sacraments and the Incarnation."[11]

The Third Part of the Summa. This part is devoted to Jesus Christ, the savior of all, to the sacraments which derive their efficacy from his passion, death and resurrection, and to eternal life which we attain by the resurrection. The treatise on Jesus Christ is divided into two main sections. The first deals with the mystery of the Incarnation (qq.1-26); and the second, with those things which Jesus did and suffered (qq.27-59). The treatise on the sacraments considers the sacraments in general (qq.60-65) and then each sacrament individually, that is, baptism, confirmation, the Holy Eucharist, penance (frequently now called the sacrament of reconciliation), extreme unction (also called the anointing of the sick), holy orders and matrimony (qq.66-90; Suppl.1-68). The very last treatise of the *Summa* speaks of the resurrection and eternal life (Suppl.69-101).

An Outline of the Summa

The contents of the *Summa Theologiae*

- 1. The nature of sacred doctrine (1a.1) (ch. 1)[12]
- 2. The subjects of sacred doctrine
    - 1. God (1a.2-119)
        - 1. The one God (1a.2-26) (ch. 2)
        - 2. The Holy Trinity (1a.27-43) (ch. 3)
        - 3. God the creator (1a.44-119) (ch. 4-8)
    - 2. The advance of the rational creature toward God (1a2ae and 2a2ae)
        - 1. The ultimate end of human life (1a2ae.1-5) (ch. 9)
        - 2. Human acts (1a2ae.6-114 and 2a2ae.1-189)
            - 1. In general
            - 2. In particular
    - 3. Christ who, as man, is our way to God (3a and Suppl.)
        - 1. The Savior (3a.1-59)
            - 1. The Savior (3a.1-26) (ch.18)
            - 2. What Jesus did and suffered (3a.27-59) (ch. 19)
        - 2. The sacraments (3a.60-90 and Suppl.1-68)
            - 1. In general (3a.60-65) (ch. 20)
            - 2. In particular (3a.66-90; Suppl.1-68)
        - 3. The resurrection (Supl.69-99) (ch. 22)

Chapter numbers refer to chapters of this book.

1. Human acts (1a2ae. 6-48) (ch. 10-11)

2. Principles of human acts (1a2ae.49-114) (ch. 12-13)

1. Virtues (2a2ae. 1-170)

1. Theological virtues (2a2ae.1-46) (ch. 14)

2. Cardinal virtues (2a2ae.47-170) (ch. 15-16)

2. Special gifts and states (2a2ae.171-189) (ch. 17)

1. Baptism, confirmation, Holy Eucharist (3a.66-83) (ch. 20)

2. Penance, extreme unction, holy orders and matrimony (3a.84-90; Suppl. 1-68) (ch.21)

The First Part of the
SUMMA THEOLOGIAE (1a)

Chapter 1

SACRED DOCTRINE (1a.1)

St. Thomas begins the *Summa Theologiae* with several presuppositions in mind. He presupposes that God revealed himself and his plans for the human race through the Biblical prophets and especially through his Son, Jesus Christ: "In times past, God spoke in fragmentary and varied ways to our fathers through the prophets; in this, the final age, he has spoken to us through his Son" (Heb 1:1-2). Furthermore, Thomas presupposes that this divine revelation has been preserved in the Scriptures and in the consistent teaching of the Church Fathers, and that it is the responsibility of the teaching authority of the Church to preserve, identify, and teach the true meaning of the Scriptural and patristic doctrine.

At the very beginning, Thomas is concerned with what he calls sacred doctrine. Sacred doctrine includes two things. In the first place, it includes the body of knowledge revealed by God and accepted by human beings on the authority of God. The human response or acceptance of this body of knowledge is called faith. In the second place, sacred doctrine includes the body of knowledge called theology. Theology is man's attempt to fathom and systematize the body of revealed truth. Theology is a human science employing both reason and revelation to do its work.

Men and women need supernatural and revealed knowledge such as sacred doctrine for two reasons. First, God has destined human beings for a supernatural end, namely, the eternal vision of

God. If men and women are to direct their actions toward this end, they must know about it and the means to achieve it. God had to reveal this information, for it could not be learned in any other way; and in this sense the revealed and supernatural knowledge of sacred doctrine is absolutely necessary. Second, even in those matters which human beings can learn for themselves, they need the illumination of sacred doctrine so that those divine realities, which are by their very nature accessible to human discovery, can be known by all with ease, solid certitude, and no trace of error. In the latter case, for example, Thomas holds that God's care for his creatures can be discovered by reason alone. Nevertheless, God has chosen to reveal this truth through his Son Jesus so that all can know it with ease, solid certitude, and no trace of error. In this sense too, sacred doctrine is necessary.

The principles with which sacred doctrine works have been revealed by God. Sacred doctrine accepts these principles on the authority of God who is incapable of error or falsehood. Sacred doctrine takes these absolutely certain principles, systematizes them and draws conclusions from them. In this sense, it is a science. This is the sense in which Aristotle understood the term "science." Moreover, sacred doctrine is one science rather than a group of related sciences because it studies all things, God and creatures, precisely as they are known through divine revelation.

Sacred doctrine is both a speculative and a practical science. A speculative science seeks the truth for its own sake. Perhaps astrophysics and paleontology are examples of a speculative science. A practical science, such as medicine and agriculture, directs human activity in a specific area. Sacred doctrine is a practical science because it directs human activity toward the goal of life; but it is also above all a speculative science because it is principally concerned with God rather than with human activity. As a speculative science, sacred doctrine excels other speculative sciences in the sense that it relies on divine revelation rather than fallible human reason for its certitude and in the sense that it is concerned with divinity rather than with natural questions. Moreover, sacred doctrine excels other practical sciences because it is concerned with the ultimate goal of human activity, namely, God and eternal happiness, whereas the other practical sciences look to more immediate goals.[1]

St. Thomas characterizes sacred doctrine as wisdom par excellence inasmuch as it judges all things in relation to God, the highest standard of judgment; and it does so with the help of divine revelation and human reason.

God is the principal object of theology, but theology is also concerned with creatures insofar as God is their beginning and end.

Sacred doctrine cannot argue about its principles, for these have been revealed by God and have to be accepted on his authority. Just as we must accept the structure of the atom on the word of the physicist, so we have to accept the principles of sacred doctrine on the word of God. For example, the fact that Jesus Christ is true God and true man has been revealed by God and must be accepted on his authority. Sacred doctrine can, however, point out the weaknesses in the arguments which someone might offer to contradict what God has revealed. Just so the Fathers of the Church pointed out the weaknesses in the arguments of the ancient heretics who denied either the divinity or the humanity of Christ. Sacred doctrine does argue about the conclusions to be drawn from the principles of faith. Here it tries to employ human reason to the fullest advantage.

The principles of sacred doctrine are taught in Sacred Scripture by reference to material things because it is natural for human beings to rise from the knowledge of sensible things to the knowledge of spiritual things. For example, Jesus described the kingdom of heaven in terms of joy (Mt 25:21), life (Mk 9:42), and light (Lk 16:6). Thomas distinguished two main senses in Sacred Scripture, the literal sense and the spiritual sense. The literal sense is that which is expressed by the words according to their primary meaning. Thus, the crucifixion of Jesus which is described in the gospels is to be understood literally. The spiritual sense is based upon the literal sense and supposes it. It is the sense whereby one thing in the Scriptures points to still another thing. The author of Hebrews, for instance, was convinced that the Old Law given through Moses prefigured the New Law given through Christ (Heb 10:1).

Chapter 2

THE ONE GOD (1a.2-26)

Having studied the nature of sacred doctrine, St. Thomas takes up the specific subjects with which sacred doctrine is concerned. Immediately he turns his attention to the one God who is the principal object of sacred doctrine and the beginning and end of all things. Thomas is concerned first with the existence of God and the divine essence—with what God is, or, rather, with what God is *not*—and with the divine operations.

The Existence of God (1a.2)

To begin with, Thomas asks if it is possible to recognize the existence of God simply by analyzing the idea of God. Is not the existence of God included in the idea of God as, for example, the idea of roundness is included in the idea of a circle? As soon as we understand the idea of a circle, we understand that it must be round. So too in the case of God, as soon as we understand the idea of God, do we not understand that he must exist? Thomas agrees that existence is part of the idea and essence of God, a fact that he will demonstrate later on; but at the outset of our inquiry, Thomas maintains, we do not know the divine essence sufficiently well to assert the fact of God's existence.

Related to this discussion is the question about the validity of the so-called ontological argument for the existence of God. The ontological argument for the existence of God was proposed by St. Anselm of Canterbury and proceeds from an analysis of the concept of God to the existence of God somewhat in this way: God is the most perfect being of which we can conceive. As such, God must be endowed with the perfection of existence; otherwise, we could conceive of a more perfect being, one that actually exists. Therefore, God exists. Descartes (1596-1650), Leibniz (1646-1716), and others accepted this argument as valid; but Thomas and many others have rejected this argument as invalid because it involves an illegitimate transition from the world of ideas to the world of reality.

Thomas was convinced that the existence of God can and must be demonstrated by an examination of what he effects, just as the existence of fire is demonstrated by the smoke it effects. Subsequently, the First Vatican Council (1869-70) taught that "God, the origin and end of all things, can be known with certainty by the natural light of reason from the things that he created."[1] This teaching was reaffirmed by the Second Vatican Council (1962-65).[2] Thomas offered five "ways" to demonstrate the existence of God. These five ways proceed from a fact of experience and invoke the principle of causality. As far as the first three of Aquinas' ways are concerned, the process of reasoning is quite simple. A being that changes supposes a being that does not change; a being that is caused supposes a being that is not caused; a contingent being supposes a necessary being. As a matter of fact, there are beings that change, that are caused, that are contingent. Hence, there must be a being that does not change, that is uncaused and necessary. This being we call God.

To clarify these arguments we might look more closely at the argument from contingency. Some beings, e.g., the flowers of spring, are contingent; that is to say, they come into existence and perish. They are not necessary beings; they do not exist of themselves; they are dependent upon other flowers and seeds for their existence. All beings, however, cannot be contingent beings.

If all beings were contingent beings, if there were no necessary being which exists without dependence upon other beings, there would be nothing at all. There must be a necessary being to explain why contingent beings come into existence.

Two observations about the first three proofs must be made at this point. First, in the case of each proof Thomas argues that an infinite series of changing or caused or contingent beings is impossible. He is not thinking of a series without a beginning, a ''horizontal'' series, as it were. Thomas admitted the possibility of God's creating a contingent series without a beginning. Rather, Thomas denies the possibility of an infinite series in the order of dependence, an infinite ''vertical'' series. A dependent series demands the existence of a being which is not itself dependent. Second, Thomas immediately calls that being which does not change, which is uncaused and necessary, by the name of God. In a sense, this designation is premature because it is not immediately evident that an unchanging, uncaused, and necessary being is the personal God whom theists acknowledge. Subsequently, however, Thomas will show that the being discovered by his five ways is the personal and omnipotent being whom we call God.

Thomas' fourth way of demonstrating the existence of God proceeds from the gradation which is found in the things of this world. Thomas argues: ''We find in things something which is more and less good, true, noble, and so on. But 'more' and 'less' are predicated of different things insofar as they approach in varying degrees that which is the maximum. Thus, that which is hotter approaches more closely that which is hottest of all. There is, therefore, something which is truest, best, most noble, and, as a consequence, being in the highest degree; for those things which are true in the highest degree are beings in the highest degree, as Aristotle writes in *Metaph*. 2. But that which is the maximum in a particular category is the cause of all those things which participate in that category. So, for example, fire, which is the maximum of heat, is the cause of the heat in all things warm and hot, as Aristotle also writes. There is, therefore, something which is the cause of the being and goodness and perfection of all other beings, and this we call God.'' This fourth proof was suggested by some observations in Aristotle's *Metaphysics* and is found substantially in Augustine and Anselm. The strength and precise meaning of this proof are not immediately evident. The argument is Platonic in origin and presupposes the idea of participation. Thomas uses the illustration from fire and heat because it is more vivid to the senses.

The fifth way proposed by Aquinas reasons from the order observed in the universe to a supreme intelligence from which the order is derived. In some cases, things lacking intelligence act with purpose and constancy for the attainment of a goal. Activity of such a nature is characteristic of intelligent beings and not of chance. If beings lacking intelligence act in such a manner, there must be a supreme intelligence directing them, as ''the arrow is directed by the archer.'' This supreme intelligence is God.

By itself this proof leads to a governor or architect of the universe. Further reasoning is required to show that this architect is also the creator of the universe.

The example of an orrery, although St. Thomas did not use it, seems to illustrate the argumentation of the fifth way. An orrery is an apparatus that shows the relative positions and motions of bodies in the solar system. When the wheels turn and the arms move, one can see just how the planets move around the sun and their relation to one another. Common sense tells us that some intelligent being made the orrery. So too, common sense tells us that some intelligent being directs the solar system of which the orrery is a model. This intelligent being we call God.

St. Thomas stated his proofs for the existence of God only in bare outline. Perhaps we wish that he had developed them in greater detail. We must remember, however, that St. Thomas was writing for believers and that he wished only to prove in summary fashion one of the preambles of the faith. (A preamble of the faith is a truth which can be known by natural reason, one that faith supposes.) Had Thomas been writing for atheists, we might have expected a much fuller treatment of the proofs for the existence of God.

The existence of an absolutely necessary being means that God continually sustains every other contingent being in existence; otherwise, it would lapse into nothing. The existence of an absolutely necessary being means that we cannot contact any reality without confronting divinity, that God is supremely active in the history of the world.

Possibly the most serious objection to the existence of God is the fact of evil. Millions of human beings, children and adults, go hungry and even starve to death. Other millions are the victims of disease, war, exploitation and deception. Still others suffer and perish in natural catastrophes such as floods, earthquakes and storms. Beyond this, there is the moral evil of human sinfulness with all its dreadful consequences for the sinner and his victims. Some have been so impressed by the enormity of human suffering that they have denied the existence of God. A good and omnipotent God, they say, could not permit suffering on such a scale. St. Thomas replies to the objection by saying what Augustine said before him: Since he is supremely good, God could permit no evil to mar his works, unless he was so powerful and good that he could bring good even out of evil.

The book of *Wisdom* says: "From the greatness and beauty of created things their original author is seen by analogy" (13:5). Paul writes: "Since the creation of the world, the invisible realities of God's eternal power and divinity have been made known through the things he has made" (Rm 1:20). Thomas' arguments for the existence of God show how God can be known from his works, as transcending his works.

What God Is Not and What He Is (1a.3-13)

The five proofs for the existence of God demonstrate the existence of a first mover, a first cause, an absolutely necessary being, a supreme being, and an architect and governor of the universe whom we are wont to call God. Analyzing the concepts of a first mover, a first cause, an absolutely necessary being, and so on, we can come to know God better in our limited way by recognizing what he is not and what he is. For this analysis Thomas employs the famous *via negativa* or way of negation and the *via affirmativa* or way of affirmation. Negatively, Thomas denies to God all those attributes of creatures which are incompatible with the concepts of a first mover, a first cause, an absolutely necessary being, a supreme being, and a governor of the universe. Positively, Thomas affirms of God all those attributes of creatures which are demanded by the concept of the being revealed by the five ways; but he affirms them analogously and not univocally, as we shall see. In this manner, Thomas arrives at the theistic conception of God. To begin with, Thomas concludes that God is simple, utterly perfect, good, infinite, present everywhere, unchangeable, eternal and one. Then Thomas draws some conclusions about the knowledge, will and power of God.

We hear an echo of Thomas' teaching about God's attributes in the words of the First Vatican Council: "The holy, catholic, apostolic Roman Church believes and professes that there is one true and living God, the creator and lord of heaven and earth. He is all-powerful, eternal, unmeasurable, incomprehensible and limitless in intellect and will and in every perfection. Since he is one unique spiritual substance, entirely simple and unchangeable, he must be declared really and essentially distinct from the world, perfectly happy in himself and by his very nature, and inexpressibly exalted over all things that exist or can be conceived other than himself."[3]

To say that God is simple is to say that he is in no sense composite. There can be no composition in God either of matter and form, or of substance and accident, or of essence and existence. There can be no composition in God because every composite is dependent on its parts, and it is necessarily caused because its parts do not come together as a whole without the intervention of an extrinsic cause. An automobile, for example, is composed of many parts, and it must be assembled by many workers and machines. Now to be dependent and caused is obviously repugnant to the divine nature. Therefore, God is altogether simple. We can form no adequate idea of the divine simplicity because it is beyond our experience; but it differs from the simplicity of creatures. Among creatures, simplicity, such as that of the amoeba, is regarded as a lower level of existence; in God, however, simplicity is a sign of the highest level of existence.

God is limitless in every perfection. He possesses within himself in an eminent manner and to an infinite degree every positive aspect of being. Thus, God is all-knowing, all-powerful, perfectly just, completely truthful, and so on. Because of God's unlimited fullness of being, he is said to be utterly perfect and infinite. The reason for the infinite perfection of God is that there is no principle of limitation either *outside* or *within* God, which restricts his being. A thing may be limited from *outside* itself by the one who produces it. A loaf of bread, for example, may be limited to one pound in weight because the baker or machine made it that way. However, the being of God cannot have been limited in this way because no one produced him. Nor can the being of God have been limited from *within* itself, that is to say, by itself. The reason is that limitation is a deficiency or lack of being; consequently, it cannot arise from the being to which it is opposed. Just as light does not give rise to darkness (which is the absence of light), so being does not give rise to limitation (which is the negation of being). Therefore, limited neither from without nor from within, God possesses the fullness of being without limitation. He is infinite; he is limitless in every perfection.

To say that God is good means that God is desirable, lovable. Every creature in the universe seeks its own perfection, the completion of its nature. A human being, for example, seeks food and drink, knowledge and love, and a host of other things, as the fulfillment of his or her existence. Even animals and inanimate creatures are driven by instinct or physical necessity to seek the perfection or goal consistent with their nature. This goal is nothing but a similitude, an image, a memory of the goodness of God, for God possesses within himself every creaturely perfection in an eminent manner. Hence, God is desirable, lovable, and, in a word, good.

God is present in all things and everywhere in the sense that he communicates existence to every creature within the universe. It is an existence that God must and does impart continually. At each moment of its existence, the creature remains a contingent being deriving its existence from God. Just as the sky is illumined only as long as the sun shines, just as the song lingers only as long as the singer produces it, so the creature exists only as long as God sustains it. Thomas concludes that God is in the world and in everything—by his power insofar as all things are subject to him, by his presence insofar as all things are visible to his eyes, and by his essence which causes all things. We live in a world pulsating with divinity. To look at the world is to see God.

God is immutable, that is to say, he is in no way subject to change. An object changes when it acquires or loses something. A person changes when he or she gains or loses weight, acquires a skill or loses it, gets sick and then gets better, and so on. God, however, is not subject to gain or loss, for he possesses the fullness of being to a limitless degree which leaves nothing to be gained. Nor can God lose anything, for, inasmuch as he has not been caused, he exists necessarily and not contingently. Consequently, God cannot cease to be in any respect; there can be no change in him; he is immutable. We must not conceive this immutability as a state of inertia; it is rather a state of intense activity analogous, perhaps, to the intense activity of the sun which is constantly emitting light and heat.

If God is immutable, he is eternal. Boethius, the Roman philosopher, defined eternity as the simultaneously complete and perfect possession of life without beginning or end. Eternity is the measure of an unchanging being, while time is the measure of a being subject to change. God is eternal because he continues to exist of himself without having begun and without the possibility of ceasing, neither acquiring anything nor suffering the loss of anything. God's eternity, therefore, supposes his immutability which excludes all change in God. God is at any moment what he always was and what he always will be. In this respect, God differs completely from human beings who not only begin to exist, but progressively mature from infancy to adulthood until they reach the grave.

The infinity of God explains the fact that there is only one God. Thomas makes the point in this way: God possesses the fullness of being without limitation. If there were many gods, one would necessarily differ from another. As a consequence, one would have something which another did not have. If this were a privation, one of them would not possess the fullness of being. If, on the other hand, this were a positive reality, one of them would lack it. Hence, there cannot be many gods. Therefore, Thomas adds, those ancient philosophers who admitted an infinite principle always felt constrained to assert at the same time its uniqueness. Because of this view about the oneness of God, theists differ from polytheists and the ancient dualists. The polytheists maintained that there was a pantheon of gods. The ancient dualists, in order to explain the origin of evil, placed a first principle of evil alongside a first principle of good.

At this point (1a.12), Thomas goes off on a different track. Breaking off his study of the divine attributes for the moment, Thomas asks how God is known by his creatures. Thomas recognizes three different ways. First, God can be known through created realities. As Paul puts it, "God's eternal power and divinity have been made known through the things he has made" (Rm 1:20). Second, God can be, and is, known through revelation. His Son, Jesus Christ, and the prophets have told us much about God

(Heb 1:1-2). Third, Thomas holds that the blessed in heaven contemplate the essence of God: they see God as he is, to use the words of 1 Jn 3:2. The possibility and the fact are made known through revelation. The vision of God is necessarily an intellectual vision. For this vision the human intellect must be fortified by what Thomas calls the light of glory. The light of glory corresponds to the degree of charity which an individual acquires in this life. It follows that one person sees God more perfectly than another, although total comprehension of God is impossible. Nevertheless, through the vision of God, we shall understand clearly what is now unclear about God, and we shall be happy beyond imagination.

Then Thomas asks how we speak about God while we are on this earth. We can speak of God because we can know him. Sometimes we say what God is not; for example, we say that God is not mutable. Sometimes we say what God is; thus, we say that God is good. This means more than the fact that God is the cause of goodness in creatures; it means that the good in creatures preexists in God in a more excellent and higher way. The words that we apply to God, such as wise, loving and good are derived originally from creatures; and they are predicated of God and creatures analogously. This is to say that both God and creatures have the perfections signified by these words, but with a profound difference. God has these perfections of himself, whereas creatures have them from God. The notion of simultaneous similarity and difference is fundamental in analogy. Thomas believed that the most perfect predicate or name for God is the one which he applied to himself in the book of Exodus (3:14). There God said to Moses: "This is what you shall tell the Israelites: '*He who is* has sent me to you.' " The name, *He who is*, expresses the very essence of God which is to exist; and it suggests God's infinity and eternity.

The Divine Operation (1a.14-26)

Next Thomas treats of God's operation. One kind of operation is immanent, remaining within God. In God the operations of intellect and will are immanent, for understanding is in the intelligent agent and willing is in the one who wills. Another kind of operation produces an external effect, and in this case Thomas considers the power of God which is the principle of the divine operation having an external effect.

Thomas could have demonstrated the existence of intellect and knowledge in God in several ways. He could have appealed to the fifth way of demonstrating the existence of God. The fifth way reasons from the order observed in the universe to a supreme intelligence from which the order is derived. Or Thomas could have argued from the infinity of God. Intellect and knowledge are surely realities that must be comprehended by the fullness of God's being. Or Thomas could have argued from the divine causality. If God has created intellectual beings, he must be possessed of intellect and knowledge. It is a fundamental principle with Thomas that the perfections of creatures must be found in the creator in a more excellent and higher way. Actually, Thomas argues for the presence of intellect and knowledge in God in none of these ways. Rather, he reasons, to know supposes a certain amplitude of nature or the capacity to take the ideas of other things into oneself, for the idea of the thing known is in the knower. Amplitude of nature follows upon immateriality, since, for Thomas, matter is a principle of restriction and limitation. For example, plants do not know because they are wholly material. Since God is in the highest degree of immateriality, it follows that he occupies the highest place in knowledge.

Like all the attributes of God, the knowledge of God is infinite; hence, God knows himself and all else perfectly. The simplicity of God demands complete identity between the divine intellect and essence, between the knower and the known; and this identity makes for total comprehension. As the salt penetrates the water, so the divine intellect penetrates the divine essence. Moreover, God knows all else other than himself; for God knows himself perfectly, so that he knows how far his causal activity extends, how far it has been exercised, and how far it will be exercised. Knowing himself, God knows other things as in a mirror. God's knowledge is necessarily individual because individual differences depend upon God's causal activity; God's knowledge coupled with his will to act is the cause of all else. So, for example, God knows that Henry weighs two hundred pounds and that Mary's hair is red. God knows what is possible but will never be realized. His knowledge of the good necessarily involves a knowledge of the way in which good can be, and is, defective; and this is a knowledge of evil.

Thomas goes on to say that there must be ideas in the divine mind. Just as a human architect constructs a building according to the ideas in his or her mind, so the divine architect has made the world according to the ideas in his mind. In a sense there is a plurality of ideas in the divine mind in accordance with the plurality of created things of which the ideas are exemplars. However, this plurality must not be seen as something opposed to the divine essence as imitable outside itself, as the exemplar of this or that object.

Consideration of the intellectual activity in God leads Thomas to conclude that he is alive or living. The sense in which Thomas understands that God is living can be gathered to some degree from a consideration of those things which are manifestly alive, such as animals. An animal is alive insofar as it manifests those activities that spring from itself and tend to its own completion and perfection. Nutrition and sensation are examples of vital activity. As soon as the animal fails to manifest activites of this nature, it is said to be dead. When, therefore, we attribute to God activity that springs from himself and contributes to his perfection, the activity of understanding and willing, we attribute to him vital activity; consequently, he is said to be, and is, alive.

The subject of the divine intellect leads naturally to the subject of the divine will, for it is impossible to have intelligence without will. Again, it seems, Thomas might have argued from the infinity of God to the existence of will in God. A will is surely a reality that must be comprehended by the fullness of God's being. Instead, Thomas argues in a different fashion. In all creatures, he maintains, there is a tendency, a thrust, a driving force toward that which perfects, and is good for, the creature in question. The creature is inclined to acquire the good if it is not possessed, and, if it is possessed, the creature rests therein. In those things which lack knowledge, this tendency or thrust is called a natural appetite. Plants, for example, naturally put down roots into the soil in search of minerals and water. In those creatures which have sense knowledge, this tendency or thrust is called an animal appetite. Lions, for example, go after the prey detected by their senses. In those things which have intellectual knowledge, this tendency or thrust or driving force is called an intellectual appetite or will. Thus, human beings will those good or desirable objects apprehended by their intellects. So too in God, Thomas concludes, will follows upon intellect. Indeed, God is his intellect and will.

God necessarily wills or loves himself, since the divine intelligence cannot fail to recognize what is supremely good. God freely wills things other than himself, that is to say, his creatures, in order to share his good with them as much as possible. The will of God acting in conjunction with the divine intellect is the cause of all else. The will of God is immutable; God's knowledge embraces everything from the beginning so that the divine will is not subject to change. Thus, it is possible for God to will one thing now, say rain, and its contrary afterwards, fair weather, without changing his will.

The will of God is always fulfilled; it always achieves its objective. No creature can thwart the will of God, since every creature depends upon God for its activity. Even the sinner, who seems to thwart the will of God by sinning, does the will of God by suffering the consequences of his sins according to the divine plan. How is one to reconcile the infallibility of the divine will with human freedom? Both revelation and reason assert the factuality of both. The divine will is infallible because it is the first cause of every created effect including the free human act. Human beings are free because they are able to choose among created goods. Created goods are limited in their appeal and do not inexorably draw the human will after them.

How can God's will be supreme and infallible when human beings are free? Thomas answers by saying that the causality of God extends not merely to the acts men and women perform, but also to the mode of the act, its freedom or necessity. God wills some things to come about by necessity and some things to come about freely. How can God move human beings so that they remain free? It is a mystery.

Does God will evil? Not directly, because evil is opposed to the good which alone is desirable. In no way can God will the evil of sin which draws his rational creatures away from him. In other cases, though, God may will some good to which evil is attached, as, for example, God wills the preservation of lions who must eat other animals to live.

Because God has a will, God is capable of, and does, love, for love is the fundamental act of the will. To love anything is nothing else than to will good to that thing. God loves all that exists. If God is the cause of all that exists from gnats to angels, then whatever good things creatures possess, whether it be their very existence, their characteristic properties, gifts, and so on, these come from God. The love of God for all things consists precisely in this, that God wills and causes the good which they have. Whereas human love is elicited by the good which it finds in others, divine love is the cause of good in others. Obviously, God loves some creatures more than others. For example, the greater gifts conferred upon rational creatures indicate that God loves them more than brutes or plants.

The divine will is also just and merciful. God is just in the sense that he gives to each thing what is required by its nature and condition to fulfill its role in the universe. It is the kind of justice that characterizes the just leaders of states who see to it that everyone has what he or she needs and deserves. At work too in the universe is the mercy of God which removes the failings and deficiencies of his creatures. Thus, the bestowal of good things upon creatures, absolutely considered, pertains to God's goodness; the bestowal of good things in due proportion, to his justice; and the giving of good things to remove defects, to his mercy.

The providence of God supposes both his intellect and will. Divine providence has, roughly, the same relation to the universe that the plan of the architect has to a building under construction. Divine providence is the plan according to which all things are directed to a particular end and serve a particular purpose. Providence supposes the existence of this plan in the divine mind and the will of God to carry it out. Providence is eternal; but the actual implementation of God's plan, which is called divine governance, is temporal. The providence of God extends as far as his causality, even to the smallest detail of a creature's existence and activity. In this regard, the words of Jesus are memorable: "Are not two sparrows sold for next to nothing? Yet one of them does not fall to the ground without your Father's permission" (Mt 10:29). While the whole providential plan exists in the divine mind, God executes his plan in some instances through others; so, for example, God provides for children through their parents. In this way, God allows creatures to share in his own causality. God's providential plan, despite its infallibility, does not impair the freedom of his rational creatures, as we noted earlier without being able to explain the mystery before us.

The providence of God brings all things to their appointed end. According to the providence of God, some men and women will achieve the beatific vision of God. God's plan for *them* is predestination and is executed in the lives of the predestined. Thomas recalls the words of Paul: "Those God predestined, he likewise called" (Rm 8:30). In his providence God permits some to fall short of the beatific vision. This is reprobation which means permitting some to fall into sin and condemning them for their sin.

In this sense God elects some in preference to others. God does not predestine some in view of their merits; indeed, our merits are the result of predestination. Predestination achieves its effect certainly and infallibly without destroying human freedom. In this difficult matter, Church doctrine insists on several things: that God is the author of our salvation, that we must cooperate with the grace of God in order to be saved, and that no one is condemned unless it be through his own fault. The names of those who have been predestined are said to have been entered by God into the book of life (Ps 69:29).

The power of God, which is identical with his essence, is the capacity of God to act on other things. Divine omnipotence means that God can do all things that are possible, that is, whatever does not involve a contradiction. For example, God cannot make a square circle; such a thing cannot exist; its conceptual and constitutive elements are mutually destructive. Similarly, God cannot render the past as though it had never been. Surely God can make things other than those which he has made, such as the fabulous unicorn. He is able to make better things than those he has actually made; and he is able to improve those things which now exist. In any event, what God makes is admirably suited to the purpose it is meant to serve, and thus it is worthy of God to the extent that a finite being can be.

Thomas concludes this section about the one God by speaking about his happiness. God is perfectly happy in himself and by his nature. God understands his own nature perfectly because he has the perfection of knowledge, and this intellectual comprehension affords him supreme happiness.

Just as a mother delights in gazing at her baby, just as a biologist is happy in his study of living things, just as a gardener finds satisfaction in contemplating her beautiful flowers, so God is supremely blessed in the possession and contemplation of his own essence, the supreme good.

Chapter 3

THE HOLY TRINITY (1a.27-43)

Having studied the one God, Thomas considers the three divine persons in the one God. This is the mystery of the Holy Trinity. The three divine persons are Father, Son and Holy Spirit. The three divine persons are really distinct from one another, eternal and perfectly equal; yet, they are one and the same God because all have one and the same divine nature. Of these three persons, the Son proceeds from the Father by an eternal generation; and the Holy Spirit proceeds from the Father and the Son by an eternal spiration, as it is called.

There is absolutely no way in which we could have come to the knowledge of the Holy Trinity by ourselves. We know about the three divine persons in the one God only because God has chosen to reveal them to us. Even after the revelation of this mystery, we cannot understand it fully; but we believe it because we have God's word for it. In heaven, we shall see God face to face, and then we shall understand how there are three divine persons in the one God.

God did not reveal the mystery of the Holy Trinity in a single blinding flash, but only gradually. There was a development between the Old and New Testaments. In the Old Testament God spoke to the nation of Israel and stressed his oneness. God commanded Moses to say: "Hear, O Israel, the Lord our God is one Lord. Therefore, you shall love the Lord, your God, with all your heart, and with all your soul, and with all your strength" (Dt

6:4-5). In the New Testament Jesus acknowledged that commandment as the first and greatest of the Lord's commandments (Mt 22:34-40). Jesus, the new Moses, preached an unyielding monotheism. At the same time, the word of God enshrined in the pages of the New Testament identifies three distinct persons with the one God. There is the person whom Jesus calls his Father and is the Lord of heaven and earth (Mt 11:25-27; Lk 10:21-22). There is a second person, Jesus himself, who, being in the form of God, emptied himself, taking the form of a servant (Ph 2:6-7). John wrote: "In the beginning was the Word, and the Word was with God, and the Word was God" (Jn 1:1); and this Word who became flesh and dwelt among us (Jn 1:14) was Jesus.

There is also a third divine person, the Holy Spirit. Jesus commands baptism in the name of the Father, Son, and Holy Spirit (Mt 28:19). More than a cosmic force, the Spirit teaches the apostles all things (Jn 14:26), and he glorifies Jesus, because he receives of what is his and declares it to the apostles (Jn 16:14). The Spirit is sent by the Father in the name of the Son (Jn 14:26), and is unmistakably distinct from each of them. Thus, the New Testament propounds a mystery for our belief: three distinct persons are divine, but they are not three gods, only one God.

The mystery of the Holy Trinity was expressed in the creeds of the Church. For example, the Athanasian Creed of the fifth or sixth century puts the matter in this way: "The Father is God, the Son is God, and the Holy Spirit is God. But there are not three gods, only one God. The Father is Lord, the Son is Lord, and the Holy Spirit is Lord. There are not three lords, but one Lord. For according to Christian truth, we must profess that each of the persons individually is God; and according to the Christian religion we are forbidden to say that there are three gods or three lords. The Father is not made by anyone, nor created by anyone, nor generated by anyone. The Son is not made nor created, but he is generated by the Father alone. The Holy Spirit is not made nor created nor generated, but proceeds from the Father and the Son."[1]

Frequently we resort to examples to clarify the mystery of the Holy Trinity as far as we can. Just as the three angles of a triangle are distinct from each other, yet each angle seems to take in the whole area of the triangle, so the three persons of the Holy Trinity are distinct from each other, yet each person is identified with the nature of God. Or another example. Just as the child is the expression of the love between father and mother, so the Holy Spirit is the expression of the love between Father and Son. A third example. Just as the mind, the hand and the instrument of the musician produce the musical sound, so Father, Son and Holy Spirit have created and sustain the harmony of the universe. Even though we use these examples to clarify the mystery of the Holy Trinity, we realize that they are deficient in some way. Fortunately, what is required of us is acceptance of this mystery, and not understanding. It is this mystery with its revealed presuppositions that Thomas wishes to probe in his *Summa*. Reason can offer some clarification of it, even though the basic mystery will remain with us while we are pilgrims on this earth.

Thomas' treatise on the Holy Trinity takes up three subjects: the origin or procession of the divine persons, the relations which are the basis for the distinction of the divine persons, and the persons themselves.[2]

The Origin or Procession of the Persons in God (1a.27)

To explain the origin of the second and third persons of the Holy Trinity, to the degree that an explanation is possible, Thomas points to the vital activities of knowing and loving God. Whoever knows an object, there proceeds within the knower an idea of that object, a mental image or word, whereby the thing known is in the knower. Moreover, if the object is apprehended as good, there also proceeds within the lover an impulse, an affection, an inclination toward the object whereby the thing loved is in the one who loves.

However, God knows and loves himself perfectly. Hence, there are two processions or emanations in God. Insofar as God knows himself, he originates the Son who is the image or word of the Father. The Son is God Known. The procession of the Son is called generation because it bears some resemblance to the biological procession of generation whereby like begets like. Insofar as God loves himself, he originates the Spirit who is the thrust or impulse of God to love himself. The Spirit is God Loved. The procession of the Spirit is called spiration. The Son and Spirit are distinct from the Father and each other in personality by reason of generation and spiration; yet, they are identical with the divine essence by reason of the simplicity of God.

This psychological argument, as it is called, was suggested by the names Word and Spirit which the New Testament applies to the second and third persons of the Trinity. The argument was first proposed by Augustine; it was developed by medieval theologians and adopted by Thomas. It is an argument from analogy and not a rational proof of the mystery.

The Divine Relations (1a.28)

The two processions in God, generation and spiration, set up real relations in God between that which proceeds and the principle from which it proceeds—between the one generated and the one generating on the one hand, and between the one spirated and the one spirating on the other. Here a relation means the reference of one thing to another. Three conditions are required for a real relation: a subject (for example, a father), a term of the relationship (in this case, a son), and a reason why the subject is related to the term of the relationship (the act of generation). Each procession in the Trinity sets up two opposed relations, one in the principle of the procession, the other in the one proceeding. In the case of generation, the relations are paternity and filiation; in the case of spiration, spiration and procession. In the latter case, the names, spiration and procession, are also applied to the relations, even though these two names were used earlier with a different meaning.

The real relations in the Trinity have to be identified with the divine essence which is characterized by unity and simplicity. Still, these relations imply opposition and distinction between a father and his son. It does not follow that the relations are identical with each other just because each one must be identified with the divine essence, since each relation implies opposition to its term.

The Persons of the Trinity (1a.29-43)

The Father, Son and Holy Spirit of the Blessed Trinity are divine persons. With Boethius, Thomas defines a person as an individual substance of a rational nature, or, in other words, an individual, intellectual substance. Thomas recognizes human, angelic and divine persons. The word, person, is rightly predicated of God in a super-eminent way because it represents a perfection, and God is the fullness of perfection. In God, the term "person" signifies the subsistent relations, such as paternity and filiation. It is these relations which are individual and distinctive in the divine nature and merit the name of person.

Because there are several subsistent relations in the Trinity, there are several persons. Distinction arises in the Trinity where the relations are opposed to each other. Paternity and filiation are opposed to each other; spiration and procession are opposed to each other; but spiration and procession are not opposed to paternity and filiation. Of the four relations in God, three are numerically distinct and thus constitute the three divine persons. The divine paternity is the person of God the Father, the divine filiation is the person of God the Son, and the divine procession (the relation) is the person of God the Holy Spirit. When we speak of God as one, we are referring to the one divine nature. When we speak of the persons as three, we mean that each one of them is really distinct from the other as a person, but not as God.

The word, Trinity, signifies the three persons in the one God. In speaking of the Holy Trinity, we must avoid any statement that suggests a difference in nature among the three divine persons. We may say, for example, "The Son is other than the Father," to express the distinction of persons, but not a difference in nature. So too we may say, "To the king of ages, the immortal, the invisible, the *only* God, be honor and glory" (1 Tm 1:17) and "God *alone* is eternal," for these statements reflect the unity of the divine nature. However, it would be misleading to say, "Before there were creatures, God was *alone*," since this statement could be understood as a denial of the Holy Trinity. We may say, "The Son *alone* is generated," because this statement is true only of the Son.

The mystery of the Holy Trinity cannot be discovered by reason alone because our natural knowledge of God rises from the creatures to their creator and cause. However, the causal activity of God is common to the whole Trinity; hence, this activity pertains to, and reveals the unity of the divine nature, but not the distinction of persons.

A notion is the distinctive way in which we know a divine person. The persons are distinct by reason of their origin; and so by reflection upon their origin we can identify five notions or distinctive predicates: (1) unbegottenness and (2) paternity which are proper to the Father; (3) filiation which is proper to the Son; (4) spiration which is common to the Father and the Son; and (5) procession which is proper to the Holy Spirit. Obviously, the notions, with the exception of unbegottenness, have the same names as the relations.

By way of summary, we may say that in God there are five notions, four relations, three persons, two processions, and one nature; and there is no proof from reason for the mystery of the Holy Trinity. It must be accepted on the authority of God who revealed it.

In virtue of all that has been said up to this point, Thomas holds that the first person of the Blessed Trinity is rightly called Principle, Father and Unbegotten. The name, Father, is primarily a distinctive personal name in God, referring to the first of the divine persons; but it is also an essential name, referring to the three divine persons in the undivided nature of God. We use the name in the latter sense when we say, for example, "God is the father of us all." The second person of the Blessed Trinity is rightly called Word of God, and Son and Image of the Father. The third person is rightly called the Holy Spirit or the Holy Ghost because he proceeds from the Father and the Son, both of whom are holy and spirits. The Holy Spirit is also rightly called Love and Gift because these names suggest that he proceeds by way of love which has the nature of a gift.

The procession of the Holy Spirit has been a source of controversy among Christians. The Orthodox Church holds that the Holy Spirit proceeds only from the Father; but the Roman Catholic Church holds that the Holy Spirit proceeds from both the Father and the Son. To make this point, the Roman Catholic Church has inserted the *Filioque* into the Nicene Constantinopolitan Creed, the one said at Mass, so that the creed says, *Qui [Spiritus] ex Patre Filioque procedit*, which means "The Spirit proceeds from the Father and the Son." If the Holy Spirit did not proceed from the Father *and* the Son, Thomas argues, the Spirit could not be distinguished as a person from the Son, for it is procession in the Trinity that sets up opposition and distinction among the divine persons.

Because the Son has from the Father that the Holy Spirit proceeds from the Son, it can be said that the Father spirates the Holy Spirit through the Son, or that the Holy Spirit proceeds from the Father through the Son, which is the same thing. Since the Father and the Son are one in all things in which relative opposition is not a factor, it follows that the Father and the Son are one principle of the Holy Spirit, because there is no relative opposition in this matter.

Each person of the Holy Trinity is to be identified with the divine essence, even though the persons are really distinct. This fact governs our way of speaking about the Trinity. Sometimes, the word, God, signifies the divine essence, when, for example, we say, "God creates"; sometimes, however, it signifies a divine person, when, for example, we say, "God begets." Those things which are proper to the persons by which they are distinguished from each other must be predicated judiciously. Thus we may say that the three persons are one God, that there are three eternal beings, that God (Father and Son) spirates; however, we may not say that essence begets essence.

To manifest the divine persons more clearly, it is legitimate to "appropriate" attributes of the divine essence to the individual persons. Following the lead of Augustine, Thomas held that all divine activity touching creatures is common to the three persons; only in the internal life of God is there a distinction of personal activity. When, for example, we say that the Holy Spirit overshadowed Mary (Lk 1:35), it was really the Trinity that overshadowed Mary, with the Spirit being named according to appropriation. We need to remind ourselves, however, that the appropriation of essential attributes to divine persons, while helpful to our understanding, is not a perfect expression of the truth. In general, we appropriate to the Father all that is connected with beginning, like creation and omnipotence; to the Son what is related to the intellect, like wisdom and light; and to the Holy Spirit what is related to love and sanctification like grace and indwelling.

In God, Thomas maintains, the relations are the persons. It is the relations of paternity and filiation, spiration and procession that distinguish the persons. We cannot think of the Father except as the one generating or begetting the Son, nor can we think of the Son except as the one who is generated or begotten. If we abstract the idea of the relationship from the idea of the person, we radically alter the idea of the person. The idea of the person who is a subsistent relation logically precedes the idea of the "notional act" by which we conceive the person as acting. The human mind thinks first of the person, the subsistent relation, who acts, and then of his action.

The term, notional act, was used in the preceding paragraph. The notional acts correspond to the notions mentioned earlier. The notions are the distinctive ways in which we know each of the divine persons. There are five notions: unbegottenness, paternity, filiation, spiration and procession. The notional acts correspond to the notions and there are two of them, generation and spiration. The two notional acts coincide with the two processions which are the generation of theWord and the spiration of the Holy Spirit. To describe the order by which the divine persons originate, it is necessary to attribute the notional acts to the divine persons and not to the essence. Thus we must say that it is the Father and not the divine essence who generates. Further, we must say that the Father generated the Son not by free choice, but by the necessity of his nature. The Son was generated from the substance of the Father and not from nothing. The power of God is the principle of the notional acts. The power to generate refers directly to the divine nature and indirectly to the relation of paternity. The notional acts can terminate at only one person.

The divine persons are equal and co-eternal, for each is identified with the divine nature. There is an order of nature among the divine persons in the sense that one originates from another, but not in the sense that one is before the other. The Son is in the Father, and the Father is in the Son; and the same holds true for the Holy Spirit. All the divine persons are equal in power and greatness, for all have the same divine nature.

A divine person has a mission insofar as he proceeds from another divine person and begins to be present in a new way in someone or something else. Thus Jesus said that he was sent into the world by his Father (Jn 8:16, 18). The missions of the divine persons come about in time as the divine persons begin to exist in a new way among creatures. There is an *invisible* mission when the

Son and the Holy Spirit are present in the souls of the just through sanctifying grace. As to the Father, though he dwells in us by grace, still it does not belong to him to be from another, and consequently he is not sent. There was a *visible* mission when the Son was sent into the world by his Father, and when the Holy Spirit descended upon Christ at his baptism and upon the apostles on the day of Pentecost. Since the Father does not proceed from anyone, he cannot have a mission in the defined sense; only the Son and the Holy Spirit can have missions.

Chapter 4

CREATION (1a.44-49)

After he has studied the one God and the three divine persons in the one God, St. Thomas takes up the procession of creatures from God. Creatures came from God by the act of creation; and creation is the subject of this chapter.

The ancient dualists explained the existence of creatures by positing the existence of two first principles: one completely perfect and the other completely imperfect. The completely perfect principle made creatures from the completely imperfect principle. Dualism attempts to explain the perfection and imperfection in the world by a diversity of principles. However, a completely imperfect principle or being is a contradiction in terms. Imperfection is the absence of being; and a completely imperfect being would necessarily be a non-entity.

Some of the ancient dualists saw the creation of the material world as the response of God to a hostile evil principle. Augustine said of them: "They prefer to believe that God was driven, by sheer necessity of quelling the evil one in rebellion against him, to build the bulwarks of a material universe, and thus mingle the goodness of his nature with evil in order to coerce and conquer evil. Now God labors to cleanse and purify the divine nature which is so shamefully polluted, cruelly oppressed, and held captive—and with only partial success despite his pains."[1]

In radical opposition to the dualists, monists explain the world on the basis of a single principle. There are three fundamental forms of the monistic explanation: pantheism, evolution and creation. Pantheism identifies the world with God. There is a materialistic form of pantheism which denies the spirit and spiritual values and identifies God with matter and material forces. A spiritual form of pantheism reduces all reality, even material, to spirit and its activity. The world is conceived as an internal evolution of divine substance. However, pantheism is to be rejected because it identifies the infinite with the finite. God is absolute being, one, eternal and immutable. The world, on the contrary, is obviously multiple, participated, finite, changeable and temporal. Thomas' analysis of the proofs for the existence of God makes these points.

The second monistic explanation of the world is the theory of evolution. The modern theory of evolution arose as the result of the work of the French botanist, John de Lamarck (1744-1829), and, more importantly, as the result of the work of Charles Darwin (1809-82), the English botanist and naturalist. In his *Origin of the Species* (1859), Darwin postulated that living forms result mainly from the variations occurring from generation to generation, usually gradually but sometimes abruptly. Whereas forms unsuitable to the environment tend to die out because they have a relatively poor chance of survival, those forms that do suit the environment tend to be perpetuated through successful individuals. This is the process of natural selection. In its scientific form, the theory of evolution offers a highly plausible explanation of *how* the universe developed; but it does not explain the origin of the universe in the first place.

Creation, the third monistic explanation, is proposed for belief by the Catholic faith and is forced upon us by our reason. The author of the Priestly account of creation in the book of Genesis (1:1-2:3) declares that "in the beginning God created heaven and earth," and that the earth "was void and empty." Probably the author did not think of God as creating from nothing—such an idea was totally unfamiliar to him; but he did have an idea of absolute divine supremacy which is reducible to the idea of creation. In the Apostles' Creed, the Catholic says, "I believe in God, the Father Almighty, creator of heaven and earth." For the philosopher and theologian, creation is the act by which God made all things out of nothing. Whereas a carpenter makes a chair out of wood, God used no raw material to fashion the world. There is no other way to explain the existence of the world. God is an uncaused being, infinite and unique. All else besides God has the characteristics of an effect, that is, of being *ab alio* ("from another"), because it is finite, mutable, contingent and multiple. Hence, prior to the act of creation only God existed; and when he produced beings other than himself, he had to make them out of nothing in the sense that there was no preexisting raw material.

Creation (1a.44-46)

Thomas establishes the fact of creation by appealing to the nature of God. Analysis of the proofs for the existence of God reveals that God is an uncaused being, infinite and unique. All else is finite and multiple. However, the finite and multiple necessarily derives its existence from the infinite and unique. Hence, God created all things other than himself. God himself is the model of his creation; he understands all the ways in which creatures can share and reflect his perfection; in the divine mind there are ideas according to which creatures are produced—as the building is in the mind of the architect; and these ideas, though multiplied by their relation to things, are not something distinct from the divine essence. And if one asks why God created, the answer must be that God acted for himself. This answer does not mean that God created other things in order to acquire something; rather, God created other things in order to share his perfection and goodness with creatures.

Thomas thinks of creation as an act by which God produces the *whole* being of a thing. As the efficient cause of beings other than himself, God necessarily produces them in their entirety and, therefore, from nothing. Creation relates the creature to God who is the principle of its being. The carpenter uses tools or instruments to make a chair; but, according to Thomas, God does not and cannot employ an instrumental cause when he creates. Creation is an action proper to God alone. Perhaps we find a suggestion of this teaching in the Scriptures. The word which is used for creation in Genesis 1 is bārā'. This word is predicated only of the deity in the Old Testament; hence, it indicates a work which is distinctively divine, which no agent less than God can accomplish. Further, creation is an action common to the whole Trinity. Creation is the communication of existence which is to be identified with the divine essence. However, the divine essence is common to Father, Son and Holy Spirit. Nevertheless, one finds an image of the Trinity in rational creatures because one finds in them too the genesis of a mental word in the intellect and the impulse of love in the will. Even in all other creatures one finds a vestige of the Trinity because they reflect the power, intelligence and love of God which are reminiscent of the Father, Son and Holy Spirit.

God did not have to create the world from eternity; indeed, God did not have to create at all. In the matter of creation God was and is free. Nothing constrains him to create this or that creature. Still, God could have created the world from eternity, since his creative power is eternal. However, even a world without a beginning would need a creator. As a matter of fact, we are lead by faith to affirm that the world had a beginning in time. In the beginning, we are told in the book of Genesis (1:1), God created the heavens and the earth.

The Diversity of Things (1a.47-49)

The multiplicity and diversity of things are directly intended by God who desires that all creatures share and represent his perfections in a particular way. The world of creatures shares and represents the infinite goodness of God to a far greater degree than any creature could by itself. So God created the earth and the heavenly bodies, all living things, men, women and angels in extreme variety rather than a relatively few creatures. It follows that there are inequalities among creatures or degrees of being, goodness and perfection; and this by the will of the creator himself. Thus, human beings with their capacity to think are more perfect than animals who lack that capacity. Despite the diversity among creatures, Thomas thinks of them as one world in the sense that all of them display a marvelous unity, being ordered to each other and ultimately to God.

Connected with the diversity of things is the distinction between good and evil. For Thomas, evil is not a thing, an essence, or a nature in itself, as the ancient dualists held; rather, evil is the absence of some good which a person or thing ought to have. Thus, blindness in a man is an evil, because he ought to be able to see; but his inability to fly like a bird is not an evil, because he is not supposed to have wings. It follows that evil afflicts what is essentially good; it is the privation of something good in a subject which is itself good. All evil is either physical or moral. Physical evil, such as death and blindness, is not related to morality, that is, to right and wrong conduct; but moral evil has to do with conduct which is bad or sinful. Moral evil is worse than physical evil because moral evil makes a person bad and turns him or her aside from God.

Good is the cause of evil in the sense that an agent, which is good by reason of its being, causes a privation or a deficiency in something else. For example, a lioness causes evil when she kills a zebra in order to feed herself and her cubs. Actually, this physical evil is reduced to God as its cause, although he does not cause it per se or for its own sake, but incidentally. As the supreme agent and the supreme good, God wills the order and perfection of the universe, and this entails the corruption of some creatures which is a physical evil. So God wills the preservation of predatory animals for the perfection of the universe, and this entails the killing of prey.

In no sense, however, is God the cause of moral evil which withdraws the rational creature from his final end. Moral evil is the total responsibility of the intellectual creature who acts in a sinful manner. God does inflict punishment on the sinner, and this, of course, is an evil. Thomas concludes this discussion by noting that there cannot be a first principle of evil as there is a first principle of good. Evil is the privation of goodness and being. The existence of absolute evil is a contradiction in terms.

Chapter 5

ANGELS (1a.50-64)

In the previous chapter we were concerned with creation, and now we begin to study what God has created. God created three categories of creatures: purely spiritual beings or angels, corporeal creatures such as animals and rocks, and creatures that are both spiritual and corporeal, that is, human beings. Thomas discusses angels first. Angels are created spirits, without bodies, having intellect and free will. The word, angel, means "messenger" and describes not so much the nature of an angel as his function.

Angels are mentioned frequently in the Old Testament. They exist in great numbers (Gn 32:1-3; Dn 7:10); they are members of the heavenly court (Is 6; Jb 1:6; 2:1); and they do God's will (Tb 12:18). In obedience to God's will, they communicate divine messages (Gn 31:11); they destroy and punish (2 K 19:35; 2 S 24:16); and they save and help (1 K 19:5-8). According to the New Testament, Jesus himself accepted the popular belief in angels. For him, angels are spiritual beings (Mt 22:30); they constantly behold the face of the heavenly Father (Mt 18:10); and they will accompany him at his second coming (Mt 16:27). Angels announce his conception (Mt 1:20) and his birth (Lk 2:9-15); they minister to him in the desert (Mt 4:11) and strengthen him in his agony (Lk 22:43); they are prepared to defend him when he is captured (Mt 26:53); and they are witnesses to his resurrection (Mt 28:2-7; Jn 20:12). Some angels have sinned (2 P 2:4; Jude 6). There are ranks and gradations among the angels (Lk 1:19; Ep 1:21; Jude 8-9). The worship of the angels in heaven is the prototype of the worship of the Church (Rv).

The existence of angels has been solemnly taught by the magisterium of the Church. The Fourth Lateran Council (1215), the twelfth ecumenical council of the Church, declared: "We firmly believe and profess without qualification that there is only one true God . . . , the creator of all things visible and invisible, spiritual and corporeal, who, by his almighty power, from the very beginning of time has created both orders of creatures in the same way out of nothing, the spiritual or angelic order and the corporeal or visible universe. And afterwards he formed the creature man, who in a way belongs to both orders, as he is composed of spirit and body."[1]

The Second Vatican Council (1962-65), speaking of the communion of saints, declared: "The Church has always believed that the apostles and Christ's martyrs . . . are closely joined with us in Christ, and she has always venerated them, together with the Blessed Virgin Mary and the holy angels, with a special devotion."[2] In his *Credo of the People of God* (1968), Pope Paul VI includes the holy angels in the heavenly realm where Christ reigns in glory.

One may wonder that Thomas was able to say so much about angels. The reason is that he was able to draw upon the teaching of the Church and the Fathers and employ the philosophical principles bearing upon purely spiritual beings.

The Nature of Angels (1a.50-53)

The existence of angels has been revealed by God. Although reason can demonstrate the existence of God, reason cannot demonstrate the existence of angels. However, reason can explain the sublime fittingness of angels. Thomas holds that the perfection of the universe requires the existence of angels. God made creatures so that they might share and represent the being of God in various ways. Angels reflect the being of God insofar as they are purely spiritual beings, just as God is a purely spiritual being. Thus, we see a gradation among God's creatures: the corporeal, the simultaneously corporeal and spiritual, and the spiritual. Just as the table of atomic weights suggested the existence of certain undiscovered elements, so the gradation among creatures suggests (without demonstrating) the existence of angels. An angel is the missing grade between God and creatures dependent on matter.

Angels are creatures; they have been created by God, for God has created all things other than himself; and the angels continually depend upon God for their existence. Faith teaches us that the angels were created in time, and not from eternity. Thomas believes that the angels were created in incomparably greater numbers than any other creatures. The reason is that angels reflect the divine beauty more perfectly than other creatures do; and so the creation of angels achieves the purpose of creation more effectively than the creation of other creatures. Thomas also holds that each angel is specifically distinct from every other angel, just as human beings are specifically distinct from brute animals. There is only one individual in whom the angelic species is complete. As spiritual beings, angels are incorruptible by their nature.

Angels have no bodies; they do not have to acquire knowledge through bodily senses, as human beings have to acquire knowledge through their bodily senses. According to Holy Scripture, angels sometimes assumed bodily forms. Thomas timidly suggests that the bodies assumed by angels were made of compressed air. Obviously he was only speculating. If the angels walked and talked, they used the bodily organs as instruments; but they did not make the body live or make it their own.

Angels are not in place as bodies are in place; angels do not have the material dimensions of bodies. But angels are in a place when they exercise their power there. So, for example, if an angel stirred up the water of a pool, the angel would be in that place (see Jn 5:4-5). An angel passes from place to place by ceasing to apply its power in one place and by beginning to apply it in another place. Since intellect and will are the roots of an angel's power, an angel can change his place with the speed of thought and desire.

Angelic Knowledge (1a.54-58)

Thomas holds that the angelic act of knowledge is distinct from its nature, existence, and intellect. Only in God are all these the same. Angels have no sense knowledge because they have no senses; they have only intellectual knowledge.

The knowledge of angels is innate. God provides the angels with the knowledge he wishes them to have. Angelic knowledge differs from angel to angel, their intelligible species being fewer and more universal the higher we go in the angelic order of perfection. The knowledge of the angels extends to themselves, other angels, and God. It extends even to individual material things, but not to the future except insofar as angels can conjecture about the future in virtue of what usually happens. An angel cannot know the secret thoughts of a man and his inner acts of free will; these are known only to the man himself and to God. By their natural powers angels cannot know the mysteries of grace such as the incarnation of the Son of God and the elevation of creatures to a supernatural state. These mysteries depend upon the free will of God and can be known only if God reveals them. As a matter of fact, angels come to know these mysteries in the beatifying vision of God.

While angels have a store of innate knowledge, they do not always consider everything they know innately. In this way they are like human beings who do not always think about everything they know. However, angels always consider what is known to them through the vision of God. In this lies their eternal happiness.

The angels do not reason from principle to conclusion. Their knowledge is intuitive. They see at once the implication of any piece of knowledge they choose to consider. There can be no error or falsehood in the natural knowledge of the angels or in their vision of the divine essence. Following Augustine, Thomas accepts the distinction between the "morning knowledge" and "evening knowledge" of the angels. The former refers to the angelic knowledge of creatures as angels know them in the vision of the divine essence. The latter refers to the angelic knowledge of creatures as angels know them in their own nature.

The Angelic Will (1a.59-60)

In accordance with a principle which he developed earlier, Thomas holds that where there is an intellect, there is a will. In other words, where there is an apprehension of the good, there is a tendency or inclination toward the good as something desirable. In intellectual creatures, this tendency or inclination is called the will. The will strains to possess the good and rests in it once it is possessed. Because angels are intellectual creatures, they have wills. In a sense, the will is a blind faculty, depending upon the intellect for its direction. The angelic will is distinct both from the angelic nature and intellect. The will of the angels is free. The intellect can recognize the goodness as well as the limitations of particular things, and the will can choose among them. There is neither a concupiscible nor an irascible appetite in the angels, since both of these presuppose an animal nature which the angels do not have.

Because angels have an intellectual appetite which is the will, they are capable of love which is the fundamental act of the will. The angels love themselves and what is good for them; they naturally love each other because of all they have in common; and they naturally love God more than they love themselves because he is the universal good, and they belong to him.

The Creation of Angels (1a.61-64)

To repeat what was said earlier, angels are creatures; they have been created by God; and they continuously depend upon God for their existence. Faith teaches us that the angels were created in time, and not from eternity. Only Father, Son and Holy Spirit have existed from eternity. It seems that the angels were created simultaneously with the rest of creation so that the universe with all its parts might function perfectly from the beginning. It was fitting that the angels, the noblest of God's creatures, should be created in the noblest of places, which in ancient and medieval cosmology was the empyrean or highest heavenly sphere.

From the first moment of their creation, the angels possessed perfect natural happiness, that is to say, they knew and contemplated God as well as he can be known and contemplated with one's natural powers. But above this happiness there is still another which we look forward to in the future; this is the vision of God whereby we shall see him as he is, face to face, as it were. This vision is beyond the nature of every created intellect. To achieve this supernatural goal, the angels required the grace of God moving the angelic will to seek it. It is likely that the angels were created in the state of sanctifying grace, that they had faith, hope and charity from the beginning. However, they had to use these splendid gifts in order to merit their eternal happiness. The angels were given a choice, a choice between life with God or without him. The choice was made quickly. By a single act of charity, in accordance with the angelic nature which is not given to gradualism, some of the angels merited life with God, never to relinquish it. In proportion to their natural gifts, angels shared in the gifts of grace and glory. The blessed angels can neither sin nor advance in the degree of glory which they have achieved.

As creatures, the angels were able to sin, for the angelic nature and will are not the ultimate measure of right and wrong; God's nature and will are the ultimate norm. The angels were capable of only two sins, namely, pride or the refusal to subject themselves to God, and envy or grief over the good fortune of others. The angels could commit no fleshly sins because they have no bodies. Lucifer, the prince of devils, wished to be like God (Is 14:13-14). Possibly this means that he rejected the supernatural end offered him by God for the created good which he could attain by his own powers. The devils are not naturally evil; they are evil by their perverse wills. The devil and his companions did not sin at the moment of their creation, but immediately afterwards. Possibly Lucifer was, in the natural order, the greatest of all the angels, good or bad, since the greatest of the angels had the most reason for pride. By example, suggestion, or even persuasion, Lucifer was able to draw the other angels into sin. St. Thomas holds that the angels who remained faithful to God outnumber those who rebelled, for sin is something contrary to the angelic nature.

The fallen angels retain their natural knowledge, but their splendid wills are forever confirmed in sin. In their fallen condition, the devils regret the loss of heaven, the salvation of the blessed, the curbs placed on their wicked wills, and the pain of hell. Thomas believes that the fires of hell torture the demons because they somehow limit the activity of the demon's spiritual nature. Even when the demons beset men and women on earth, they carry with them their own gloomy atmosphere and continue to suffer the other penalties of their sin.

Chapter 6

CORPOREAL CREATURES (1a.65-74)

St. Thomas distinguishes three categories of creatures: purely spiritual creatures or angels, purely corporeal creatures such as animals and rocks, and creatures that are both spiritual and corporeal, that is, human beings. Having studied the angels, Thomas now turns his attention to corporeal or material creatures. He is concerned with three things: their creation, their distinction, and their adornment. The treatise on corporeal creatures is really a systematic exposition of the Biblical hexaemeron, the work of the six days of creation recorded in the book of Genesis.

What is to be said about the account of creation in Genesis (1:1-2:4a) and Thomas' exposition of it? The description of creation together with the enumeration of the works of division and ornamentation in Genesis presupposes the same picture of the visible world which is seen in the *Enuma Elish*, an ancient Mesopotamian epic. The order of enumeration in Genesis is obviously schematic and has no reference to the chronological development of the earth, of which the author had no knowledge. The author of Genesis wished to refute the Mesopotamian and Canaanite myths of creation. The author wished to teach that God is the sole creator, the source and origin of all things. He wished to deny the dualism implicit in pagan mythology. He never intended to write a scientific account. Commenting upon this account, Thomas makes it clear that he is not approaching it in search of scientific explanation. Thomas accepted the science of his day and used it to exemplify certain ideas; but his interest as a theologian was centered on a metaphysical truth, that God is the beginning and end of all things.

The Creation of Corporeal Creatures (1a.65)

Certain heretics maintained that the visible world had not been created by the good God, but by an evil principle. St. Thomas insisted that God is the creator of the visible world too, since he is the cause of all being, invisible and spiritual, visible and corporeal. Scripture teaches that God "made heaven and earth, the sea and all that is in them" (Ps 146:6); and after making each kind of corporeal creature, "God saw that it was good" (Gn 1). The visible universe of corporeal creatures was created to share in, and reflect, the goodness and perfection of God.

Thomas explains: "The universe is made up of creatures, as a whole is made up of its parts. If, however, we wish to discover the purpose of some whole and its parts, we shall find, first of all, that the individual parts exist for the sake of what they do, as the eye exists to see. We shall find, secondly, that the less noble parts exist for the sake of the more noble ones, as the senses exist for the intellect, and the lungs for the heart; and thirdly, that all the parts exist for the perfection of the whole, as the matter for the form, for the parts are, as it were, the matter of the whole. Furthermore, the whole man exists for some extrinsic purpose, that purpose being the fruition of God.

"So, therefore, as far as the parts of the universe are concerned, each creature exists for its own activity and perfection; and the less noble creatures exist for the nobler ones, as the creatures which are below man exist for him. What is more, individual creatures exist for the perfection of the whole universe. Finally, the whole universe is ordained to God as its end or purpose, insofar as it imitates, as it were, and shows forth the divine goodness to the glory of God. Rational creatures, however, have God for their end in a special and higher manner, because they can attain him by their own operation through knowing and loving him. And so, it is clear that the divine goodness is the end of all corporeal creatures'' (1a.65.2)

Only God could create corporeal creatures; no creature, such as an angel, could share this power even as an instrument in the hands of God.

The Division and Adornment of Corporeal Things (1a.66-74)

The division and separation of material things began on the first day of the Biblical account of creation (Gn 1:1-2:4a). According to the book of Genesis, the earth was a formless wasteland at the beginning, in the sense that it was covered by darkness and water and lacked plants and animals. God created light on the first day so as to distinguish day and night and render his works visible. God made the firmament on the second day. For the author of Genesis, the firmament referred to the starry heavens and the sky with its air and clouds. He thought of it as a kind of dome separating the waters above the dome from the waters below it. On the third day God gathered the waters below the sky into a single basin so that the dry land might appear. God called the dry land ''the earth'' and the basin of the waters ''the sea.'' On the third day too, the earth brought forth every kind of plant and tree. From this account and from other places in the Bible, we gain a picture of the ancient Semitic cosmogony. In the beginning there was a primordial ocean, the abyss of Genesis 1:2. After God's creative activity, part of this vast ocean became the salt-water seas, and part of it became the fresh water under the earth which wells up as springs and fountains. Part of the primordial ocean is held up by the dome of the sky from which rain descends upon the earth.

The work of adornment began on the fourth day. On that day

God placed the light-giving bodies in the sky, that is to say, the sun, the moon, and the stars. The light that was created on the first day was not the light of the luminous heavenly bodies which appeared only later. On the fifth day God produced the birds of the air and the fish in the waters. Just as the firmament was adorned on the fourth day, so on the fifth day the elements of air and water beneath the firmament were made fruitful with living things. On the sixth day God created terrestrial animals and man, the latter being made in the divine image. All this contributed to the adornment of the earth, the lowest body of all. Finally, on the seventh day God rested from his labor, not as one tired by his work, but as one who ceases from his activity and rests in himself. By the seventh day creation was complete; God created no more creatures; that is to say, he made nothing afterwards that had not existed previously, in some degree, in the first two works. According to Genesis 2:3, "God blessed the seventh day and sanctified it." Of course, God continues to preserve and govern the things he has made. Finally, Thomas asks just what the term, day, in the Biblical account of creation means. Some, according to Thomas, think it is without temporal significance, referring only to the order in which things were made. Others, however, think that the term does have a temporal significance.

Chapter 7

HUMAN BEINGS (1a.75-102)

It remains for Thomas to study the third category of creatures, namely, human beings, who are a composite of spiritual soul and material body.

In the Priestly account of creation (Gn 1:1-2:4a), the author of Genesis sets forth the work of God in six days followed by a sabbath for rest. Thereupon the author tells the story of creation a second time, drawing upon another ancient source, the Yahwist (Gn 2:4b-25). By this repetition, the author wished to teach his readers that men and women are superior to the other things created by God, being made in the divine image and likeness. In this second account of creation, it is the man who gives names to all the cattle, the birds of the air and to every beast of the field. This is the author's way of saying that the man is the lord of them all. The author of Genesis also wished to say that the woman shares in the dignity of the man. She is indeed bone of his bones and flesh of his flesh.

The Second Vatican Council appealed to these passages in Genesis and in other books of the Bible to substantiate its own teaching about men and women. According to the council, Scripture teaches that men and women were created in the image of God, that they are capable of knowing and loving their creator, that they were appointed by him to be the masters of all earthly creatures (Gn 1:26-27; Ws 2:33), in order that they might subdue them and use them to God's glory (Si 17:3-10). Hence, all things should be related to men and women as their center and crown. The council went on to say that each individual is one person, even though he or she is composed of body and soul. The body is good and honorable, being a kind of microcosm of the material world. The soul is spiritual and immortal. By their intellects, human beings surpass the material world. The intellect can know reality with certitude, and not only observable data. By their wills, human beings are free and reflect the divine image in a remarkable way. Human dignity demands that men and women act knowingly and freely. They achieve their dignity when they pursue their end by a spontaneous choice of what is good and employ apt means to that end.[1]

Thomas' theological anthropology is divided into two main sections: the predominantly philosophical exposition of human nature (1a.75-89) and the dogmatic discussion of the creation of the first man (1a.90-102). As far as human nature is concerned, human beings are composed of soul and body. The body was of interest to Thomas only insofar as it was related to the soul. Therefore, in speaking of human nature, Thomas treated of the human soul, its nature, faculties and activity. The discussion of the creation of the first man concludes Thomas' study.

The Nature of the Soul (1a.75-76)

For Thomas, the soul is the first principle of life. It is the difference between a living body and a dead body. A soul vivifies a plant or an animal or a human being. The soul of a person is also the principle of his or her intellectual activity; and it is incorporeal and subsistent. It can exist and operate even when it is separated from the body. The soul of a plant or animal, however, cannot exist and operate independently of its bodily structure. The soul of a plant or animal is not self-subsistent. While the human soul is self-subsistent, it is not a complete human being, as Plato (427?-347 B.C.) held. A complete human being is composed of body and soul. The human soul is not a composition of matter and form, nor is it corruptible, as plant and animal souls are. Human souls and angels are not of the same species, as Origen (185?-254?) held, since each angel differs specifically from every other spiritual substance.

What is to be said about the union of soul and body? The soul, the principle of intellectual life, is the form of the body. Every human being has his or her own soul; and there is not one universal soul for all human beings, as some erroneously thought. There is just one soul in every human being; but the intellectual soul in men and women is capable of the sensitive and nutritive activity of plant and animal souls respectively. There is no other substantial form in human beings except the intellectual soul. The soul is united to its body because the soul derives its knowledge initially through the bodily senses. The human soul is joined immediately to its body, there being no connecting link between the two. The soul is present in the whole body and in every part of the body.

The Faculties of the Soul (1a.77-83)

A faculty is the power of the soul to perform a specific operation. The faculties of the soul are distinct from its essence. There are several faculties of the soul which are distinguished according to the operations which they produce and the objects toward which they are oriented. Some faculties serve the others; in humans, for example, the senses serve the intellect which draws its ideas from the data furnished by the senses, and the intellect serves the will by guiding it. Some faculties, like the intellect and will, are to be found only in the soul; but the vegetative and sensitive faculties are rooted in the composite of soul and body. The latter can be exercised only as long as the composite lasts, that is, until death.

Thomas distinguishes five general categories within the faculties of the human soul: the vegetative, the sensitive, the appetitive, the locomotive and the intellectual faculties. Humans have some faculties in common with plants and animals; but some are proper to themselves. Humans have vegetative faculties in common with plants and animals. The vegetative faculties have, as their primary purpose, the inception and protection of life through generation, growth and nutrition. Humans have sensitive faculties in common with animals. They are the five external senses comprising the senses of sight, hearing, smell, taste and touch, and the four internal senses which are the common sense, the imagination, the estimative faculty and the sense memory. The operations of the estimative faculty and sense memory are analogous to those of the intellect, but they differ by reason of the particular character and material limitations of their objects.

Over and above the vegetative and sensitive principles of activity, men and women have two faculties which are the operational powers of intellect and will, of knowledge and volition. Actually, men and women have two intellects, the passive or "possible" intellect and the active intellect. Both are faculties of the soul. The passive or "possible" intellect is called by this name because it *receives* its knowledge. It is, as it were, a *tabula rasa*, a blank page, on which nothing is written at the beginning of an individual's existence. The active intellect abstracts the universal content of the data presented by the senses and impresses it upon the passive intellect. Perhaps we might compare the active intellect to a secretary who transcribes information from a book (sense data) onto the pages of a notebook (the passive intellect). However, it is the passive intellect which actually knows in virtue of the universal content abstracted from the sense data by the active intellect.

There are several things which seem to be distinct intellectual faculties, but really are not. Memory is one of them. Memory is a function of the passive intellect which preserves the ideas of things. Intelligence and reason do not denote separate intellectual faculties, but rather different acts of the passive intellect. Intelligence is a simple, direct knowledge of the truth, like understanding that the whole is equal to the sum of its parts. Reason is the gradual apprehension of the truth whereby the intellect proceeds from one thing known to another, like reasoning from the contingency of creatures to the existence of God. The higher and lower reasons which Augustine distinguished are not separate faculties. The higher reason, according to Augustine, contemplates eternal truths while the lower reason thinks on temporal things. The speculative and practical intellects are not different faculties; rather, the former designates the intellect insofar as it simply considers the truth, while the latter denotes the intellect insofar as it directs human activity. Synderesis is the habit of the first principles of morality by which we are inclined to do good and avoid evil. Conscience is an act of the intellect, the faculty of knowledge; it is the application of knowledge to act, the practical judgment of the intellect as to what is right and wrong.

Next Thomas turns to the appetitive powers in human beings. In all creatures, he maintains, there is a tendency, a thrust, a driving force toward that which perfects, and is good for, the creature in question. In those things which lack knowledge, this tendency is called a natural appetite. In those things which have sense knowledge, such as animals, this thrust is called a sensitive appetite. In those things which have intellectual knowledge, such as men and angels, this thrust, or driving force is called an intellectual appetite or will. Thus, men and women have two appetites following upon their knowledge: an intellectual appetite or will, corresponding to their intellectual knowledge; and a sensitive appetite, corresponding to their sense knowledge. As a matter of fact, there are two different sense appetites, the concupiscible and irascible appetites. The concupiscible appetite is a simple tendency toward that which is sensed as good and away from that which is sensed as evil. The irascible appetite is a tendency to overcome difficulty or hindrance in attaining the good and avoiding evil.

There can be conflict between the will and the sensitive appetites. Self-control is achieved when the sense appetites obey the will.

The human will necessarily seeks what is good, that is to say, what fulfills desire and affords happiness. However, the will is free to choose among particular goods presented to it by the intellect. These particular goods are not good from every point of view; hence, they do not draw the will irresistibly. The intellect moves the will in the sense that it presents to the will what is good and desirable and moves it as an end. On the other hand, the will moves the intellect in the sense that it applies the intellect to the consideration of this or that object. Thomas finds no reason to distinguish a concupiscible and irascible appetite in the will.

If the human will were not free, then advice, exhortation, commands, rewards and punishment would be useless. Human freedom means the capacity to choose among the means to an end. For example, if one wishes to travel to a distant city, he or she is free to choose between several means of transportation—auto, bus, train or airplane. Free will was given to humans, so that they might choose the means leading to their eternal destiny. If humans choose something that leads them away from their eternal destiny, that is to say, if they sin, they abuse their freedom. There is a difference between freedom of exercise and freedom of specification. Freedom of exercise is the freedom to act or not to act. So, for example, I have the freedom to travel to a distant city or to remain at home. Freedom of specification is the freedom to choose among objects. So, for example, I am free to travel to a distant city by auto, bus, train or airplane. The free will is an intellectual appetite, acting in the light of the knowledge furnished by the intellect.

The Activity of the Soul (1a.84-89)

The activity of the soul proceeds immediately from the faculties of the soul. At this point, however, St. Thomas considers only the activity of the intellect. Because of its ethical significance, the activity of the will and sensitive appetite is dealt with later in the treatise on morals in the second part of the *Summa*.

How does the soul understand material things which are beneath it? The process of knowing begins when we contact a material object through the external senses, that is to say, when we see or hear or touch it. What we sense in this way is singular and concrete. A sensible image or phantasm of the object is produced in the imagination. It is the work of the active intellect to abstract from the phantasm the universal content of this sense data, to make the universal stand out from the particular. So, for example, it is the work of the active intellect to abstract what is common to roses and horses, after we have had experience of them. This common element is represented by an *impressed* species or form which is impressed upon the passive or "possible" intellect by the active intellect. Whereas this form exists physically in the object itself, it exists intentionally or cognitively in the mind. The impression of the impressed species upon the passive intellect enables the latter to produce the *expressed* species or idea. The expressed species or idea is the means by which we know the object. For St. Thomas the universal exists fundamentally or potentially in things and formally in the mind.

Thomas insists that ideas are not that *which* is known; rather, they are that *by which* an object is known, just as light is that by which a material object is seen. The intellect is not directly aware of its own ideas; it is directly aware of that which the ideas represent. Of course, the intellect is capable of reflecting upon its own ideas if one chooses to do so. The intellect can occupy itself with only one idea at a time; but it is capable of understanding the content of that idea at one time, even if it includes several elements. Similarly, the eye can view a single field and see many cows in it without seeing what is in adjoining fields. The intellect arrives at understanding by passing judgments, that is to say, by affirming or denying that such and such is the case. Falsehood can creep into human judgments, as experience testifies. One human being can understand something better than another human being because, Thomas believes, the bodily organs employed by the intellect of the one are better disposed to its activity. We know first in a general way, and then with greater particularity. For example, we know first what a dog is, and then we come to know the different breeds of dogs.

Two or three things remain to be said about the intellect and its knowledge of material things. The intellect knows the universal primarily and directly through the intelligible species; but it also knows the singular secondarily and indirectly through the phantasm from which it abstracts the universal and to which it turns for help in order to understand the universal. Therefore, the intellect is capable of such judgments as "Socrates is a man," because it knows both the universal and the singular, although in different ways. The intellect knows contingent things indirectly, just as it knows the singular indirectly. Finally, the intellect knows the future only if it can be known in its cause. Thus, the intellect can foresee the birth of a baby once a woman has become pregnant.

How does the intellectual soul know itself? The soul knows itself, its nature and its faculties, by its activity. If I have some idea of what it means to understand, I already have some knowledge of the soul and its faculties; and further reflection upon the whole process of understanding will deepen my knowledge. Thomas also recognizes the existence of habits, virtues and vices, in the soul; but these too are known only by the act proper to the habit. In coming to a knowledge of itself, the intellect is aware first of some object other than itself, then of the act by which that object is known, and lastly of the intellect itself through its act. The intellect knows the act of the will and, consequently, the nature of the will from which the act proceeds.

How does the human soul know the immaterial substances above it? Since the intellect is directly dependent upon sense data for its knowledge, it can have no direct knowledge of immaterial substances, such as angels. We can gain some knowledge of immaterial substances by abstracting from the conditions of matter; but such abstraction remains quite imperfect in its results. As an immaterial substance, God is not the first thing known by the human intellect, as some have said; rather, the intellect rises from the knowledge of creatures to the knowledge of God.

Up to this point Thomas was concerned with the knowledge of souls united to their bodies; but now he has a word to say about the knowledge possessed by souls separated from their bodies. He is concerned primarily with the natural knowledge of separated souls and not with the knowledge they have through the vision of God. At the moment of death, the soul is separated from its body; hence, it can no longer acquire knowledge through the senses and phantasms, and its manner of acquiring knowledge is necessarily altered. Separated souls know other separated souls perfectly, for their mode of existence is the same as that of other separated souls; but they have only an imperfect knowledge of angels whose mode of existence is superior. A separated soul knows not only by intelligible species gathered in this life, but also by new species infused by God. Souls separated from their bodies have no natural knowledge of what is happening on earth, but they can learn of affairs on earth from other souls who join them or from angels and demons or even from the Holy Spirit. The souls in heaven have knowledge of earthly affairs through the vision of God.

Thomas does not take up the acts of the sensitive and intellectual appetites at this point. He will discuss these in the second part of the *Summa*.

The First Man (1a.90-102)

Concluding his anthropological study, Thomas takes up the production of the first man. Here Thomas employs the Biblical data to a greater extent. Among other things, the Biblical account of creation in Genesis teaches that human beings are creatures of God, made in his image and likeness; they are the lords of visible creation under God; they are male and female, the woman sharing in the dignity of man, and with her husband she becomes one flesh. In the beginning, Adam and Eve walked familiarly with God, and they were free of concupiscence, a special privilege that transcends the order of nature (Gn 3). But the couple sinned; they fell from grace; and their sin was not theirs only; somehow it infects the entire human race descended from them. For the moment, Thomas is concerned with the parents of the human race as they were before their fall; he will discuss their sin and its consequences later. Speaking of the production of the first man, Thomas argues sometimes strictly, sometimes only plausibly, to complete the picture of man's original state.

Thomas holds that the soul of the first man was not made from the substance of God, for the substance of God is not divisible. The human soul is created by God. There is no preexistence of created souls; the soul begins to exist when it is united to the body for which it is destined. According to Genesis (2:7), "the Lord God formed man out of the clay of the ground and blew the breath of life into his nostrils, and so the man became a living thing." Man's body is material, being made from the clay of the ground, and his soul is spiritual; therefore, man is a kind of microcosm, a little world which is the epitome of the larger world or universe. Thomas holds that the body of the first man was produced immediately by God. God made the human body in accordance with its purpose, which is cooperation with, and service to, the soul. In describing the production of the first man, Genesis indicates that all other things were made to serve him.

According to Genesis 2:18, "it is not good for man to be alone," so God made a suitable partner for him in the person of the woman. Through the union of man and woman God provides for the propagation of the human race. It was appropriate that the first woman should be made from the first man. In this way God conferred a certain dignity upon the first man consisting in this, that as God is the principle of the whole universe, so the first man was the principle of the whole human race. Further, the fact that the woman has come from the man encourages the man to love his wife as part of himself. The first woman was made from the rib or side of the first man to signify the nature of their social union: she was not made from his head to show that she is not supposed to dominate him, nor from his feet to show that she is not supposed to be his slave.

According to Genesis 1:26, God said, "Let us make man to our image and likeness." An image is a copy of something else, resembling it in some specific way. For example, the image of Abraham Lincoln appears on American coins and bills. Men and women are imperfect images of God, who infinitely transcends them, because they have a specific likeness to God in virtue of their spiritual operations of understanding and willing. Angels are more perfect images of God than human beings are. In ascending degrees, the image of God is found in all men and women, in those who have been justified by grace, and in the blessed in heaven, in accordance with their increasing capacity to know and love God. Human beings image both the divine nature and the Blessed Trinity of Father, Son and Holy Spirit. Human beings image the Blessed Trinity, first and chiefly, when they form a mental concept of God and break forth in love for him.

Reflecting on the state of the first man prior to his fall, Thomas holds that the first man did not contemplate the essence of God, as the blessed in heaven do. Had he done so, he could not have sinned as he did. The first man did not have greater knowledge of the angels than we have. Furthermore, he was supplied with all the knowledge necessary for him to lead his life properly, including knowledge of his supernatural end and other truths necessary to attain it. In accordance with the goodness of the primitive state, the intellect of the first man was immune from the evil of error. He was created in grace, and with sanctifying grace he had all the virtues.

Adam and Eve had all the human passions which have good for their object; but they lacked those which presuppose evil, since evil was neither present nor imminent in the primitive state of the human race. Adam's passions were totally subject to reason. Because he possessed the supernatural life of grace, he was capable of meriting in the sight of God, indeed, even more powerfully than after his fall.

In the state of innocence, Adam ruled the animal world and used other creatures, such as plants, without hindrance. In the state of innocence, human beings would have differed in sex, physical proportions, virtue and intellectual gifts; but there would have been no deficiency in any way. There would have been need of a social order in paradise, of rulers and subjects; but there would have been no injustice, no oppression.

Adam and Eve were immortal in their state of innocence and immune from suffering and the ravages of old age. They needed food, for God told Adam to eat from any tree in the garden of paradise except one (Gn 2:16). By eating regularly from the tree of life, Adam and Eve could sustain their physical immortality (Gn 3:22). There would have been generation in the garden of paradise; and generation would have been accomplished by coitus without any disorderly passion. Children born in the state of innocence would have grown up as children do now—through childhood and adolescence to adulthood. Both sexes would have been born for the propagation of the human race. Children of a sinless Adam and Eve would have inherited the righteousness of their parents; but they would have been capable of sin, just as their parents were. In the state of innocence, children would not have been born knowing many things; rather, they would have acquired their knowledge without difficulty through the senses, being taught by others and learning for themselves. Children would not have had the use of reason from earliest childhood, but they would have acquired it gradually. There would have been work in the garden of paradise; and it would have been a source of pleasure.

Chapter 8

GOD'S GOVERNMENT OF CREATION (1a.103-119)

Having studied the different kinds of creatures, St. Thomas now considers God's government of his creatures. God maintains them in existence and directs them to the goal for which he created them. In some cases God acts immediately, and in others he acts through the agency of creatures.

The Government and Conservation of Creatures (1a.103-104)

Just as a well-ordered house reveals the existence of a housekeeper, so the order of the universe reveals the existence of a divine governor. The universe is, in a sense, a community. A community is a group of individuals striving together for a common goal. When individuals strive for separate goals, the result is not a community, but anarchy. Individuals work together for a common goal as the result of government. For example, a football team works together to execute a play because the coach or quarterback has chosen one; but without such direction the players would not know what to do and the result would be confusion. God created and governs the universe for one purpose, that creatures might share his goodness and perfection in some way. There is nothing which is not subject to the government of God, for it is God who maintains all creatures in existence and moves all things, including subordinate causes, in accordance with his will. The plan of government, which we call providence, exists in the mind of God; but in the execution of this plan, God governs some things by means of others. Nothing can thwart the government of God. There is no cause which can impede his action, because there is no cause independent of him. Even the sinner, who seems to defy the government of God, comes within the provisions of God's plan for dealing with sinners. Out of evil God draws good, governing all things well (Ws 8:1).

The first effect of God's government is to preserve them in existence. Preservation in existence maintains what creation began. Just as the song is continually dependent upon the singer if it is to be heard, so the creature is continually dependent upon God if it is to exist. Sometimes God preserves human beings by means of light, air, warmth and food. Of course, God is himself present in these means, so that they can produce their proper effect. God could withhold existence from the things he has made; but, as a matter of fact, he does not do so, since his goodness is manifested by preserving creatures rather than by annihilating them. Even material things are not annihilated in the sense that matter is incorruptible.

God's Movement of Creatures (1a.105)

A second effect of God's government of his creatures is that he moves them. God moves all creatures to act. It is movement deriving from God that rouses creatures from inactivity to activity. But God is not the only cause of movement; creatures too cause movement in other creatures. God is the first cause, and creatures are a second cause, God working through them. God moves some creatures immediately and others through the agency of still other creatures. God moves the created intellect and will immediately.

He rouses the will to act by inclining it to the good. As Paul writes, "It is God who makes us both to will and to do" (Ph 2:13). God moves the created will in a manner consonant with its freedom. Only God can move the will without destroying its freedom. How can he do so? God moves each thing in accordance with its nature, and it is the nature of the will to act freely.

St. Thomas admits the possibility of miracles. A miracle is nothing more than God's action outside the natural order established by him. For example, God can produce the effects of created causes without employing the causes themselves. Thus, God could immediately change water into wine without employing grapes and the natural process of fermentation. Or, to use another example of the miraculous, God could immediately heal a broken limb without any lapse of time. Why would God choose to work outside the natural order? We can think of several reasons: to identify those who speak in his name, to reveal his will to mankind, to answer prayer, and to show his love and mercy. Thus, we recognize Jesus as one sent by God to speak in his name through the miracles that accompanied his teaching. Through a miracle, a power exceeding all the limits of nature makes itself known. One miracle is greater than another to the degree that it surpasses the powers of the created universe.

The Angels' Movement of Creatures (1a.106-114)

God acts through angels upon other creatures in a variety of ways. In this case, God is the first cause of movement and change, while angels are a secondary cause. A higher angel can enlighten a lower angel by manifesting some truth to him, as a teacher enlightens a pupil; but a lower angel cannot enlighten a superior angel, just as a pupil cannot enlighten his teacher. One angel can "speak" to another angel simply by choosing to manifest the ideas in his mind to the other. Of course, such speech is not a matter of sounds. One angel speaks to another by directing his thoughts to the other. No other angel can overhear if the angel speaking wishes to exclude him from the conversation. Neither time nor distance can keep angels from speaking to one another. An angel can even speak to God in order to learn his will for the angel or just to express his admiration.

The angels are divided into hierarchies. Thomas thinks of a hierarchy as a graded or ranked series of individuals under a prince. There are three hierarchies of angels which are distinguished according to their degree of understanding, that is to say, insofar as they know the ideas of things as these proceed from God or from the most universal created causes or from their particular causes. Within each hierarchy there is a diversity of orders arising from a diversity of offices and functions, as there is a diversity of offices and functions in a city. There are three orders in each hierarchy of angels, the highest, middle and lowest orders. Within each order there are many, many angels. With the help of Sacred Scripture we are able to name the following hierarchies and orders (in descending order of rank) among the angels: (1) Seraphim (Is 6:2); (2) Cherubim (Ezk 1; 10:15, 20); (3) Thrones (Col 1:16); (4) Dominations; (5) Virtues; (6) Powers (Ep 1:21); (7) Principalities (Ep 1:21); (8) Archangels (Jude 9); and (9) Angels (mentioned in many places of Scripture). Human beings can be taken up into the angelic orders (Mt 2:30) in the sense that they can merit glory to a degree comparable to that of the angels, even the highest ones.

Thomas holds that the angelic orders are preserved in hell, because the demons retain the natural gifts upon which the orders are based. There is, therefore, precedence among the bad angels, one demon being subject to another. The demons can "speak" to one another, since this ability belongs to the angelic nature which they did not lose. The demons remain subject to the good angels, for superiority is measured by closeness to God.

Thomas was convinced that the angels are active in the visible universe; indeed, he goes so far as to say that God has placed them in charge of all corporeal creatures, such as plants and animals, for God governs the lower through the higher. The superior nature of the angels empowers them to influence the activity of lower, material beings. Angels can move bodies from place to place. The Bible tells us how an angel of the Lord seized the prophet Habakkuk by the hair of his head and carried him with the speed of the wind to deliver lunch to Daniel in the lions' den (Dn 14:36-37). Of themselves, angels can work no miracles, although they can serve God as the instruments of his miracles.

Angels can enlighten human beings by strengthening the intellect and presenting the truth to it in some sensible way. Angels have the power to impress images upon our imagination. In this regard, we think of the angel who appeared to Joseph in dreams (Mt 1:20; 2:13, 19). An angel can also affect our senses with external stimuli. Then the intellect abstracts the idea from the sensible image or phantasm. Of course, we don't always know when we have been enlightened by an angel, even though we experience the effect of his influence. Angels cannot act directly upon the human will, but they can influence it indirectly by presenting desirable images to the intellect or by rousing the passions to draw the will after them. Still, the will ever remains free to consent to, or resist, the passion.

The angels are ministers of God at whose nod and by whose authority they work. One of the ministries of angels is to guard human beings. Each human being has his or her own guardian angel throughout the course of life. The reason is again that God cares for the lower through the higher. Probably each social entity, such as a city or country, has its own guardian angel, so that each individual, who is a member of a larger body, has the protection of more than one angel. The guardian angel does not desert his charge at any time, even when, in the providence of God, his charge suffers some trial or falls into sin. At these moments, the guardian angel does not grieve, because the will of the angel is totally conformed to the will of God.

In their malice, the fallen angels or demons tempt human

beings to sin. Still, not all sins can be attributed to the temptation of the devil, for some temptations derive from unruly human appetites and the world in which we live. Demons cannot perform miracles in the strict sense of the term, but they can perform certain wonderful feats which have the appearance of miracles. In this regard, we think of the feats performed by Pharaoh's magicians with the help of demons. Even when the temptation of the demon has been repulsed, he can return to the attack, but only after the lapse of some time. God's mercy, as well as the craftiness of the tempter, seem to suggest as much.

The Action of Bodies and Humans (1a.115-119)

Through movement ultimately derived from God, one body acts upon another. A saw cuts wood; meat nourishes an animal; a virus causes death. Every body is capable of affecting another body by the very fact that it exists. Every corporeal substance, even a rock, has an activity by which it functions for the purpose assigned to it by divine providence. The direct action of the celestial bodies upon the human intellect and will is impossible; but celestial bodies can influence the intellect and will indirectly by acting directly upon the bodies of human beings. For example, the full moon can influence some persons to act in a strange way. Celestial bodies, like corporeal substances, can have no influence upon the non-corporeal angels and demons. The sun cannot warm an angel.

Finally, Thomas takes up the action of one human being upon another. Surely one person can teach another. To be effective, a teacher must have knowledge of the subject he or she wishes to teach; and the teacher must proceed from what the student knows to what he or she does not know. A human being cannot teach an angel about the things of God; but by means of speech he or she can make known to the angel the thoughts of the heart, something that the angel could not otherwise know. A human person cannot move or affect other corporeal creatures simply by an act of the will. Thus, when her hands are full, a woman cannot open the door to her house simply by willing to do so; rather, she has to put down her packages and use her hands for that purpose. By death the soul is separated from its own body, and so it can no longer move other bodies by commanding its own.

Plant souls and animal souls are derived from matter, and they cease to exist when their bodies perish; but the human soul is not derived from matter; it is immediately created by God, for a spiritual soul cannot come from matter. The human body is generated by parents, and by a single act God creates the human soul and unites it to its body. The soul does not exist until it is united to its body and enlivens it. By the process of nutrition, a man assimilates food into his own living substance, and the living substance produces the seed by which the race is propagated.

The First Part of the Second Part of the SUMMA THEOLOGIAE (1a2ae)

The prologue of St. Thomas to this part states: "Because, as Damascene says,[1] man is said to be made to the image of God, image signifying an intellectual being who is free and self-determining, now that we have spoken of the exemplar, that is, of God, and of those things which have come forth from the divine power according to the will of God, it remains for us to consider his image, that is, man, insofar as he too is the principle of his actions, having free will and control over his actions."

Chapter 9

THE ULTIMATE END OF HUMAN LIFE (1a2ae.1-5)

With this chapter we begin our consideration of the second part of the *Summa Theologiae*. In the first part of the *Summa*, St. Thomas treats of God; and in the second part, he treats of the rational creature's advance toward God. The first part of the second part of the *Summa* considers God as the ultimate end of human activity (qq.1-5) and, in a general way, the human acts by which man tends toward, or deviates from, this end. This general consideration of human acts is divided into two main sections: the section on human acts in themselves (qq.6-48) and that on the principles of these acts, including habits, law and grace (qq.49-114). These larger sections will be further subdivided and considered in the following chapters.

In his preface to the first part of the second part of the *Summa*, St. Thomas writes that the first part was devoted to God, the exemplar of man. Now it remains for him to consider the image of God, that is to say, man. In the first part, God, the supreme intellect and will, was studied as he is in himself and as the principle from which all things flow. In this part, man, the image of God possessed of intellect and will, is studied as the principle of his own activity, with control over his own acts.

In this chapter, we are concerned with Thomas' teaching about the ultimate end of human life, which is beatitude or perfect happiness. Boethius defined beatitude or perfect happiness as "a state made perfect by the aggregate of all that is good."[1] Objectively, beatitude is the supreme good, which is capable of rendering an intellectual creature perfectly happy. In this sense, beatitude refers to God, the uncreated good, who is the cause and object of an individual's perfect happiness. Subjectively, beatitude is the perfect happiness experienced by an individual who possesses the supreme good. In this sense, beatitude is something created, because it is the activity of a creature. Beatitude belongs to God in the highest degree, inasmuch as he knows and loves himself, the supreme good, in an infinite way; and so God is supremely happy. For Thomas, the beatitude of human beings cannot be found in any created good, but only in the vision of God, whereby a man or woman sees God "face to face." Still, beatitude is the ultimate perfection of the whole person and includes the resurrection of the body and its reunion with the soul, the removal of all evil, and the company of the saints.

Reason can take us only so far in this matter. Reason alone enables us to draw the conclusion that beatitude or perfect happiness cannot be found in any created good, but only in the possession of God, the universal good. But faith teaches us that we can and do achieve final and perfect happiness through a supernatural vision of God, which we call the beatific vision. The beatific vision is described in the New Testament as knowledge of God as he is, face to face without a mirror, as vision in contrast to faith (1 Jn 3:2; 1 Cor 13:12; Mt 5:8; 18:10; 2 Cor 5:7). Paul draws a parallel between this knowledge and our being known by God (1 Cor 13:12). All these texts suggest that the vision and knowledge of God in heaven are immediate and clear as opposed to the analogous knowledge of God which is mediated in this world by the knowledge of finite beings different from God. A half century or so after Thomas' death, Pope Benedict XII (1334-42) solemnly taught that through the beatific vision the blessed in heaven see the divine essence plainly, clearly, openly and, as it were, face to face; they take great joy from it, and because of this vision they possess life and eternal rest.[2]

The Ultimate End of Human Life (1a2ae.1-5)

Men and women achieve their eternal destiny by acting in a truly human way. A truly *human act* is one that is performed with knowledge and freedom, one over which a person has control. It is to be distinguished from an *act of man* which is performed without knowledge and freedom, one over which a person has no control, an act such as digestion or involuntary sneezing and coughing. A human act is performed for some reason; it is directed to some goal, to some good. Some creatures are directed to a particular end by nature, as an arrow is directed to a target by an archer; but human beings are able to choose an end for themselves when they act. Men and women act for something desirable either in itself or for another purpose. I may drive an auto simply because I enjoy driving or because I wish to go somewhere. But there is always some goal which is the ultimate explanation of my activity. Actually we are always seeking what is good for us and, in the long run, that which affords complete and enduring satisfaction and fulfillment. Such fulfillment is called *beatitude* or happiness. However, all men and women do not agree where and how this perfect happiness is to be found. In fact, it is to be found only in God, the supreme good.

Thomas was convinced that complete and enduring happiness is not to be found in any created good, even though it may afford a limited measure of happiness for a time. The rich man may rejoice in his wealth; the successful woman in the honor paid to her; the politician in the power he wields; the athlete in his physical prowess; the hedonist in his pleasures; and the scholar in his learning; but all these things afford only a limited measure of happiness; they are more or less transitory; they do not exclude unhappiness in other respects; and those who possess them may lack many another good thing, such as wisdom and health. Perfect happiness or beatitude cannot lie in any created good which always leaves something to be desired. Perfect happiness can be found only in God, the universal good. The horizon of human beings is too broad, their appetites are too extensive to be satisfied with anything less. Our hearts are restless, until they rest in God, as Augustine (354-430) testifies in his *Confessions*.

The happiness of human beings in heaven includes the direct and intuitive knowledge of God on the part of the intellect, and the delight of the will at rest in the possession of the supreme good. Beatitude or perfect happiness supposes the total conformity of the will to God's will. The soul can be happy without the body, since it is able to contemplate the divine essence without the body. However, the reunion of body and soul at the general resurrection will add to the happiness of heaven. In heaven the body will be spiritualized and have no need of the food and drink and other things that serve animal life. The blessed in heaven will enjoy the company of their friends.

While all the blessed find their happiness in God, one finds greater happiness in him than another does. One's measure of happiness is determined radically by one's degree of charity or love. We cannot be truly happy in this life, because we are exposed to too many unavoidable evils; moreover, we cannot have the vision of God in this life. One cannot turn away from God once he or she beholds him in the beatific vision, since the goodness of God is seen too clearly and the happiness it entails is experienced too intensely to be rejected. The vision of God is supernatural and it can be attained only with the help of divine grace. With the help of divine grace a person can act in such a way as to merit the beatific vision.

Chapter 10

ACTS PROPER TO HUMANS (1a2ae.6-21)

By their acts, human beings tend toward, or deviate from, their end. However, the acts performed by human beings are of two kinds: those which are proper to them by reason of the spiritual part of their nature, and those which they have in common with animals by reason of the sensitive part of human nature. Here we are concerned with the former, that is, with those acts which are proper to human beings.

The Bible takes human actions very seriously. Sometimes the works of men and women are characterized as deeds of darkness (Rm 13:12) or deeds of the flesh (Gal 5:19). On the other hand, the followers of Christ are called to fulfill the two great commandments, the love of God and neighbor (Mt 22:36-40), to practice good deeds (Jm 2:14-17), and to build up the Church, the body of Christ (1 Cor 1:9; 15:58). Christians enjoy the great privilege of freedom. They have been freed from sin (Rm 6:18-23), from death, the inevitable companion of sin (1 Cor 15:56-57), from concupiscence (Rm 7:3-25), and from the Jewish Law (Rm 7:3-6; Gal 4:21-31). In the Christian community all enjoy equal freedom through baptism (1 Cor 12:13). The Bible holds human beings responsible for what they do. The prophets of Israel held the prince and people responsible for the good or evil they had done. Ezekiel wrote: "The virtuous man will be credited with his virtue; and the wicked man, with his wickedness" (Ezk 18:20). In the first three chapters of Romans, Paul describes the depravity of the pagan world; and he says that it was the evil will of the pagan world that provoked God's anger upon it. The Bible holds out rewards and punishments to good and evil men respectively. God rewards every person according to his merits (1 S 26:23; Pr 12:14). At the last judgment, the Son of Man will sit on his throne; and he will reward and punish individuals according to their works (Mt 25:31-46).

General Considerations (1a2ae.6-7)

Every truly human act is voluntary. An act is voluntary, when it is freely willed by a human being in the light of the knowledge which he or she has. A voluntary act is one over which a person has control and for which a person is responsible. Thus, a person who reads a book acts voluntarily, because he or she acts knowingly and willingly. But a person who turns over in bed while asleep acts involuntarily. A failure to act when a person can and ought to act is voluntary; accordingly, the failure of a parent to correct an erring child is voluntary on the part of the parent.

Thomas lists four classical impediments to human activity: force, fear, concupiscence and ignorance. *Force* is the external violence which compels a person to do something to which he or she is opposed internally. An external act performed against one's will is not a human act. A person may be forcefully carried from his or her home when he or she chooses to stay. In this case, leaving one's home is involuntary. We are not responsible for what we are forced to do, because in such cases the consent of the will is withheld. Force or violence can make us do something against our will; but it cannot compel us to will what we are forced to do. *Fear* arises from the threat of an impending evil. That which is done out of fear is *simply* voluntary, because the person wishes to hinder a great evil which is feared; but *in a way* the act is involuntary, because the person would have acted differently had he or she not been afraid. As an illustration, Thomas points to a captain who throws cargo overboard in a storm to lighten his ship. In the circumstances, jettisoning the cargo is *simply* or essentially voluntary, although involuntary *in a way*.

Concupiscence is a movement of the sense appetite toward a good that affords pleasure. The sexual drive is an example of concupiscence. Concupiscence, if it draws the will after it, can render an act even more voluntary. On the other hand, concupiscence can render an act less voluntary, if it diminishes knowledge and freedom. Finally, there is *ignorance*. We can distinguish three types of ignorance. Antecedent ignorance goes before our actions and renders them involuntary. For example, a man can take his life involuntarily, if out of antecedent ignorance he takes a lethal drug to cure an illness. Concomitant ignorance affects our actions very little, for even if we had not been ignorant, we would have done the same thing. St. Thomas gives this example: a hunter may kill an enemy whom he wishes to kill, thinking at the same time that he is killing a stag. In this case, the hunter's ignorance is concomitant; and what happens is not *in*voluntary, but *non*-voluntary, since that which is unknown cannot be actually willed. Consequent ignorance is that which we tolerate or even protect, because it allows us to slide out of things. Our ignorance is consequent, when, for example, we neglect to find out the laws that affect us so that we won't be burdened. What we do out of consequent ignorance is voluntary, although there may be some diminution of culpability, because we may not have acted as we did, had we realized what we were doing.

The circumstances of a human act have an important bearing upon the morality of that act. They are extrinsic to the substance of the act, but touch it in some way. The circumstances of an act can be determined by the answers to such questions as: Who did this? What was the result? Where? By what means? Why? How? When? Circumstances affect the morality of an action. For example, the amount of money stolen by a thief determines the gravity of his crime. The most important circumstance is the intention of the one acting, the reason for which the person acted.

Acts Elicited and Commanded by the Will (1a2ae.8-17)

Acts *elicited* by the will are those which proceed immediately from the will itself and are completed in the will. An act of love of God is an elicited act of the will. Acts *commanded* by the will are those which originate in the will and are completed by another human faculty. Eating and drinking are acts commanded by the will. First, then, the *elicited* acts of the will.

Speaking of the elicited acts of the will, St. Thomas describes those which spring from the will as it strives for a goal and employs the means to achieve it. Thomas enumerates six acts of the will: three of them (volition, fruition and intention) are concerned with the goal itself; and three of them (consent, choice and use) are concerned with the means to achieve it. Let us suppose that a lady wishes to buy a new coat. She needs a new coat and the idea of a new one pleases her (volition). Still, she doesn't have the new coat until she buys it; but when she has bought it, she will be glad she has it (fruition). Prior to buying the coat, she must make up her mind to buy it (intention). All these acts of the will have to do with the new coat, the goal which the lady has in mind.

Having decided to buy a new coat, the lady must now employ the means to complete her purchase. She could take a bus or drive an automobile to the department store; she could shop in this store or in that one or in all of them; she could pay by check or pay cash or use a credit card to buy the coat. In other words, she recognizes and accepts the means to accomplish her purpose (consent). Next she chooses among the means available to her. She will drive her auto to the department store where coats are on sale, and she will purchase one with her credit card (choice). Finally, the will applies all the lady's faculties to make her purchase—getting into the car, driving it, selecting the coat and paying for it (use).

St. Thomas looks at each of these elicited acts in some detail. *Volition* is the act of the will by which it seeks some real or apparent good. Volition has to do primarily with an end and secondarily with the means to achieve the end. Because the will seeks an end, it is prepared to take the steps necessary to achieve the end. For example, a sick person who wishes to recover his health is prepared to take the medicine prescribed by the doctor.

The will is moved by the intellect insofar as it presents the good which is the object of the will. The will can be moved by the sensitive appetite insofar as it changes the disposition of the subject. For example, something may seem good to a man who is angered, which does not seem good to him when he is calm. Through its volition of the end, the will moves itself to will the means. The will can be attracted by an external object, as we have seen; but St. Thomas is unwilling to admit any direct influence of the stars upon the will, since the corporeal cannot act directly upon the incorporeal. The will is utterly dependent upon God, the first mover, who rouses it out of its inactivity without impinging upon its freedom. The will tends naturally toward the good in general and all those particular goods which belong to men and women by their very nature, such as life, knowledge, and so on. The will necessarily seeks the perfect good; but it is not constrained to seek any particular good whose deficiency the intellect can always recognize. For example, the intellect can always recognize the advantages and disadvantages of taking a vacation in the summer or winter, of going to this resort or that resort or staying at home, of traveling by this means or that means. Hence, the will is not constrained to choose any of these particular goods. Nor is the will constrained to follow the impulse of the passions, as long as these do not totally suppress the use of reason.

Fruition or enjoyment is the act of the will by which it delights in the actual possession of the longed-for end, as the woman delights in the coat which she has purchased. While the will delights to some degree in the possession of particular goods, especially insofar as these bring one to his or her true end, it delights fully only in the possession of God, the supreme good. Even in the quest for good, there is a certain measure of delight.

Intention is the act of the will by which it proposes to seek an end or goal by using the proper means. For example, a person may say, "I intend to regain my health by taking medicine." The intention may focus upon an intermediate or final goal, upon one goal or several goals simultaneously, provided that they are not incompatible with each other. Quite clearly, a person may wish for something without intending to use the means to achieve it. Thus, a person may wish to be chaste without intending to avoid the near occasions of sin. Intention is characteristic of rational beings only, since they alone can direct their activity toward a goal in a knowledgeable, rather than instinctual, manner.

Having spoken of the elicited acts of the will which focus upon the end, that is to say, volition, fruition and intention, Thomas takes up the acts which have to do with the means to the end; and these are consent, choice and use. However, Thomas singles out and describes one act of the intellect which goes before these acts of the will focusing upon the means. This is the act of counsel. When a person takes counsel, he or she undertakes an inquiry into all the means available to achieve a certain goal. Think of the lady who must decide what she must do to purchase her new coat. We take counsel about matters of free choice and some importance. Counsel is a kind of analysis; it considers the end to be achieved and the means to be employed here and now to achieve it.

Consent is the act of the will corresponding to the act of the intellect which is counsel. Consent is the act of the will accepting the means recognized by the intellect as suitable to the goal; but at this point there is no choice of a particular means. The will gives consent to the judgment of the intellect about the suitability of the means.

Choice or election is the act of the will by which it selects one means to an end in preference to other means that might be available. Think once again of the lady who chooses a particular department store in preference to other ones in order to purchase her coat. The means can be viewed as a goal or an end, but one pointing to a more remote goal. Choice too is always concerned with something that is possible to ourselves. The will is not free with respect to our ultimate end; but no particular goal or end is so perfect as to compel the will to tend to it. Thus, in a particular choice, the will may go either way. This is what is meant by freedom of choice.

Finally, *use* is the act of the will by which it applies itself and other human faculties to the pursuit of a goal by the use of the chosen means. While use is an act of the will, it supposes the direction of the intellect. Use follows choice in the sense that it is the application of the chosen means: means are chosen and then the will sets them in motion.

Commentators on the *Summa* have devised a schema which graphically presents the acts of the intellect and will involved in the double process of making up our minds and carrying out our intentions. As Father Walter Farrell, O.P., writes in his *Companion to the Summa*, "the interaction of intellect and will is like the steady interaction of the different cylinders of the gas engine."

Acts of the Intellect	Acts of the Will
	I
	Order of Intention
	1. *Dealing with the End*
1. Simple Apprehension	2. Simple Volition
3. Judgment Proposing the End	4. Intention
	2. *Dealing with the Means*
5. Counsel	6. Consent
7. Judgment	8. Choice

II

Order of Execution

9. Command	10. Active Use
11. Passive Use	12. Fruition

At this point in his *Summa*, however, Thomas is particularly concerned with the acts of the will and not with the acts of the intellect.

Next Thomas takes up acts *commanded* by the will—those which originate in the will and are completed by another human faculty. Jogging is an act commanded by the will. Reading and writing are acts commanded by the will, and there are many others too. But the matter is somewhat more complicated than it may appear. According to the schema which appears above, command is an act of the intellect and not of the will. Still, Thomas speaks of acts commanded by the will. How can this be? The answer is this: Like a general who commands or directs a soldier to go forward, so the intellect may command or direct the eyes and feet to jog or do something else. Soldiering and jogging are intelligent, directed activities; and they reveal the activity of the intellect. However, the act of the will called choice precedes the actual command and gives it the capacity to move what is subject to command. In this sense, the actions of the other human faculties are said to be commanded by the will. To command is really an act of the intellect which presupposes, however, an act of the will.

The command and the commanded act are one human act, just as a whole is one, yet many in its parts. Even other acts of the intellect and will can be commanded. So, for example, the intellect can command prayer and renunciation. In varying degrees the acts of the sensitive appetite are subject to command; but the acts of one's vegetative nature are not. The members of the body are obedient to the commands of reason. As Augustine writes: "The mind commands a movement of the hand, and so ready is the hand to obey, that one can scarcely discern obedience from command."[1]

Morality (1a2ae.18-21)

Next St. Thomas takes up the ethical aspects of human acts. He treats of the moral goodness and badness of human acts and their essential relationship to merit and guilt, reward and punishment.

Without stating it in so many words, Thomas works with the principle, *Bonum ex integra causa, malum ex quocumque defectu.* This principle means that goodness springs from wholeness, while evil is the result of some deficiency. In other words, an action is good if it is good in every respect, while an action is evil if it is defective in some way. The sources of goodness and badness in a moral action are the object of the act, its purpose, and the circumstances that surround it. The primary goodness or badness in moral actions is derived from the object. The object of an act is its subject matter, the act in itself. The object has to do with the essential goodness or badness of the action itself. Honoring one's parents is an essentially good action; abusing a child is an essentially bad action. Sometimes the object of an action is essentially indifferent, like wearing black or brown shoes. In this case we must look to the circumstances of the action and the intention of the agent to determine the morality of an action.

The circumstances give an added moral dimension to an action morally specified or unspecified by its object. For example, stealing is an evil act, but the amount of money stolen, an important circumstance, determines the gravity of the theft. A circumstance can change the character of an act by introducing a new element. Thus, stealing a *sacred* object changes the character of a theft by adding the element of sacrilege. The circumstances of an action have to do with such matters as the identity of the person who acts, the place where he or she acts, the means he or she uses, the time and the purpose of the action. The intention of the agent is one of the circumstances of a human act, but it has a special prominence because it prompts the action.

As we have said, one source of goodness and badness in moral actions is the object of the act, the act in itself. An act is good by reason of its object, if it is in accord with reason; and it is bad by reason of its object, if it is not in accord with reason. An action which is good by reason of its object becomes evil, if the intention of the agent is evil. Thus, if I help a poor person out of pride, my act ceases to be a good act (Mt 6:1-4). Sometimes an act is neither morally good nor morally bad by reason of its object, like wearing black or brown shoes. Such an act is said to be morally indifferent. But when a person performs such an act, the act loses its indifference and becomes morally good or bad in virtue of the circumstances that surround it and the intention of the agent performing it.

While we can distinguish the interior act of the will and the exterior act commanded by the will, in reality they go to make up one complete moral action. Sometimes, the purpose of the one who acts coincides with the object of the exterior act, as in the case of one who gives an alms to help a poor person. Sometimes, however, the purpose of one who acts does not coincide with the object of the exterior act, as in the case of one who steals in order to commit adultery. In the latter case, the wrong-doer is more adulterer than thief.

For Thomas, reason is the immediate norm of morality in the sense that what is reasonable is good, and what is unreasonable is bad. However, reason is the norm of morality only to the degree that it reflects the eternal law of God. (Thomas will have more to say about this later on.) Conscience is the judgment of reason about the goodness or malice of a proposed course of action. When the will acts in accordance with conscience, the act is morally good; but when the will does not act in accordance with conscience, the act is morally bad. An inculpably erroneous judgment about the morality of an action does not vitiate the goodness of the will; but a culpably erroneous judgment does.

Moral good and evil depend primarily upon the will; however, the external act does, for better or worse, bring the interior act of the will to its natural conclusion and perfection. Still, there are external actions which are evil in themselves by reason of their objects; and the good intention of the will cannot render them good. For example, one who robs a bank to help the poor is nonetheless guilty of theft. An external act can increase the intensity of the will act. And it can have other consequences too, consequences that follow naturally from an external act and in the majority of cases cannot be disowned. On the other hand, if the consequences follow by accident and seldom, they are not imputable. Thus, a man who drives his auto at a reckless speed is morally responsible for an ensuing wreck; but a man who drives his auto at a safe speed is not morally responsible for an ensuing wreck.

An act is good insofar as it conforms to right reason and the eternal law of God; and it is sinful insofar as it does not. Morally good acts are worthy of praise, and morally evil acts are worthy of blame. Human acts are meritorious or demeritorious insofar as they are good or evil. Every human act, both good and bad, acquires merit or demerit in the sight of God.

Chapter 11

THE PASSIONS (1a2ae.22-48)

Having discussed those actions which are proper to human beings, Thomas now studies those actions which are common to human beings and animals. Thomas calls these actions passions; moderns call them emotions. Thomas' study of the passions or emotions is largely psychological, although he pays some attention to their ethical, metaphysical and theological dimensions. Initially, Thomas considers the passions in general—their subject, the differences between them, their morality, and their mutual relationship. Then he takes up the individual passions of the sensitive appetite, those of the concupiscible part and those of the irascible part. In this connection, he considers their nature, causes, effects and ethical significance.

The Passions in General (1a2ae.22-25)

Passion is the movement of the sensitive or animal appetite in a human being. The passions are rooted ultimately in the soul, since the soul is the ultimate principle of human activity. Proximately, however, the passions are rooted in the sensitive appetite, which human beings have in common with animals. Like all sense activity, the passions involve some bodily changes. A man will flush with anger; his face will glow with excitement; he will tremble with fear. Similarly, an animal may growl when threatened or freeze with fear. The passions presuppose the knowledge of the senses and follow upon it; they are movements of the appetitive part of human beings, and more properly of the sensitive, rather than the intellectual, part. The passions are an integral part of human nature, as they are an integral part of an animal's nature. A passion is a response to a stimulant; and it is something active rather than passive, even though the term, passion, seems to suggest *being acted upon*. All the passions start from love or hate and terminate at delight or sorrow.

Thomas distinguishes the passions of the concupiscible appetite from those of the irascible appetite. The former have to do simply with some sensible object apprehended as good or evil, no other consideration coming into play. The passions of the concupiscible appetite are love, hate, desire, flight, delight and sorrow. Delight, for example, arises in the concupiscible appetite when a person possesses some sensible, good object, such as a warm coat in winter. The passions of the irascible appetite have to do with some sensible object apprehended as good or evil, but under the aspect of difficulty or arduousness, as difficult to obtain or avoid. The passions of the irascible appetite are hope, despair, daring, fear and anger. Fear, for example, arises in the irascible appetite when a person is confronted by an evil that is difficult to avoid. Thus, a person may experience fear of catching a contagious disease. With the exception of anger, all the passions are paired off with a contrary passion with respect to good and evil. Some passions, like love and delight, have reference to the same object, but in a different way.

We can understand the passions of the concupiscible appetite by the reactions of a lady who is driving her auto in the heat of a summer day. She sees one sign advertising a cold drink and another sign advertising a hot drink. At that moment, a cold drink appeals to her (love), but a hot drink repels her (hate). She stops her car at a restaurant, because she craves a cold drink (desire); but she does not enter the restaurant, because it is too crowded (flight). So she goes to another restaurant where she orders and enjoys her cold drink (delight). If her cold drink had been warm, she would have been sorry (sorrow).

In the concupiscible appetite, therefore, there are six passions or operations: (1) love is the tendency of the appetite toward the good, while (2) hate is the aversion of the appetite from evil. (3) Desire is the inclination of the appetite to the good apprehended as absent, but future, while (4) flight is the aversion of the appetite from evil apprehended as absent, but future. Finally, (5) delight is the repose of the appetite in the apprehension and possession of the good, while (6) sorrow is the grief caused by the apprehension and presence of evil.

The following schema illustrates the relationship of the passions of the concupiscible appetite to their objects and each other:

Concupiscible Appetite

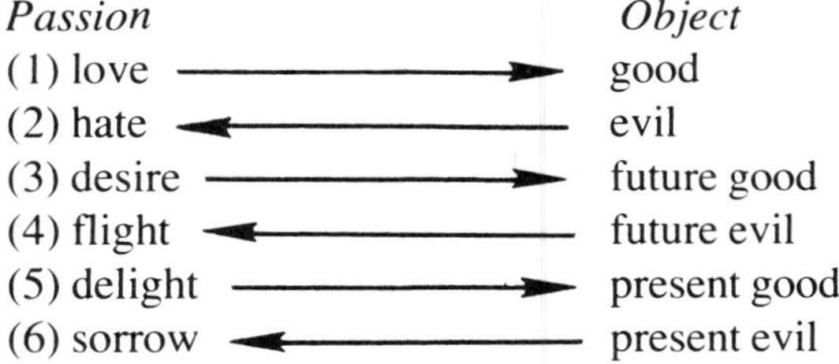

The arrows indicate the appetite's motion toward (——►) or retreat from (◄——) the object.

We can understand the passions of the irascible appetite by imagining ourselves in one of the game parks of Africa. Let us suppose that a cheetah is stalking an antelope to secure food (hope). When the cheetah chases the antelope, the prey escapes and the cheetah gives up the chase (despair). Let us suppose that in another part of the park a wildebeest is attacked by wild dogs. The wildebeest may choose to fight (daring) or to run away (fear). All the animals in the park are protected from poachers who are punished by the state (anger).

Thus, there are five passions or operations in the irascible appetite: (1) hope is the movement of the appetite toward a good apprehended as difficult, but possible to obtain, while (2) despair is the retreat of the appetite from the good apprehended as impossible to obtain. (3) Daring or boldness is the movement of the appetite in response to an evil apprehended as terrible and imminent, but superable, while (4) fear is the retreat of the appetite from an evil apprehended as terrible and imminent, but insuperable. Finally, (5) anger is the inclination of the appetite to inflict punishment on a guilty party.

Irascible Appetite

Passion		*Object*
(1) hope	⟶	arduous, absent, *possible* good
(2) despair	⟵	arduous, absent, *impossible* good
(3) daring	⟶	arduous, absent, *superable* evil
(4) fear	⟵	arduous, absent, *insuperable* evil
(5) anger	⟶	inflicts punishment on a guilty party

In themselves, the passions are neither morally good nor morally bad; they are movements of an essentially irrational appetite. For example, we cannot say immediately that love and desire are good, and hate and flight are bad. The passions are good or bad in virtue of their relationship to the will. When they are under the control of the will and directed to a good object (one in accord with reason), they are good. When, however, they are under the control of the will and directed to a bad object (one not in accord with reason), they are bad. Thus, a husband's desire for his own wife is good, but his desire for another man's wife would be evil. The orderly activity of the passions contributes to a person's moral perfection. It belongs to his or her moral perfection to be moved to the good not only in respect to the will, but also in respect to the sensitive appetite.

The Passions of the Concupiscible Appetite (1a2ae.26-39)

Having looked at the passions in general, St. Thomas next considers the passions of the soul in particular, and first those of the concupiscible appetite. At the very root of the passions are love and its opposite, hate.

Love is something pertaining to an appetite, since good is the object of both. However, there are three kinds of appetites. First, there is the natural appetite of things lacking knowledge, like plants, for the things that are suitable to them according to their nature. Thus, plants have a natural appetite for minerals and water, and the tendency of the appetite toward these things is called a natural appetite. Then there are the movements of love in the sensitive appetite and will following upon the apprehension of some sensible or intellectual good, as the case may be. These two kinds of love involve knowledge and awareness in the subject itself. Consequently, love may be understood as a passion, as a movement of the concupiscible appetite, or, in a wider and extended sense, as a movement of the will.

Thomas distinguishes the love of concupiscence from the love of benevolence (which he calls the love of friendship). The love of concupiscence is the love of a person or object for the good which they can bring to the one who loves. A patient may love his or her physician simply because he is able to effect a cure. This is the love of concupiscence. The passion of love is always of this type; and rational love, the response of the will to good, can be of this type. However, the love of friendship loves another simply because it finds in him or her another self. It is the kind of love that can exist between God and human beings, among the members of a family, between neighbors, and in other cases too. Love of friendship can exist only in the will.

There are three causes of love. The first cause is the goodness of the object which is loved. A woman may love her pet because of the companionship it affords. The second cause of love is knowledge, for the good cannot arouse the appetite unless it is known. Thus, one cannot love beautiful music unless he or she has heard it. Finally, similarity begets love. A creature necessarily loves itself; hence, it is natural for it to love what is similar to itself. We love the members of our families because we have so much in common. Love cannot be caused by any other passion; rather, love is at the root of all the other passions, because all the other passions suppose complacency in some good, which is characteristic of love.

What are the effects of love? One of the effects of love is union, because love moves a person to desire and seek the presence of the beloved whom he regards as another self. A second effect of love is a kind of inherence whereby the beloved is in the lover, and the lover is in the beloved. John said, "He who abides in love abides in God, and God in him" (1 Jn 4:16). A third effect of love is a kind of ecstasy whereby someone is carried outside oneself insofar as one's affection is centered on one's friend. A fourth effect of love is zeal, which attempts to exclude everything that is opposed to the good of a friend. Zeal resents what is hurtful to our friends. Love of a suitable good perfects the lover; but love of a good which is unsuitable to the lover wounds and worsens him. Every agent, whatever it be, always acts out of love of some kind, for every agent acts for an end, which is the good desired and loved by each one.

Just as the object of love is the good, so the object of *hate* is what is evil. Hate arises from love, for we hate that which is opposed to that which we love. We hate sin because we love God. Love is stronger than hate, because the effect cannot be stronger than its cause; and, as we have said, hate arises from love. Sometimes, however, hate is felt more keenly than love and so seems stronger. Properly speaking, it is impossible for someone to hate herself, for she naturally desires what is good for herself; but sometimes she can seek what is evil for herself, because it appears to be good. Someone can hate the truth insofar as it is repugnant. Hate can be directed to everything of a certain kind, as sheep hate all wolves, to use the example of St. Thomas.

Desire is a craving for a sensible good which is not possessed. It is an act of the sensitive appetite. Because desire is concerned with an absent good, it is a passion specifically distinct from love (whose object is good in general) and joy (whose object is the good which is possessed). Corresponding to the passion of desire in the sensitive appetite is the act of desire in the intellectual appetite or will. Natural desires reach out for the goods nature must have, such as food, drink and the like; yet, men and women are capable of acquiring an infinite number of other desires, like those for fame, wealth, social position and power.

Unexpectedly, Thomas omits consideration of the passion of *flight* or aversion, possibly because his remarks about the irascible passion of fear will be, for the most part, applicable to flight. In any event, flight is the turning away of the appetite from the disagreeable or evil. We simply do not like it. We might think once more of the lady who did not enter the restaurant because it was too crowded. Mice and snakes and cockroaches might arouse similar feelings of aversion. Quite clearly, these feelings of aversion can be accompanied by a bodily reaction, such as a disgusted look or a shrinking back from the disagreeable object.

Delight or pleasure is a passion of the sensitive appetite. It is the reaction of the appetite to the possession of a material good. The child experiences delight as it eats a piece of candy; the couple experiences delight upon the birth of their baby; and the actor delights in the applause of an audience. The intellectual appetite, the will, delights in the possession of an intellectual good; but St.

Thomas reserves the name of joy for this kind of delight. In themselves, spiritual joys are far greater than anything the senses have to offer, because they are more noble and enduring. For example, the joy of friendship is more noble and enduring than the pleasure of eating. Still, for many of us sensible pleasures are usually greater, because they are more known to us. If we compare sensible pleasures, it seems that the pleasures of touch are the greatest, as in the case of eating and sexual union. Some pleasures are natural, as in the case of eating, some are unnatural, as in the case of a homosexual union. In other words, even a corrupt action can sometimes bring delight or pleasure.

What are the causes of delight or pleasure? St. Thomas enumerates several. There is real delight in the exercise of our faculties; and what we do well, we enjoy doing. Those who play golf well, those who swim well, those who play the piano well—all these derive great pleasure from their activity. Change is a cause of pleasure by coping with satiety and sparking interest in new things. Travel can have this effect. Hope and memory can be a source of delight or pleasure. For example, those who look forward to a vacation and those who look back to one can experience pleasure. Even sadness or sorrow can be a cause of pleasure. Sadness brings to mind that which is loved, but absent; and yet the mere thought of it gives pleasure. So too the recollection of deliverance from that which caused sadness affords pleasure. The action of another may cause pleasure, insofar as we obtain some good through the action of another. Doing good to others causes us pleasure, for whatever we do or suffer for a friend is pleasant, because we look upon a friend as another self. Likeness causes pleasure, because human beings enjoy association with their kind, as young people enjoy being with young people. Things that arouse wonder are a source of pleasure, because they give a pleasing knowledge of striking facts together with a desire for further knowledge.

What are the effects of delight or pleasure? One of the effects is a certain expansion of the human spirit so that, as it were, one's heart overflows (Is 60:5). Another effect of delight or pleasure is the desire that it may continue. This is especially true of spiritual pleasures, although bodily pleasures, such as eating, may become disagreeable if they are carried to excess. The joy that is involved in using our minds facilitates mental activity by fostering greater attention; but bodily pleasures can impede mental activity, as in the case of drunkards. A final effect of delight or pleasure is the improvement of our work, for we work better when we enjoy what we are doing.

Certain pleasures are good, and certain ones are evil. The difference between the two has to do with the object that affords pleasure. Thus, the pleasure derived from legitimate sexual union is good, but the pleasure derived from illegitimate sexual union is evil. The joy that awaits God's rational creatures at the end of their lives, when they see God face to face, is the greatest human good of all. The objects in which a person delights reveal the moral character of an individual. The good person delights in virtuous works; the bad person, in evil ones.

Sorrow or sadness is to be found both in the sense appetite and in the will. The passion of sorrow is the reaction of the sense appetite to the presence of a particular evil. Often the existence of sorrow is reflected in the face and demeanor of one who is sad. Most of our sorrows are opposed to the passion of pleasure. The desire for pleasure is stronger than the desire to avoid sadness or pain, because one flees evil only because it is opposed to the good. Interior sorrows are more intense than exterior ones, because they affect the appetite more directly, and not only indirectly through the body.

What are the causes of sorrow or pain? The presence of a particular evil rather than the loss of some good is more properly the cause of sorrow. Sometimes the frustration of a desire can be the cause of sorrow, as in the case of a business executive who is denied a promotion he was seeking. St. Thomas says that the natural craving of a creature for the integrity of its being, as opposed to its division and corruption, is a cause of sorrow. Sorrow also results when the will or the sensitive appetite resists a stronger power. As an example, we might think of a swimmer who wishes to swim in one direction, but is swept in a different direction by a strong current.

What are the effects of pain or sorrow? One of the effects is to deprive a person of the capacity to learn. A severe toothache, for example, can prevent a person from studying. A second effect of sorrow or pain is a sense of being burdened and depressed. A third effect is to impede activity, just as pleasure improves it. Generally we do better when we act with pleasure than with sorrow. Thus, we derive greater benefit from reading when we find it interesting than when we find it dull. St. Thomas considers sorrow to be more harmful to the body than the other passions of the soul.

What are the remedies for sorrow or pain? Just as weariness is relieved by rest, so sorrow, no matter what the cause, is relieved by pleasure of any kind. Thus, a sick person is cheered by good news. Tears and weeping mitigate sorrow and pain, because they afford a measure of release from the hurt, which hurts even more if we keep it shut up. The sympathy of friends relieves the burden of sorrow, since they seem to carry the burden with us and show that we are loved, a pleasurable experience. The contemplation of truth, which Thomas regards as the greatest of all pleasures, mitigates sorrow, just as any pleasure does. Finally, an immediate and practical remedy for sorrow is sleep and a bath.

In itself, sorrow is an evil. Still, it is a sign of a good person, if he or she is in pain or sorrow on account of the presence of evil. Sorrow can be useful, when it leads one to avoid what is evil or what is an occasion of evil. Thus, sorrow for sin is useful, when it leads one to avoid sin. Bodily pain may at times seem to be the greatest of evils, because it is so repugnant to human nature; but that which harms the soul, like sin, is worse than that which afflicts the body.

The Passions of the Irascible Appetite (1a2ae.40-48)

The passions or emotions of the irascible appetite have to do with some sensible object apprehended as good or evil, but difficult to obtain or avoid. The five passions of this appetite are hope and despair, daring and fear and anger. There are corresponding movements or acts of the will. With the exception of anger, the passions of the irascible appetite are grouped in pairs: one seeks the thing, while the other surrenders before it. Hope, for example, seeks the good despite its difficulty; but despair gives up on it.

Hope is a passion of the irascible appetite. One hopes for some good thing that is difficult and arduous to obtain, for as St. Thomas notes, we do not speak of anyone hoping for trifles, which can be had at any time. Hope presupposes desire, since the wish or longing for something goes before the surge of hope. For example, we desire a particular career, before we hope to follow it. There is even a kind of hope in animals, as we see in a dog pursuing a rabbit or in a hawk pursuing a bird.

Despair, on the other hand, is not the mere absence of hope; rather, it is the retreat of the appetite from the good which is impossible to obtain. Despair is contrary to hope, as withdrawal is to approach. Perhaps the fox in Aesop's fable illustrates the point. As we know, the fox disparages the grapes as sour, when he could not reach them.

What are the causes of hope? Experience is a cause of hope. The more experienced a person is, the more easily he or she can do something. Moreover, experience often reveals possibilities, which otherwise would have remained hidden. An educational experience in a school or college can have this result and arouse hope. Sometimes, however, experience discloses what is impossible, and so it causes a lack of hope. Young people and drunkards abound in hope: young people, because they have not experienced many setbacks; and drunkards, because their judgment is blurred. Hope causes love, in the sense that we begin to love someone from whom we hope for some benefit. Hope intensifies our efforts in pursuit of some object, and it affords pleasure which is also conducive to action.

Fear is a passion of the irascible appetite which recoils in the face of an imminent and grave evil, one that can hardly be resisted. There is a corresponding emotion of fear in the will too. There is a natural fear which shrinks from whatever corrupts one's nature; so, for example, there is a natural fear of death or the loss of a limb. But there is also an acquired fear, whose object is an evil opposed to a good we have learned to love and desire. In this way, one may fear the loss of his job or good name.

What is the object of fear? As a movement of the irascible appetite, fear has evil for its object. However, one can fear the loss of the good, which is a kind of evil, or even the good itself, which may be able to inflict punishment. Thus, a person may fear God who punishes sinners. That which corrupts our nature, such as death, can be an object of fear, if it is imminent. The evil of sin, properly speaking, cannot be an object of fear, because it lies in our power either to sin or not to sin. Fear itself can be feared. Unusual and sudden things are especially feared, because they seem greater and deprive a person of the chance to seek a remedy. Those evils, for which there is no remedy, inspire the greatest fear because of their seemingly endless duration.

What is the cause of fear? Thomas regards love as the cause of fear. Because we love some good object, we regard as evil, and fear, that which can deprive us of that good object. For this reason, we fear a contagious disease, because it can deprive us of health and even life, which we love. A lack of personal resources, such as wealth, strength, power and a multitude of friends, can inspire fear, because we seem to be more vulnerable in these circumstances.

What are the effects of fear? Thomas holds that one effect of fear is a certain contraction of spirit or withdrawal into oneself.

Fear makes one more willing to seek advice. It may cause one to tremble. However, a moderate fear can stimulate productive activity. Think of the student who pays more attention to her studies for fear of failing the examination.

Daring or boldness is contrary to fear. Whereas fear turns away from some terrible and imminent danger, daring strives to overcome the danger. Daring results from hope, since one attacks the threatening object boldly through hope of overcoming it. Whatever stimulates hope and reduces fear automatically contributes to daring. The passion of daring may not be as enduring as the intellectual motion of daring, because the latter can be more circumspect and thus successful in dealing with the evil at hand.

Anger is a passion of the irascible appetite which seeks to punish the one by whom we have been offended. It is concerned with the punishment to be inflicted and the person who is guilty. Since anger is not concerned with trifling matters, but with matters of some magnitude, it pertains to the irascible appetite, and not to the concupiscible appetite. So that justice is preserved, reason has to draw a comparison between the injury done and the satisfaction to be demanded. The difference between hatred and anger is that hatred wishes evil as evil, whereas anger wishes evil as a means of just punishment. Anger becomes unjust when it inflicts excessive punishment.

The motive of anger is always some injury done to the one who is angry; otherwise, there would be no reason for anger. The real root cause of anger is another's contempt for us. Excellence makes a person prone to anger. The more a person excels in some respect, the more he or she is offended by a slight in that regard. Unmerited contempt more than anything else provokes anger; and the insignificance of the person with whom we are angry tends to increase our anger, because that person has less reason for despising us.

What are the effect of anger? One of the effects is pleasure, in the sense that the angry man finds pleasure in the thought and hope of punishment for the guilty party. Anger often produces a physical reaction: the blood rushes to the face, the eyes flash, and the body tenses. Obviously, anger can upset the judgment or reason, if it is not controlled. We can become so angry that we become speechless.

Chapter 12

HABITS (1a2ae.49-89)

After considering the acts proper to human beings and the passions, Thomas considers the principles of human acts. They are intrinsic and extrinsic to them. The intrinsic principles of human acts are the human faculties and habits. Thomas discussed the human faculties in the first part of the *Summa*; so now he takes up habits. He will take up the extrinsic principles of human acts later.

Habits in General (1a2ae.49-54)

Thomas' treatise on habits in general deals with the nature of habits, their subject in the human soul, the cause of their formation, growth, and corruption, and finally the distinction and division of habits.

Thomas places habits within the general category of quality. A habit is a quality which disposes a person for better or for worse either in regard to himself or to another. An entitative habit, such as beauty or health, affects the nature of its possessor. On the other hand, an operative habit, such as speaking a foreign language or habitually lying, influences the activity of the possessor. Three conditions are necessary for the possession of a habit: first, that the subject of a habit be capable of further development; second, that he or she be capable of developing in several ways; and, third, that a number of factors play a role in this development. For example, we see these conditions verified in the development of a young person's character. A young person is capable of developing many different personality traits; and many factors, such as family background, schooling, and social relationships, play an important role in this development. Under these circumstances, the young person develops habits which influence his or her actions for better or worse.

Certain habits, such as health and beauty, the so-called entitative habits, can modify the body; but these are more like habitual dispositions, since they are relatively unstable. Those habits which affect the actions of human beings are found in the soul and above all in the faculties of the soul, for these are the source of human activity. Habits are to be found in the sensitive powers of a person, insofar as these are subject to the direction of reason. The intellect is the subject of habits called intellectual virtues. Habits in the will are the moral virtues and vices. Angels have habits too, because they are creatures with intellects and wills.

How are habits formed? Nature and temperament can dispose an individual to certain habits. Thus, some people are naturally inclined to be extroverts, while others are naturally inclined to be more reserved. Personal acts can engender habits; for example, the studious person has learned the habit of study by studying faithfully. One act does not cause a habit; only the repetition of acts does. Thus, one becomes an habitual liar by telling lies repeatedly. What has been said about the formation of habits up to this point is true of the natural order; but in the supernatural order there is a whole range of habits, which are not acquired by our actions, but are infused by God. These are the supernatural habits of grace and the virtues. These habits help human beings achieve their supernatural destiny. When an infant is baptized, the child is adorned with the whole panoply of supernatural virtues, even though the child is not yet able to exercise them. So, too, the adult sinner puts on the whole armor of supernatural virtues at the moment he or she repents and makes a confession of sins.

How do habits grow? Habits grow in two ways. A habit, such as purity or justice, can grow by taking deeper root in the subject, so that it can be eradicated only with greater difficulty. An intellectual habit can also grow by extension to more objects. Just so one's science can grow by extending to more objects. Habits grow by acts which are more intense than the habit itself. For example, a habit which has an intensity of 5 grows by an act having an intensity of 6. Habits are corrupted or weakened by contrary habits. Even mere neglect or laziness can weaken a habit. Thus, the habit of generosity can be weakened by a repeated failure to give to others; and one can lose the ability to speak a foreign language by a lack of practice.

Many habits can be located in the same subject. Thus, the intellect can be the seat of various sciences. Habits are distinguished according to the subject in which they are located, as justice, which is located in the will, is distinguished from fortitude, which is located in the irascible appetite. Habits are distinguished according to their objects, some having to do with knowledge, and others with goodness. Finally, we must distinguish between good habits or virtues and bad habits or vices.

Virtues (1a2ae.55-67)

Since habits are either good or bad, Thomas proposes to speak in the first place of good habits or virtues and in the second place of bad habits or vices. Speaking of virtues, Thomas discusses the nature of virtue, its subject in the human soul, the kinds of virtue, the cause of virtue, and certain properties of virtue. In this matter, Thomas draws not only upon the *Nichomachean Ethics* of Aristotle, but also upon Biblical and patristic sources.

Virtue is a certain kind of habit, namely, a good habit. Aristotle said, "Virtue is that which makes its possessor good, and his work good likewise."[1] We may say further with Peter Lombard, "Virtue is a good quality of the mind by which men live rightly, one which they cannot use badly, and, in the case of the infused virtues, one which God puts in them gratuitously.''[2]

Since a virtue is a habit by which we work well, it resides in a faculty of the soul. A virtue can reside in one faculty only, and not in several faculties at the same time. The intellect can be the subject of virtues. Intellectual virtues confer an aptness for a good work, namely, the consideration of truth, which is the good work of the intellect. Intellectual virtues make good grammarians, scientists, artists, and the like. The concupiscible and irascible appetites can be the subject of virtues like temperance and fortitude. If these appetites are to be guided by reason in an habitual way, they too must be perfected by virtues. And, of course, the will can be the subject of virtues. The virtues in the will, such as charity and justice, direct a person's affections toward God and neighbor.

Thomas has more to say about the intellectual virtues. Habits in the intellect are virtues in the sense that they confer an aptness for a good work, such as the scientific investigation of truth. Still, the intellectual virtues do not guarantee the right use of that aptness. We can all conjure up visions of the evil scientist and venal artist. If a person makes good use of the aptness conferred by the intellectual virtues, that is due to the will, which puts all the powers and habits to their respective use. Consequently, a virtue which perfects the will, such as charity and justice, confers the right use of these speculative habits.

There are five intellectual virtues in all. Three intellectual virtues perfect the speculative intellect in the consideration of truth. They are understanding, which is concerned with the first principles of knowledge; science, which deals with the truth known through demonstration; and wisdom, the virtue which sees the relationship of all truth to the ultimate truth, which is God. In the latter case, wisdom is theology if it relies upon God's revelation; and it is philosophy if it relies solely upon human reason.

The other two intellectual virtues are seated in the practical intellect which has to do with human activity. Art is the *recta ratio factibilium*, "right reason regarding things to be made"; and prudence is the *recta ratio agibilium*, "right reason regarding things to be done." Art guides human activity in making things; it is the virtue of the artist and craftsman. Prudence guides human activity in choosing means to an end and making decisions. Prudence is the helmsman of human life; and it presupposes right ends and goals. Justice, for example, inclines us to give each person his or her due; but it is prudence that determines the means of achieving justice. Connected with the virtue of prudence, but distinct from it, are *eubulia* (the virtue of good counsel), *synesis* (the virtue of common sense in practical affairs) and *gnome* (the ability to judge rightly regarding extraordinary matters in life). Eubulia is the virtue of taking counsel; synesis is the virtue of judging well; and gnome is the virtue of commanding action aright.

The moral virtues are found in the appetites of the soul. Just as an appetite is distinct from reason, so the moral virtues are distinct from intellectual virtues. If we set the theological virtues of faith, hope and charity aside for the moment, we must say that all virtues are either intellectual or moral. Moral virtues can exist without the intellectual virtues of wisdom, science and art; but they cannot exist without the intellectual virtues of understanding and prudence, since understanding and prudence have to do with the moral principles and choice of means to the end, upon which the moral virtues depend. The intellectual virtues, with the exception of prudence, can exist without the moral virtues. However, there can be no prudence without the moral virtues, just as there can be no moral virtues without prudence. The moral virtues incline the appetite toward the good that is in accord with reason, which is a due end; and prudence counsels, judges and commands aright what is suitable to the end. For example, temperance inclines a person to be moderate in eating and drinking, and prudence determines how much and what a person is to eat and drink in order to be moderate. Without the other, both temperance and prudence would cease to exist.

Moral virtues are to be distinguished from the passions, because a virtue is a principle of operation, while a passion is an operation or movement of the sense appetite. Obviously, the virtuous person does not consent to, and tries to restrain, those passions, which are not in accord with reason; but he or she consents to, and even encourages, those passions which are in accord with reason. Even the passion of sorrow is compatible with the moral virtues, in the sense that one grieves over that which is opposed to, or thwarts, those virtues. Thomas points to Jesus who, although he was perfect in virtue, experienced sorrow (Mt 26:38). Some moral virtues, like charity and justice, govern the operations of the will; and some, like temperance and fortitude, govern the operations of the sense appetite or passions. By a kind of overflow, the virtuous operations of the will, such as the practice of justice, can produce certain passions, such as joy, in the sense appetite.

There is more than one moral virtue, because the moral virtues modify the appetites which are several in number. Some moral virtues, such as justice, regulate one's conduct in relation to others. They are social virtues. Other moral virtues, such as temperance and fortitude, regulate one's conduct in relation to oneself. They are personal virtues. The moral virtues connected with justice, such as religion, piety and gratitude, have a common note, one of debt, of what is due another. The personal moral virtues regulate different passions, as meekness regulates anger, and temperance regulates desire.

Four moral virtues are called cardinal or principal virtues: prudence, justice, fortitude and temperance. Prudence perfects the intellect; justice, the will; fortitude, the irascible appetite; and temperance, the concupiscible appetite. All the moral virtues, many as they are, can be reduced to these four. For example, every moral virtue that curbs and represses the passions can be called temperance; and every moral virtue that prompts us to act rightly where others are concerned can be called justice. These four virtues, as distinguished from the other moral virtues, are also called cardinal virtues because of the importance of their matter. Fortitude, for example, is the virtue which strengthens us against the dangers of death.

The theological virtues are those which focus upon God as our supernatural end; they are infused by God, and they are known only by revelation. The theological virtues focus upon God, insofar as he surpasses our natural knowledge, while the intellectual and moral virtues have to do with what lies within the purview of reason. The theological virtues are faith, hope and charity. By faith we believe what God has revealed about himself; by hope we rely upon God to attain salvation; and by charity we love God above all things for his own sake. The theological virtues are infused simultaneously; but there is a certain priority in their operation. We cannot tend toward God by hope and charity, which are acts of the will, until we come to know God by faith. Still, charity is more excellent than faith and hope because, as we shall see, charity is the root and form of all the virtues. Thus, Paul wrote, "The greatest of these is charity" (1 Cor 13:13).

What is the cause of virtues? The acquired virtues are caused by repeated good acts. The supernatural virtues are infused by God. The supernatural virtues include both theological and moral virtues. The theological virtues direct us to our supernatural end; but supernatural moral virtues are also needed, because the soul needs to be perfected by infused virtues in regard to other things, yet in relation to God, our supernatural end. There is an essential distinction between the acquired virtues and infused virtues, because each is guided by a different rule, the former by reason, and the latter by faith. As an example, St. Thomas speaks of the consumption of food. The rule fixed by reason is that the consumption of food should not harm the health of the body nor impede the use of reason; but faith encourages a person to chastise his or her body and bring it into subjection (1 Cor 9:27) by abstinence in food and drink.

Does virtue observe a mean? The moral virtues do. For example, in the consumption of food and drink we act virtuously by eating and drinking neither too much nor too little. In the case of fortitude and temperance, excess and defect are to be judged in reference to the individual. For instance, what is too much or too little food for one person may be just the right amount for another. In matters of justice, however, the mean is definitely objective. Thus, in the payment of a debt, the mean is what is owed, neither more nor less. The mean of an intellectual virtue is the true, so that an intellectual virtue achieves its mean, when it is conformed to reality. The theological virtues do not observe a mean, for we can never love God as much as he ought to be loved, nor believe and hope in him as much as we should.

Are the virtues connected? In the case of the moral virtues, we may distinguish between an imperfect moral virtue and a perfect moral virtue. An imperfect moral virtue is simply an inclination to do some good work. If we take the moral virtues in this way, they are not connected. Thus, a person who is liberal may not be chaste. On the other hand, a perfect moral virtue inclines us to do a good work well. If we take the moral virtues in this way, then we must say that they are connected. For example, one cannot be truly prudent, unless one is also moderate and just and strong of mind, and so forth. The acquired moral virtues are not connected to charity: they can exist without it; but the infused moral virtues cannot exist without charity. Charity brings all the infused virtues, including faith and hope, in its train. Faith and hope can exist in an imperfect way without charity; but charity is quite impossible without faith and hope, for we cannot have friendship with God through charity, unless we first believe in it and hope for it.

What is to be said about the equality and relative excellence of the virtues? The virtues can be greater or lesser at different times in the same individual or in different individuals—and this because of more repeated acts or a better natural disposition or a greater gift of grace. For example, the same individual may be more temperate in food and drink at one time than at another. There is a certain equality in the growth of the virtues similar to the growth of the fingers on the hand of a child. In themselves, the intellectual virtues are superior to the moral virtues, because they perfect the highest faculty of the soul. Still, the moral virtues do more to achieve one's ultimate goal.

The chief moral virtue is justice, because it modifies the will, the appetite most akin to reason, and sets a person in order, not only in regard to himself or herself, but also in regard to others. The chief intellectual virtue is wisdom, because its object, God, surpasses the objects of the other intellectual virtues. The greatest theological virtue is charity, since it implies a certain union with the Beloved, whereas faith and hope imply a certain distance from God.

Both the moral and intellectual virtues will remain in the next life. As for the theological virtues, only charity will remain in the next life, since faith will give way to vision, and hope to possession.

Gifts, Beatitudes and Fruits (1a2ae.68-70)

Every individual, who has been reborn, receives the gifts of the Holy Spirit. They are infused along with grace and charity. The gifts are supernatural habits by which we become docile to the promptings of the Holy Spirit. The virtues are intrinsic principles of activity, whereas the gifts are habits that make us amenable to the external impulse of the Holy Spirit. Louis Billot, S.J. (1846-1931), compared the virtues to the motors of a ship, and the gifts to sails unfurled to receive the movement of the wind. As the appetites are made obedient to reason by the moral virtues, so all the powers of the soul are made obedient to the Holy Spirit through the gifts.

The gifts are located in the reason and appetite. In the reason, there are the gifts of understanding, counsel, wisdom and knowledge; and in the appetitive power, the gifts of piety, fortitude and fear. This enumeration of the gifts reflects the text of Isaiah 11:2-3, as it is found in the Septuagint and Vulgate. Thomas explains the nature of each gift in this way: the speculative and practical reasons are perfected in the discovery and apprehension of truth by the gifts of understanding and counsel respectively. For right judgment about the truth, the speculative reason is perfected by wisdom; and the practical reason, by knowledge. The appetitive power is perfected by the gift of piety in one's relations to others; by the gift of fortitude against dangers threatening oneself; and by the gift of fear against inordinate lust for pleasure.

St. Thomas believes that the gifts of the Holy Spirit will remain in heaven, where the soul will be especially open to the influence of the Holy Spirit. The gifts are inferior to, and dependent upon, the theological virtues which have God himself for their object; but the gifts are superior to the other virtues, intellectual and moral, because of their relationship to the Holy Spirit.

The beatitudes pronounced by Our Lord in his Sermon on the Mount (Mt 5:3-12) are the effects of the gifts of the Holy Spirit. The beatitudes are acts; hence, they differ from the virtues and the gifts, not as habit from habit, but as act from habit. To each of these acts Our Lord attached an explicit reward. The rewards assigned to the beatitudes in the Sermon on the Mount can be enjoyed in an imperfect manner even in this life, but in a perfect manner only in the next life. For example, those who hunger and thirst for holiness (Mt 5:6) shall be satisfied imperfectly in this life and perfectly in the next. The enumeration of the beatitudes in Matthew's gospel suggests a progression in the possibilities for happiness, as one withdraws from sensual pleasures and engages more fully in virtuous activity and a life of contemplation.

The fruits of the Holy Spirit are acts or good works performed under the inspiration of the Holy Spirit and affording a certain pleasure. More is required for a beatitude than for a fruit. A beatitude is a more perfect and excellent work, whereas a fruit is simply a virtuous and delightful work. A beatitude is a fruit of the Holy Spirit; but not all fruits are beatitudes. The fruits of the Holy Spirit enumerated by Paul in Galatians 5:22-23 are charity, joy, peace, patience, benignity, goodness, long-suffering, mildness, faith, modesty, continency and chastity. Paul names twelve fruits, but there are more. There is contrast and opposition between the works of the flesh, which subject human beings to sensible goods, and the fruits of the Spirit, which elevate them to a higher plane.

Vices and Sins (1a2ae.71-89)

Thomas' treatise on vices and sins has a structure similar to that on the virtues. Speaking of vices and sins, he discusses their nature, the manner in which they are distinguished, the comparison of one sin with another, the psychological seat of vices and sins, their causes and effects. Included in the treatise is a detailed exposition of the doctrine of original sin, its transmission, nature and subject. Thomas concludes the treatise by setting forth the differences between mortal and venial sin.

A vice is a bad habit, just as a virtue is a good habit. A sin is a bad act as opposed to a good act. A vice is unnatural in the sense that it is contrary to human nature, because it is contrary to the order of reason. A sinful act is worse than a vicious habit or vice, since it is more blameworthy *to do* evil than *to be able* to do evil. A mortal sin is incompatible with the infused virtues, because a single mortal sin destroys charity, which is the root of all the infused virtues. However, a single mortal sin is compatible with the acquired virtues, because a habit is not destroyed by a single act in this case. A venial sin is compatible with the acquired virtues, because a habit is not destroyed by a single act in this case. A venial sin is compatible with both the infused and acquired virtues. In the case of a sin of omission, one may positively will to neglect a duty or one may neglect the duty without any act of the will at all. Augustine defined sin as a "word, deed, or desire, contrary to the eternal law."[3]

Thomas goes on to consider the distinction between sins. The distinction is important, not only because of its bearing upon human conduct, but also because of its relevance to the sacrament of penance or reconciliation. According to the Council of Trent (1545-63), a penitent must confess his or her sins specifically and in particular, together with the circumstances which change the species of sins. The specific confession of sins is necessary, so that the priest, exercising the power granted him by Christ (Mt 16:19; 18:18; Jn 20:23), can forgive or retain sins and impose a suitable penance with full knowledge of the penitent's condition.[4]

Sins are distinguished specifically by their objects; the created objects, to which the sinner turns, differentiate his or her sin. Thus, the adulteress turns to another woman's husband, and the drunkard turns to drink; and by reason of their distinct objects, the sin of adultery is distinct from the sin of drunkenness. All sins may be classified as spiritual or carnal. Spiritual sins, like presumption, are consummated in the mind alone; carnal sins, like gluttony, defile the body. Apart from the intention of the sinner, sins are not distinguished on the basis of their causes; for example, a fearful or greedy person may proceed to a variety of sinful actions, such as theft or bodily injury or abusive language. However, these sins are distinguished by the injury done to others, and not by the fear or greed of the sinner. Sins against God or one's neighbor or oneself are distinct by reason of their distinct objects.

The different punishments due to different sins—eternal punishment to mortal sin and temporal punishment to venial sin—do not distinguish one sin from another in a specific way; rather, the measure of punishment is consequent upon the species of sin, which is determined by its object. The sins of commission and omission do not differ specifically, if they are directed to the same end. For example, the covetous man, in order to hoard money, takes what is not his, which is a sin of commission and neglects to give what he ought, which is a sin of omission. Sins of thought, word and deed, really belong to one complete species of sin, when they are related to each other, as in the case of a man who first thinks of sinning with a woman, then solicits her with words and consummates the sin by a wrongful deed. Of course, even an isolated thought can be a sin, as in the case of a lustful desire (Mt 5:28). Sins of excess and deficiency differ in kind, because they proceed from different motives. Thus, intemperance is excessive love of bodily pleasure, while insensibility is hatred of them. Finally, circumstances may or may not affect the species of sins, insofar as they do, or do not, give rise to new deformities.

Next, Thomas compares one sin with another. He does not believe that sins are connected, as one virtue is connected with another through charity and prudence. The reason is that the goods, to which the sinner's intention is directed, are of various kinds, having no mutual connection. Are all sins equal? No, one sin is more serious than another, just as one sickness is more serious than another. A sin is more serious to the extent that it departs from the rule of reason and attacks the values established by reason. The gravity of a sin is measured first and foremost by the object from which the sin derives its species; and the more reprehensible the object, the worse the sin. Thus, murder, which deprives a person of life, is worse than theft, which deprives him or her of some external good. The more grievous sin is opposed to the greater virtue, because both are about the same object. Hence, a sin against the theological virtue of faith is worse than a sin against the moral virtue of temperance.

Other factors too affect the gravity of sins. Other things being equal, spiritual sins are worse than carnal sins; and this for several reasons, one of which is that carnal sins imply a stronger temptation as the result of the concupiscence of the flesh. The more deliberate a sin is and the less it is due to a lack of knowledge and freedom, the worse it is. Circumstances can aggravate the gravity of a sin in two ways at least. In one way, circumstances can add a new species of sin; thus, adultery, which is also an injustice, is worse than fornication. Or, in a second way, circumstances can increase the deformity of the same sin; thus, the theft of a large amount is worse than the theft of a small amount. A sin is greater insofar as it does more harm; for example, the sinner who also gives scandal by his sin, commits the greater sin. Finally, it makes a considerable difference who commits a sin and against whom it is committed; for instance, to strike a parent is worse than striking a stranger.

What is the subject or psychological seat of sin? The will is the subject of sin in the sense that it is the principle of voluntary acts which are sinful. However, not only the will, but also all those human faculties which are moved or restrained from movement by the will, can also be the subject of sin. Thus, the sense appetite, which is the principle of the passions, can be the subject of sin to the degree that it is under the control of the will. The reason is the subject of sin, when it is ignorant of what it can and should know, and when it guides the lower powers improperly. The sin of morose delectation is in the reason, when it dwells upon something that should be cast aside as soon as it touches the mind, such as thoughts of lust, revenge, envy and so forth. Morose delectation means approval of the evil, but without desiring it. St. Thomas, but not all his predecessors, considered morose delectation to be a mortal sin, when it implied approval of what was seriously wrong. For example, merely to think approvingly of fornication is itself a mortal sin.

Next, St. Thomas turns to the causes of sin. A sin is an inordinate act; it implies the privation of something that should be in a human act. A sinful act fails to measure up to its norm. It must be traced back to a positive cause. The causes of sin are the causes of human activity: the intellect, the will, the senses, imagination and sense appetite. The proximate cause of sin is the will which, rejecting the rule of reason and the divine law, is intent on some mutable good in an inordinate manner. The remote cause of sin is the imagination and the sense appetite, which can influence the reason and will. Things external to the human person can be a cause of sin in some sense, because these things can stir the senses and, through them, influence the reason and will. In this way, a pornographic movie or book can be a cause of sin. One sin can cause another sin in a variety of ways; for example, by creating a disposition to that sin. So, taking drugs wrongfully in one instance might lead to further abuse.

Having spoken of the causes of sin in general, St. Thomas takes a closer look at each one of them in particular. He looks at the internal and external causes of sins, and the sins which are the cause of other sins.

What are the *internal* causes of sin? They are ignorance in the intellect, passion in the sensitive appetite, and malice in the will. Ignorance causes sin in the sense that it removes the knowledge which would prevent a sinful act. In this case, ignorance means the failure to know what one can and should know. For example, the ignorance which causes a surgeon to botch an operation is sinful. Such ignorance, if it is due to stress or other occupations, excuses the surgeon to some degree, but not entirely. Ignorance excuses from sin to the degree that it destroys the voluntariness of sin.

The passions can be a cause of sin. The passions of the sensitive appetite can move the will only indirectly, either by appropriating the energy of the soul and withdrawing it from the will, or else by impeding the judgment of the intellect. For example, when anger flares up, one's willpower is correspondingly diminished because the energy of the soul, in which all the faculties are rooted, is limited. Sometimes the passions can become so strong, that they draw the intellect in their train, as in the case of a violent desire. A sin committed through passion should be called a sin of weakness, because disorderly passions impede the use of reason and will. After all is said and done, self-love is the source of every sin, because a person seeks some temporal good inordinately when he loves himself inordinately. All the passions which are a cause of sin can be reduced to the concupiscence of the flesh, the concupiscence of the eyes, and the pride of life, about which we read in 1 Jn 2:16. The passions diminish sin to the degree that they impede the reason and will, but ordinarily they do not excuse one from sin altogether. A sin committed through passion can be a mortal sin if reason does not step in to prevent the sinful act, when it can and should.

The last internal cause of sin, which St. Thomas considers, is malice. Malice is concentrated in the will, which in this case sins of its own accord and is not influenced by ignorance and passion. The will sins through malice, when it loves some lesser good, such as riches or pleasure, in preference to a higher good, such as maintaining the rule of reason and doing the will of God. A person who sins through habit, sins through malice, since he chooses the evil, which has become connatural to him through the habit. Still, a person does not have to have a habit to sin through malice, since the will can choose evil without a habit, just as it can choose good without a virtue. Other things being equal, to sin through malice is worse than to sin through passion, which impels the will to sin, as it were.

What are the *external* causes of sin? The external causes of sin are distinct from the person of the sinner. In no sense is God the cause of sin, since God hates sin which turns men and women away from him. God is the cause of the sinful act, insofar as it is a positive entity; but God is not responsible for it, insofar as it is defective and fails to measure up to its norm. The defect and failure must be attributed to the free will of human beings. God is the cause of spiritual blindness and hardness of heart (Is 6:10; Rm 9:18), when he withdraws his grace from an individual. Sometimes this blindness and hardening redound to the salvation of the individual, and sometimes to his damnation.

The devil cannot be a direct cause of sin, because he cannot force the will to sin; he can only persuade or tempt a person to sin.

As someone has said, the devil can only offer inducements to sin, as a merchant can offer his wares for sale. Moreover, the devil can work upon the senses, the passions and the imagination in order to lead men and women into sin. In one sense, the devil is responsible for all human sins, because he tempted the parents of the human race to sin, so that their descendants are prone to sin. Still, apart from the temptations of the devil, human beings are also tempted by the world in which they live and by the unruly desires they experience within themselves.

Original Sin. Thomas' discussion of original sin is a continuation of his discussion of the external causes of sin. Like the devil, men and women can be the external causes of another's sin by outward suggestion; but they have a special manner of causing sin by propagating the human race, which is infected with original sin.

According to the teaching of the Church, the parents of the human race rebelled against their Maker at the beginning of human history. The result was that Adam and Eve and their descendants were alienated from God. This alienation consists essentially in the loss of sanctifying grace or divine life, accompanied, however, by the deterioration of human nature itself in many important respects, including suffering and death (Rm 5:12). Every infant born into this world is the victim of this alienation; he or she is infected by the original sin of Adam, which is transmitted by propagation, and not by imitation. Original sin is removed by baptism, which restores an individual to the life of grace or friendship with God through Jesus Christ, who takes away the sins of the world. The other consequences of original sin contributing to the deterioration of human nature are removed only gradually in this life, but completely in the next life. This teaching about original sin was expressed in the most complete and authoritative manner by the Council of Trent[5] in 1546, and Thomas did much to prepare the way.

The first question Thomas asks is, How is original sin transmitted? He explains the transmission of original sin by the solidarity of all men and women with Adam. Adam was constituted by God as the head and representative of the human race. All men and women are one with him, insofar as they have one common nature, which they receive from him. When Adam sinned, his sin infected the human nature which all receive from him; and in this way, original sin is transmitted to the sons and daughters of Adam. Why did God will the solidarity of Adam and his descendants in this manner? God did so with a view to the mystery of Christ and his redemptive activity (Rm 5:12-21).

Thomas uses an analogy to help in this difficult matter. All men and women who share Adam's nature may be considered as many members of one body, like the human body and its members. Just as the whole human body is held accountable for the sin of one of its members as moved by the will—think of the murderer who is punished for the sin committed by his hand—so the whole human race is held accountable for the sin of Adam, who moves all his descendants by generation. Or, to use another analogy, one that is not Thomas': Just as a parent might squander his property, which he could have left as a heritage to his children, so Adam squandered the gifts of God which he could have left as a heritage to his descendants. Fortunately, these gifts have been restored through Christ.

Thomas does not believe that any other sins of Adam, apart from the original sin, were transmitted to his descendants, because the first sin was sufficient to do the damage. Thomas notes that all the descendants of Adam, Christ excepted, contract original sin. The Church also knows that Mary, the mother of Christ, did not contract original sin because of the merits of Christ. Original sin is transmitted by the normal process of generation, so that a person, who was somehow formed miraculously from human flesh, would not contract original sin. Thomas takes the position that if Eve alone had sinned, and not Adam, their children would not have contracted original sin. Here Thomas reflects the medieval view that the man, and not the woman, is the active principle of propagation in the order of nature.

Original sin is a habit, not in the sense of a virtue or vice, but in the sense of a kind of sickness disrupting human nature and its powers. Original sin is specifically one sin in each individual, just as a fever, for example, is specifically one illness in a sick person. The formal element of original sin is the deprivation of original justice, that is to say, of grace and charity, whereby the will is subject to God; and the material element of original sin is concupiscence, whereby the other powers of the soul are inordinately attracted to created goods. Original sin is equally in all, since the formal element of original sin, the deprivation of grace and charity stemming from Adam, is not subject to degrees, just as death is not subject to degrees.

The guilt associated with original sin, which is derived from Adam's perverse will, resides in the soul; and the evil inclinations which torment the flesh are the punishment of original sin. The primary subject or seat of original sin is the essence of the soul, which is the primary objective and term of generation, by which original sin is transmitted. The first power or faculty of the soul to be infected by original sin is the will, which is the first to be inclined to sin. As far as the subordinate powers are concerned, those most corrupted by original sin and inclined to evil are those which are most involved in the act of generation: the generative power, the concupiscible appetite, and the sense of touch. And with these remarks, Thomas concludes his study of original sin, which, along with the devil and the sinful suggestions of other men and women, is one of the external causes of sin in an individual.

One more cause of sin remains to be considered, and that is sin itself. One sin can be the cause of another. Following the apostle Paul (1 Tm 6:10), Thomas notes that covetousness or the inordinate desire for money is the root of all evil. With money an individual is able to indulge all his or her sinful desires; and he or she is led in all manner of disreputable ways to secure it. With Sirach (10:13), Thomas holds that pride, which is the inordinate desire to excel, is the beginning of every sin, because it prompts one to seek all those temporal goods inordinately, by which he or she may have some advantage. Along with covetousness and pride, there are five other capital sins: lust, anger, envy, gluttony and sloth. These seven sins are commonly called capital sins, not because they are necessarily the worst sins, but because they are the chief sources from which other sins arise. Pride, for example, is the source of presumption, ambition, vainglory and boasting; and anger is the source of contumely, blasphemy, quarrels and murders.

Having completed his discussion of the causes of sin, Thomas now takes up the effects of sin. The effects of sin are to diminish the good of nature, stain the soul, and incur the debt of punishment. The first effect of sin is to diminish the good of nature, in the sense that sin diminishes the natural inclination to act reasonably or virtuously by establishing a contrary disposition. Still, this natural inclination to act reasonably or virtuously in accordance with one's nature can never be totally destroyed, as long as one retains his or her nature. Sin inflicts four wounds upon human nature: the reason is obscured, the will is hardened to evil, good actions become more difficult, and concupiscence becomes more unruly. Because of the sin of Adam, we experience death and bodily defects. In a sense, these things are natural to human beings; but in the beginning God removed these deficiencies and bestowed on human nature the gift of immortality, which was lost through Adam's sin. As Paul wrote: "By one man sin entered into this world, and by sin death" (Rm 5:12).

A second effect of sin is to stain the soul in a metaphorical sense. This stain is a kind of shadow upon the brightness of the soul, which has withdrawn from the light of reason and grace. Thomas is speaking here of the effect of mortal sin, and not of venial sin. The stain of sin remains in the soul even after the sinful act has ceased, until one returns to the light of reason and grace by repentance.

The third effect of sin is the debt of punishment incurred by the sinner. The sinner is subject to a threefold punishment: one inflicted by the sinner himself, namely, remorse of conscience; another inflicted by human beings, such as civil and ecclesiastical authorities; and a third punishment inflicted by God. A new sin can be the punishment for a previous sin, for the sinner is liable to lose the help of divine grace and so leave himself or herself open to further sins (Rm 1:24). Whatever sins turn a person away from God, so as to destroy charity, incur a debt of eternal punishment. Turning away from God, an infinite good, deserves the loss of God, an infinite punishment; and turning inordinately to a finite good deserves the fire of hell, a finite punishment. Some sins are venial and deserve only a temporary punishment.

Even after a person has repented of his or her sin, the debt of punishment can remain, as in the case of King David. He repented of an adulterous act with Bathsheba, the wife of Uriah; yet, he was punished by God with the death of the child born of the adulterous union (2 S 12:13-14). Not all that we suffer in this life is a punishment for personal or actual sins; rather, some trials are prescribed by God for our benefit, just as a physician sometimes prescribes bitter medicine for his patients. Thus, sickness is not necessarily a punishment for personal sins; it may come to us that we might grow in virtue. No one is punished in the strict sense of the term for another's sin.

Next, Thomas comes to the important distinction between mortal and venial sin; it is the distinction between death and sickness. Of course, God can restore a dead person and a sick person to life and health. Venial sin, especially repeated venial sins, can be a disposition to mortal sin, because they accustom a person to disorder. A venial sin cannot become a mortal sin, because they suppose distinct acts of the will. It is impossible for a circumstance in the strict sense to change a venial sin into a mortal sin. On the other hand, a mortal sin cannot become a venial sin, because death can never be transformed into a mere sickness.

Venial sin, unlike mortal sin, does not cause a stain in the soul, because it does not exclude the comeliness of reason and grace.

According to Thomas, Paul speaks of venial sins as wood, hay and stubble (1 Cor 3:12). These can be burned up either by the fire of trials in this life or by the fire of purgatory in the next life without loss of eternal life. Thomas does not think that Adam and Eve could have been guilty of venial sins in the state of innocence before committing a mortal sin; nor does he think that a good or wicked angel can sin venially. Finally, Thomas thinks that it is impossible for venial sin to be in a person with original sin alone.

Chapter 13

LAW AND GRACE (1a2ae.90-114)

The final section of the first part of the second part of the *Summa* is devoted to the extrinsic principles of human acts. The extrinsic principle which tempts us to do evil is the devil, about whom Thomas spoke earlier (1a.114). The extrinsic principle which moves us to embrace the good is God, who instructs us by his law and helps us by his grace. Hence, Thomas takes up at this point the two subjects of law and grace.

Law (1a2ae.90-108)

The Second Vatican Council declared "that the highest norm of human life is the divine law—eternal, objective, and universal—whereby God orders, directs and governs the entire universe and all the ways of the human community by a plan conceived in wisdom and love. Man has been made by God to participate in this law with the result that, under the gentle disposition of divine providence, he can come to perceive ever more fully the truth that is unchanging. . . . On his part, man perceives and acknowledges the imperatives of the divine law through the mediation of conscience. In all his activity a man is bound to follow his conscience in order that he may come to God, the end and purpose of life."[1] In these words of the Second Vatican Council one hears an echo of Thomas' teaching on law.

In his treatise on law, Thomas studies first the nature of law in general, the different kinds of law, and the effects of law. Then Thomas examines the different kinds of law in particular, that is to say, eternal law, natural law, human law, the Old Law and the New Law.

Reason is the guide of human actions. Because law is something that guides human actions, it is something that pertains to reason. Law directs our actions to a goal; and the goal at which law aims is usually called the common good. For example, sanitation laws seek to preserve the health of the community, and traffic laws seek to preserve the safety of the community. Obviously, the making of laws is the responsibility of the person who is in charge of the community, whether that person be one or more than one. A law must be promulgated; it must be made known to those whom it binds, for only in this way can they observe it. It does not make much difference how a law is promulgated, as long as it is effectively brought to the attention of the community. Thus, a law is a reasonable and authoritative directive, given by the person who is in charge of the community for the common good, and promulgated. Law, as an authoritative directive, supposes the guidance of the intellect, the motive force of the will, and the notification of those who are to be ruled by it.

After explaining the nature of law, Thomas distinguishes the various kinds of law without discussing them in detail. That detailed discussion will come later. The eternal law is God's plan for governing the universe. This plan is eternal, because it has existed in the mind of God from all eternity. The natural law is nothing else than the participation of the rational creature in the eternal law of God. The natural law, therefore, is God's eternal law, as it governs human beings. The natural law is reflected in the inclination of human nature to its proper activity and goal. Human law is the application of the natural law to particular cases. For example, the natural law prescribes that human life should not be endangered needlessly; and traffic laws supplement the natural law by regulating the speed of automobiles, so that human life is not endangered needlessly. The divine positive law supplies a need, which is not met by natural and human law. It directs human beings to their supernatural end; it clarifies the demands of the natural law; and it governs not only the exterior, but also the interior acts of human beings, which other human beings are not competent to judge. The divine positive law is manifested in the Old and New Laws, which are distinguished from each other as the imperfect from the perfect, as the boy from the man. St. Paul speaks of still another law in his members fighting against the law of his mind (Rm 7:23). This law is the impulse of sensuality, to which we are all subject.

The effect of law is to make men and women good, for any subject is good or virtuous when he or she pursues a worthy goal in subjection to one who rules. The law accomplishes its objectives by commanding what is good, forbidding what is evil, permitting what is indifferent and punishing what is contrary.

Next, St. Thomas takes a closer look at each of the different kinds of law. Eternal law is the plan in the mind of God according to which he directs the activity of his creatures. Just as an architect builds a house according to a plan he has in mind, so God governs the universe according to a plan he has in mind; and this plan is the eternal law. All men and women know the eternal law of God to a greater or lesser extent, because all know the common principles of the natural law to a greater or lesser extent; these principles are imprinted, as it were, on the hearts of human beings. Every law is derived from the eternal law to the degree that it is reasonable. All creatures are subject to the eternal law of God, because all of them are subject to his government. Irrational creatures obey the eternal law of God necessarily, guided as they are by divine providence through inner forces; however, rational creatures are subject to the eternal law with knowledge of it. Both good and bad persons are subject to the eternal law in different ways. Good men and women are perfectly subject to it, since they act according to it. Bad persons are imperfectly subject to the eternal law as far as their actions are concerned, because they do not act according to it in many respects. Still, bad persons do not evade the eternal law, since they suffer the penalties which the eternal law decrees for them in view of their wickedness.

The natural law is the participation of the rational creature in the eternal law of God; it is the eternal law, as it governs human beings. The natural law is, as it were, something imprinted on human nature; and it is reflected in the tendencies and propensities of human nature to its proper activity. The fundamental principle of the natural law is that good is to be done, while evil is to be avoided. A rational creature apprehends as good those things to which human nature is inclined, for example, the preservation of life, the procreation and education of children, the knowledge of God and life in society. The natural law prescribes the acts of all the virtues in the sense that it enjoins rational creatures to act according to reason, which is to act virtuously. The natural law is one and the same for all men and women, for all have the same human nature.

All men and women know the most fundamental precepts of the natural law, such as the need to do good and avoid evil. The majority of human beings also know the secondary precepts of the natural law, such as those which are found in the Decalogue. The secondary precepts are conclusions drawn from the fundamental precepts of the natural law. However, a minority of human beings are ignorant of some of these secondary precepts, because their reason is perverted by bad habits, education, or tradition. Thus, some primitive peoples did not think of theft as wrong, even though it is contrary to the natural law. Furthermore, even more men and women can be ignorant of the more remote conclusions of the natural law.

Positive law is either human or divine. Human laws promote the application and fulfillment of the natural law. For example, the natural law has it that criminals should be punished, while human laws determine how they should be punished. Human laws serve to encourage the good in the practice of virtue and restrain the wicked in the pursuit of evil. Thomas, following Isidore of Seville (560-636), describes a good human law in this way: "Law shall be virtuous, just, possible to nature, according to the custom of the country, suitable to place and time, necessary, useful; clearly expressed, lest by its obscurity it lead to misunderstanding; framed for no private benefit, but for the common good."[2]

Thomas distinguishes various forms of human law. The "law of nations," common to people wherever they have lived, is derived from the natural law; and it refers to those usages, like just buying and selling, which must be observed if people are to live together. Civil law, on the other hand, refers to the particular laws of states, according as each state decides what is best for itself. There are various categories of law, which govern certain groups, such as ecclesiastical law and military law. Then there are laws which reflect the various forms of government, such as monarchy and democracy. Finally, there are the different forms of law, which deal with specific matters, such as constitutional law and criminal law.

Human law should be made to suit the majority of instances, and not for what may possibly happen in individual cases. Human law does not forbid all the vices from which the virtuous abstain, but only the most grievous vices from which it is possible for the majority to abstain, and chiefly those which harm others. Human law must prescribe those virtuous acts which serve the common good. Human law obliges a person in conscience, because it is a just enactment looking to the common good. Human law binds all subjects equally and without exception. Generally, one should observe the letter of the law; but, in some instances, he or she should not observe it, in order to insure the common good intended by the lawgiver. For example, a traffic law forbids one to park her car in the middle of the road; but she may do so, if it is necessary to protect injured persons from oncoming cars. Often the lawgiver will give a dispensation from the law to protect an individual from harm in a particular instance.

Human laws should be changed, as their deficiencies become apparent and the condition of subjects changes. Laws that were appropriate in a feudal society are out-of-date in an industrial society. Still, frequent changes of law are to be avoided, because the custom of observing what are considered just laws contributes so much to the common good. Custom can obtain the force of law; it can abolish a law, and it can interpret a law. Custom has this significance, because it seems to proceed from a deliberate judgment of reason about what is good and useful. However, custom can never change the divine or natural law.

The Old Law. Divine positive law is divided into the Old Law and New Law. The Old Law means, in general, the law of God as it is found in the first five books of the Old Testament, the Torah or Law of the Jews. The Old Law was good, because it repressed the evil tendencies of the human person and forbade all kinds of evil actions. Still, the Old Law was imperfect in the sense that it did not confer grace, which was reserved to Jesus Christ (Jn 1:17). The Old Law disposed and prepared the Jewish people for the coming of Christ by bearing witness to him (Lk 24:44) and withdrawing them from idolatrous worship. According to Paul, the Old Law was given to the Jews by God's ministering angels at the hands of Moses (Gal 3:19) because, as Thomas explains, it was only a preparation for the perfect or New Law, given by God incarnate in the person of Jesus. The Old Law was given to the Jews, because Christ was to be born of them. Everyone was bound to obey the Old Law, insofar as it expressed the precepts of the natural law; but what the Old Law added over and above these precepts bound only the Jews. The Old Law was suitably given at the time of Moses, for at that time the people had come to realize their moral weakness without a written law, and yet they had still not given up hope by reason of their vices.

All the precepts of the Old Law were intended to prepare the Jewish people for the coming of Christ and the New Law. The Old Law contained moral precepts reflecting the natural law, ceremonial precepts regulating divine worship, and judicial precepts governing human relationships. To secure compliance with these precepts, the Old Law employed temporal promises and threats, as opposed to spiritual things, in accordance with the preparatory stage of the Jewish people at that time.

The moral precepts of the Old Law restated the precepts of the natural law. All the moral precepts can be reduced to the Ten Commandments, which have to do with one's relationship to God and neighbor. The Ten Commandments do not admit of dispensation, because they express the intention and will of God. To fulfill a law it is not necessary that a person have the corresponding virtue; rather, it suffices that he or she fulfill the law knowingly and freely. A person acting without the supernatural virtue of charity does not necessarily sin, whatever he or she does; and so, for example, a son who lacks charity for some other serious sin, nonetheless fulfills the law, "Honor thy father," when he honors his father, so that he does not commit a second sin. The Old Law prepared the people for the justifying grace of Christ, but observing the precepts of the Old Law did not of itself confer the grace of justification.

The ceremonial precepts of the Old Law were applications of the moral precepts to the worship of God. The external worship of the Old Law was figurative in many respects, looking forward to Christ, who is our way to heaven, and to heaven itself, which is the goal of earthly existence. The ceremonial precepts were intended to withdraw the people from the worship of idols and oblige them to worship the true God. The ceremonies of the Old Law were appropriately divided into sacrifices, such as the holocaust, sin-offering, and peace-offering; the use of sacred things, such as the tabernacle and instruments of worship; sacraments, such as circumcision, the consecration of priests, and the eating of the paschal lamb; and observances in matters of food, clothing, and so forth.

Even before God gave the Old Law, we read about ceremonial actions in the Bible, like the offering of fruits and animals to God

(Gn 4:3-4) and the offering of holocausts on an altar (Gn 8:20). These were inspired by devotion to God, but they did not have the force of law, since there was no legislation to that effect. The ceremonies of the Old Law did not have the power to expiate sin, but sin could be forgiven through the faith and devotion of the worshipper. The ceremonies of the Old Law ceased at the coming of Christ, for they no longer had meaning; the Christ whom they prefigured had come. It would be seriously wrong to carry out the ceremonies of the Old Law now, since such an observance would signify that Christ has yet to be born and suffer.

The judicial precepts of the Old Law governed human relationships, and they derived their binding force not only from reason, but also from divine institution. These precepts were laid down primarily to govern the people of God in relation to each other, but like everything else in the Old Dispensation they had a symbolic meaning (1 Cor 10:11). The judicial precepts no longer bind, for they lost their force with the coming of Christ; still, one could observe them for other reasons without sinning—let us say, as useful social institutions. The judicial precepts had to do with such matters as the form of government, the role of judges and witnesses, the ownership and transference of goods, dealings with foreigners and the treatment of wives, children and servants.

The New Law. This is the law of the New Testament. The New Law is chiefly the grace of the Holy Spirit, which is given to those who believe in Christ (Rm 3:27; 8:2); secondarily, however, the New Law is a written law instructing the faithful as to what they should believe and do. The New Law, as the grace of the Holy Spirit, but not as teaching and commandment, justifies the sinner. The giving of the New Law was delayed for a long time to prepare men and women for its reception and to reveal their weakness and need of grace. The New Law will endure until the end of the world, since it is the immediate preparation for this moment, and it is the state in which the grace of the Holy Spirit is possessed most abundantly.

The Old Law sought to subject human beings to God, and the New Law seeks to do the same thing; they differ, however, as the imperfect differs from the perfect. The New Law fulfills the Old Law by giving what the Old Law foreshadowed, namely, the grace of Jesus Christ. Moreover, Jesus fulfilled the Old Law by observing its precepts, explaining its true meaning and adding some counsels of perfection. The New Law was virtually contained in the Old Law, as the tree is virtually contained in the seed. As far as external observances go, the Old Law was more burdensome than the New; but the internal demands of the New Law are more difficult than those of the Old, although love eases the difficulty.

As St. Thomas has said, the New Law consists chiefly in the grace of the Holy Spirit. Accordingly, the New Law prescribes certain external actions that lead to grace, such as the reception of the sacraments instituted by Christ. Moreover, the New Law prescribes those external actions, which are necessarily in keeping with the grace of the Holy Spirit, like the confession of one's faith (Mt 10:32-33); and it forbids those external actions, which are in opposition to it, like the denial of one's faith and killing, stealing and adultery. The New Law makes no further determination about external actions. As far as one's internal actions are concerned, that is to say, one's thoughts and desires, the New Law regulates these sufficiently in Jesus' Sermon on the Mount. Over and above that which is strictly necessary to live a virtuous life, our Lord offered certain definite pieces of advice or counsels having to do with poverty, chastity and obedience, which expedite and assure the gaining of eternal life.

Grace (1a2ae.109-114)

The first part of the second part of the *Summa* is completed by Thomas' treatise on grace. As the extrinsic principle which moves us to embrace the good, God instructs us by his law and helps us by his grace.

To begin with, we may ask what the Bible and the Church have to say about grace. One finds the idea of grace in the Bible wherever it speaks of the favor which God shows his creatures. According to the Old Testament, God shows his favor to all creatures (Si 1:8), but especially to Israel. The most striking sign of God's favor was his election of Israel to be a people peculiarly his own (Dt 7:7-8). God's favor was absolutely gratuitous (Ex 33:19).

According to the New Testament, God shows favor to his people in many ways. The grace of God has appeared in Christ Jesus, offering salvation to all (Tt 2:11). We are saved by the favor of the Lord Jesus (Ac 15:11). We are undeservedly justified by the gift of God through the redemption wrought in Christ Jesus (Rm 3:24). The surpassing grace of God is within the Christian (2 Cor 9:14). In these passages, grace is something given gratuitously to the Christian as the beneficiary of God's saving will. There is an opposition between grace and works (Rm 11:6; Gal 2:21). Grace gives rise to good works (2 Cor 8:1); it enables Paul to resist temptations (2 Cor 12:9); and it is something dynamic (Ep 3:7-9).

In the Synoptic gospels, the idea of grace is bound up with the kingdom of God, which is offered as a gift to all upon the condition of repentance. In John's gospel, the idea of grace is found in Jesus' teaching about a new birth from on high (Jn 3:3), a new life (Jn 15:1-8), and a new divine presence in the soul of the believer (Jn 14:23). In all these ways, God shows favor to his people and bestows grace on them.

The Church's teaching about grace has been quite detailed. With respect to sanctifying grace, the Church teaches that justification means the remission of sins and the infusion of grace along with the virtues and gifts that accompany it. The Holy Spirit lives in the soul of the justified person, who shares in the divine life. Through grace one becomes an adopted son or daughter of God and an heir to heaven. The divine life of grace is increased by keeping the commandments and performing good works, which gain merit for eternal life. Grace is a gift of God and raises us to a supernatural level of existence. Mortal sin destroys the life of grace in the soul; but it can be recovered by repentance and the sacrament of penance.

With respect to actual grace, the Church teaches that a person can perform naturally good works without grace; but it is grace that elevates a person's works to a supernatural level. Under the influence of grace, a sinner must prepare himself for justification by acts of faith, sorrow and love; but grace does not rob the sinner of his freedom in the process. Actual grace is necessary to avoid mortal sin for a long time. To persevere to the end requires a special grace. God grants everyone the grace to keep the commandments but not to avoid all venial sin.[3]

Before we look at Thomas' teaching on grace, some definitions and distinctions may be helpful. In general, grace is a supernatural gift of God bestowed on an individual with a view to sanctification and salvation. Some graces or gifts, like prophecy or miraculous power, are given to a person for the benefit of others, and they are called charisms (*gratiae gratis datae*). Other graces are given to a person for his or her own sanctification and salvation, and these are graces in the usual sense of the term. There are three kinds of grace understood in the latter sense: uncreated grace, created or sanctifying grace (*gratia gratum faciens*), and actual grace. Uncreated grace is the abiding presence of the Holy Trinity in the souls of the just, the friends of God. Created or habitual grace, which is also called sanctifying grace, is a sharing in the life of God himself. Of itself, this type of grace is something permanent, although the life of grace can be destroyed through mortal sin. Uncreated grace and created grace are inseparable. Finally, actual grace is a transient help of God, which enlightens the mind and moves the will to do good and avoid evil. All the other kinds of grace, of which theologians speak, can be reduced to sanctifying and actual grace. Sacramental grace, for example, is a kind of sanctifying grace, and efficacious grace is a kind of actual grace.

With these clarifications in mind, we can now turn to Thomas' teaching on grace. Thomas discusses the necessity of grace and explains its nature, divisions, cause, and its effects relating to justification and the acquisition of supernatural merit for eternal life.

Just how necessary is grace? We do not need grace to know those things which we can learn through the senses; but we do need the illumination and movement of God's grace to know those truths which surpass our natural knowledge. We do not need grace to accomplish this or that good work, such as building a house or planting a tree; but we do need grace, both habitual and actual, to do all the good natural to us and to carry out the works of supernatural virtue, which are meritorious. Unless habitual grace elevates our nature and unless actual grace prompts our actions, we cannot merit the supernatural reward of everlasting life. Without actual grace, we cannot prepare ourselves for the gift of habitual grace; consequently, if the sinner is to rise from his sinful condition, he needs actual grace to move him to repentance, and habitual grace to restore him to supernatural life.

Grace is necessary in other ways too. Without the healing effect of habitual grace in the soul, one cannot avoid mortal sin for long, since the sinner is not so set on God that he or she is unwilling to be separated from him for any reason. A person in the state of habitual or sanctifying grace needs the further help of actual grace in order to act righteously, for it is God, the first mover, who rouses the person to act. To persevere in good to the end of life, one needs the help of grace. Perseverance of this kind is a special gift not given to all, for grace is given to many who do not receive the gift of perseverance in grace.

What then is grace? Grace is a gift of God; it is a supernatural reality of which God is the cause. Sanctifying grace is a quality, in the sense that it is an habitual gift infused by God into the soul. It is a created sharing in the life of God; and of itself, it is something permanent. Actual grace, however, is not a quality or habitual gift; rather, it is a transient movement of the soul by God to know or will or do something good. Actual grace enables us to *act* supernaturally. It follows, therefore, that a baptized infant, a man in a coma, or a woman fast asleep have no need of actual grace, because each one is incapable of acting responsibly under the circumstances. Grace is not identical with the supernatural virtues; grace modifies the essence of the soul, while the virtues reside in the powers or faculties of the soul.

What are the divisions of grace? The first division has to do with the distinction between sanctifying grace and gratuitous grace or charism. Sanctifying grace is the habitual grace of which Thomas spoke earlier, and it unites a person to God. On the other hand, a gratuitous grace or charism is given to a person, so that he or she may cooperate in the justification of another. The distinction between operating grace and cooperating grace applies to both actual grace and sanctifying grace. Actual grace is operating grace, when it initially rouses the will from inactivity to activity; and it is cooperating grace, when it works with the will to complete the good work commanded by the will. Sanctifying grace is operating grace, when it heals and justifies the soul, or makes it pleasing to God; and it is cooperating grace, when it is the principle of meritorious works.

Thomas also distinguished between prevenient grace and subsequent grace. To clarify the difference, he enumerates five effects of grace: to heal the soul, to desire good, to carry out the good proposed, to persevere in good, and to reach glory. Grace, inasmuch as it causes one effect in us, is called prevenient with respect to the following effect; and inasmuch as it causes the following effect, it is called subsequent with respect to the preceding effect. Gratuitous grace or charisms are listed by St. Paul as wisdom, knowledge, miracles, prophecy, discerning of spirits, tongues and interpretation of tongues (1 Cor 12:8-10). Sanctifying grace is nobler than the gratuitous graces or charisms, because it actually unites a person to God, whereas the charisms only lead to such a union.

Who is the cause of grace? God alone is the cause of grace, for sanctifying grace is a created sharing of the divine nature by a participated likeness. Is some preparation required on the part of a person for the reception of grace? The soul must be prepared for the reception of sanctifying grace, just as the soil must be prepared for the reception of the seed. However, there can be no preparation for the reception of actual grace; indeed, actual grace is something like rain, which falls on the soil without regard to its condition. The only preparation that leads infallibly to the reception of sanctifying grace is the preparation, which a person makes under the influence of actual grace. The intensity of sanctifying grace or divine life can differ from soul to soul, since God dispenses his gifts in varying degrees for the perfection of the universe. Short of a special revelation from God, we cannot be absolutely certain of having sanctifying grace; but we can have some indication of the presence of grace, if we delight in God, if we despise worldly things, and if we have no consciousness of unrepented mortal sin.

What are the effects of grace? The first effect of grace is justification. Justification is the transition of a person from a state of sin or aversion from God to a state of grace or friendship with God. Four things are required for the justification of a sinner: the infusion of sanctifying grace by God, faith by which a person turns to God, sorrow by which he or she turns away from sin, and the remission of sins. These four things occur simultaneously, although there is a certain natural order among them, beginning with the infusion of grace, which is followed by the acts of faith and sorrow and the remission of sins. In a sense, the justification of the sinner can be called the greatest work of God because it is accomplished on behalf of those who are unworthy of it. Hence, we read in the Vulgate: "His tender mercies are above all his works" (Ps 144:9). The justification of the sinner is not generally considered to be miraculous, that is, as something outside the customary order of things, because justification generally assumes a common and wonted course.

The second effect of grace is merit. A person can merit as a reward what God has ordained to be merited. A person in the state of grace, who is deified, as it were, by partaking of the divine nature, can merit eternal life as a strict right—as a son or daughter to whom the inheritance is due by right of adoption. It is grace working through charity, which makes it the principle of merit. For merit we need sanctifying grace; hence, a person cannot merit the first grace given to him or her. Only Christ can merit condignly, that is, in strict justice, the first grace given to another; he can do so in his capacity as head of the Church (Heb 2:10). However, one can merit the first grace given to another congruously or appropriately, because a person in grace fulfills God's will, and it is congruous that God should fulfill such a person's desire for the salvation of another. One who sins mortally cannot merit condignly or congruously his restoration to grace, for he lacks the principles of condign and congruous merit. One in the state of grace can merit condignly an increase of grace, which is simply a stage on the road to eternal life. One cannot merit the special grace of perseverance. One can merit temporal goods only to the degree that they are needed to attain everlasting life.

The Second Part of the Second Part of the
SUMMA THEOLOGIAE (2a2ae)

Chapter 14

THE THEOLOGICAL VIRTUES (2a2ae.1-46)

In the first part of the *Summa*, St. Thomas treats of God; and in the second part, of the rational creature's advance towards God. The first part of the second part of the *Summa* considers God as the ultimate end of human activity and, in a general way, the acts by which men and women tend toward, or deviate from, this end. The second part of the second part of the *Summa* descends to greater detail in its discussion of human activity. This second part of the second part is largely a treatise on the virtues which are reducible to seven: the three theological virtues of faith, hope and charity, which are considered first (qq. 1-46); and the four cardinal virtues of prudence, justice, fortitude and temperance, to which all the moral virtues can be reduced (qq. 47-170). While Thomas' teaching on the virtues holds good for all men and women and all states of life, he concludes the second part of the second part of the *Summa* with a consideration and appraisal of particular states of life, such as the active and contemplative lives, the episcopacy, and the religious state (qq. 171-189).

First, then, the theological virtues.

Faith (2a2ae.1-16)

In the Bible, the word *faith* has various shades of meaning. In the Old Testament the man of faith, one who believes, is a member of the community which was established by the covenant on Mt. Sinai. Faith and existence are one (Is 7:9). The man of faith believes confidently in God's justice and patiently awaits its execution (Heb 2:4). Faith is trust in God's promise (Gn 15:6; Pr 78:22). Faith and belief are understanding (Is 43:10).

In the New Testament, faith signifies the right response of the individual to God, who has revealed himself through his Son, Jesus Christ; but again there are various shades of meaning. Faith is belief in the Second Coming (Mk 13:21), belief in miracles (Mk 2:5), and trust in God (Mk 11:22). For Paul, one is justified by faith (Rm 3:22). Faith comes through hearing the word of God (Rm 10:17). Faith is a gift (Ep 2:8). Faith is hope for salvation and life (Rm 6:8). To have faith is to know God (Gal 4:9). Faith excludes boasting (Rm 3:27). For John, faith is a personal belief in Jesus (Jn 2:11; 3:16). The works of Jesus lead to faith in him (Jn 14:10-11). John wrote his gospel to beget faith (Jn 19:35; 20:31).

While the Bible uses the term faith with various shades of meaning, the magisterium uses the term in a specific and technical sense. According to the First Vatican Council, faith is a supernatural virtue whereby, under the influence of grace, we believe a truth revealed by God, not because we understand what God has revealed, but because God, who can neither deceive nor be deceived, has revealed it.[1] This understanding of faith has been accepted and reaffirmed by the Second Vatican Council.[2] Both councils used the term *faith* in the sense in which St. Thomas understood it.

In the prologue to his treatise on faith, the first theological virtue, Thomas describes the order of his treatment: first he will study faith itself, then the gifts of the Holy Spirit corresponding to the virtue of faith, followed by the vices opposed to faith, and, finally, the precepts pertaining to this virtue.

The object of faith is God and other things related to God. Faith assents to these realities, insofar as they are known by divine revelation. Actually, the object of faith is simplicity itself; but the human mind, because it is finite, can grasp the object of faith only with a multiplicity of concepts. Faith is not subject to error, because it relies on the revelation of God, who can neither deceive nor be deceived. The object of faith cannot be something seen; so, for example, when doubting Thomas saw the Risen Christ in the upper room, he was able to see his humanity, but he had to profess his belief in the divinity of Jesus, which was invisible (Jn 20:26-29). The object of faith cannot be at the same time the object of scientific knowledge. In other words, I cannot believe and understand some truth about God at one and the same time. For example, if reason convinces me that God is provident for his creatures, such rational conviction excludes assent to the same truth on the basis of divine revelation, which is the ground of faith.

The most important matters of the Christian faith are expressed in propositions called articles of faith. Often the articles of faith express truths which involve special difficulty for the believer. The articles of faith may be understood more deeply as time goes on; and, as a result, new articles of faith may be formulated, although the substance of the faith remains the same. The articles of faith are embodied in creeds, such as the Apostles' Creed and the Nicene Creed. These creeds do not differ substantially, but accidentally, by reason of their greater explicitness. A creed is useful, because it offers a summary of the faith to which one is committed. It is essential that a creed have the approval of the Pope, who is the final authority on matters of faith.

Having discussed the object of faith, Thomas takes up the act of faith which is to believe. Faith involves internal belief and external confession of that belief. To believe means to accept some truth on the authority of God, a truth which one does not understand. For example, we believe that three divine persons are one God, because God has revealed this truth to us; yet, we do not understand how three really distinct persons are one God. To achieve their supernatural destiny, human beings must believe certain truths beyond the reach of reason, so that they can direct their lives to that destiny. Moreover, God has offered for belief some truths that reason can discover for itself, so that all men and women can know these truths easily and certainly.

We are bound to believe explicitly the primary articles of faith and believe implicitly whatever God has revealed. Obviously, those who are teachers in the Church must have a fuller knowledge of the truths of faith and believe them more explicitly. Thomas holds that it is necessary to believe explicitly in the mystery of Christ and the Holy Trinity in order to be saved. Explicit belief in the mystery of Christ is necessary, because "there is no other name under heaven given to men, whereby we must be saved" (Ac 4:12). Explicit belief in the Trinity is necessary, because it is impossible to believe explicitly in the mystery of Christ without faith in the Trinity.[3] When accompanied by charity, the act of faith is meritorious. To seek out reasons in support of what one believes shows good will and increases the merit of faith.

To confess our faith externally is also an act of faith. One confesses the faith externally by words and deeds. It is never lawful to deny one's faith; but one need not confess that he or she is a Christian and a Catholic at all times and in all places, but only when the honor of God and the good of our neighbor demand such a confession. On the other hand, if Catholics are being persecuted in a certain country, they do not have to walk up to their tormentors and ask to be imprisoned. St. Athanasius (296-373) repeatedly fled from those who persecuted him.

Next Thomas discusses the virtue of faith. Paul defines faith as "the substance of things to be hoped for, the evidence of things that appear not" (Heb 11:1). One may paraphrase these words by saying that faith is a habit of the mind, whereby eternal life is begun in us, making the intellect assent to what is not apparent. The virtue of faith resides in the intellect, which assents to the truths of faith. Faith gives us a knowledge of sublime truths, but it does not make us good by itself. Faith without charity is a lifeless faith; but a lifeless faith becomes a living faith in the presence of charity.

Thus, a Catholic who commits a mortal sin has a lifeless faith; when he repents, his faith becomes a living one. Living faith is a virtue; a lifeless faith is not. Faith is one virtue in the sense that it relies simply and solely upon the authority of God as the basis of belief. By its very nature faith precedes all the other virtues, because the intellect must first grasp the ultimate end of human existence before the other virtues can function. Faith is more certain than science and the other intellectual virtues because it is founded on divine truth and not on human reason.

Who are those who have faith? Prior to their fall, both men and angels had faith, for they were created with the gift of grace, which is accompanied by faith, and they did not have the vision of God, which excludes faith. The fallen angels retain their faith, for James writes: ''The devils believe and tremble'' (2:9). The reason is that they see many evident signs that the teaching of the Church is from God. Of course, the faith of the demons is not a virtue; it is not a living faith accompanied by charity. The heretic, who denies one article of faith, such as the divinity of Christ, has neither living nor lifeless faith; he has no faith at all since he rejects the basis of faith which is the authority of God revealing. Faith permits no compromise; one must take all or have none of it. Faith can be greater in one person than in another because of greater firmness and devotion in the intellect and will respectively.

God is the author or cause of faith in a threefold manner: he has revealed what is to be believed; by his actual grace, he moves the intellect and will to assent to what he has revealed; and he infuses the supernatural virtue of faith into the soul. God is the author or cause of lifeless faith too, even if it is not vitalized by charity.

One of the effects of faith is fear. By faith we come to know about the punishment inflicted by God on sinners so that we are afraid to incur it. This is servile fear, of which lifeless faith is the cause. By faith we also come to know God as the supreme good so that we are afraid to be separated from him. This is filial fear, of which living faith is the cause. Faith also has the effect of purifying the heart by raising the mind and heart to God and withdrawing them from created goods.

Next Thomas considers the gifts of understanding and knowledge, which correspond to the virtue of faith. These gifts supplement faith. The gift of understanding is the capacity to penetrate more fully the mysteries of faith which are beyond the grasp of reason, although the gift does not afford a perfect understanding in this life. The gift of understanding can be exercised even in the area of human action when human reason, perfected by the gift, contemplates the eternal law as the supreme guide of our actions. Just as the gift of charity is in all those who have sanctifying grace, so also is the gift of understanding. The sixth beatitude, "Blessed are the clean of heart, for they shall see God" (Mt 5:8), is closely allied to the gift of understanding for understanding effects clarity by purging the mind of phantasms and errors; and it purifies our vision of God in this life by enabling us to see especially what he is not. The fruit of the Holy Spirit called faith (Gal 5:22), which Thomas takes to mean certitude of faith, is also closely allied to the gift of supernatural understanding.

While the gift of understanding gives us a sound grasp of what we are to believe, the gift of knowledge enables us to distinguish what is to be believed from what is not to be believed. The gift of knowledge is primarily speculative, since it enables a person to know what he or she ought to hold by faith; yet, the gift has practical consequences, since we are directed in our actions by faith. The gift of knowledge is allied to the third beatitude, "Blessed are they that mourn, for they shall be comforted" (Mt 5:4). Knowledge gives rise to mourning, because it makes a person realize how he or she has been duped by creatures, which are an occasion of sin.

In due sequence, Thomas takes up the sins opposed to faith and the gifts corresponding to it. Unbelief is a sin against faith. It is a voluntary lack of faith. The unbelief of those to whom the faith has never been preached is not a sin, because it is not voluntary; but the unbelief of those who reject the faith for no good reason, after it has been preached to them, is a sin. Dissent, which is the act proper to unbelief, is an act of the intellect moved, however, by the will, just as the assent of faith is. Apart from the sins directly opposed to hope and charity, unbelief is the greatest of sins because it deprives the unbeliever of the saving knowledge of God. Of course, not every action of the unbeliever is a sin for his nature remains good and capable of a naturally good action such as caring for his children or honoring his parents.

For Thomas, there were three main types of unbelief: that of pagans who resist the faith, that of the chosen people, and that of heretics. (Once more we must note that unbelief is sinful only when it is voluntary.) The unbelief of heretics is the worst because they have corrupted the faith they have received, whereas the others did not receive the faith in the first place. Arguing or disputing about the faith in public is sometimes necessary in order to refute error and strengthen others in the faith. A person who does not have the faith cannot be compelled by any power on earth to accept it, for belief must be a voluntary act. One must avoid any communication with an unbeliever that might endanger one's faith. Unbelievers should not be in authority over believers where this is a cause of scandal and a danger to the faith. Just as God allows certain evils to take place in the universe which he might prevent, lest, without them, greater goods might be forfeited or greater evils might ensue, so human governments should tolerate the religious rites of unbelievers.[4] The children of Jews and heretics are not to be baptized against the wishes of their parents, since the children belong to the parents. Of course, children who have reached the use of reason and wish to be baptized, may be baptized even if their parents are unwilling.

Heresy is a species of unbelief; it is the sin of one who professes the Christian faith, but corrupts its dogmas. The Church should be merciful to heretics while hoping for their conversion; however, Thomas is of the opinion that heretics should be excommunicated and even sentenced to death by the state, if they threaten the faith of others.[5] Penitent heretics should be accepted back into the Church; but backsliders may be punished by a sentence of death. Thomas was convinced that the corruption and abandonment of the faith was far more serious than any crime of a temporal nature, for which the state is wont to inflict death.

Apostasy is a sin of unbelief; it is the sin of one who professed the Christian faith and has rejected it completely. In Catholic countries, Thomas maintains, a ruler who proves apostate is, upon excommunication, justly deprived of the allegiance of his subjects, lest he corrupt their faith.

Blasphemy is the sin of one who disparages the divine goodness, denying to God what belongs to him or asserting of him what does not belong to him. For example, to say that God is wicked, because he did not avert some great tragedy, is blasphemy. Blasphemy can remain in the heart, or it can be expressed in words; and in the latter case, it is opposed to the external confession of one's faith. Blasphemy is always a mortal sin, indeed a very great sin, because it is a kind of unbelief. The wicked in hell blaspheme, because they detest the divine justice which punishes them in that state.

There is a particular kind of blasphemy called blasphemy against the Holy Spirit. To blaspheme against the Holy Spirit is to sin out of a certain malice by despising those things which withdraw a person from sin. St. Thomas enumerates six sins against the Holy Spirit: despair, presumption, resistance to the known truth, envy of a brother's spiritual good, the intention not to repent, and the obstinacy whereby a man hardens his purpose by clinging to sin. For example, presumption is a sin against the Holy Spirit because it removes the fear of divine justice which hinders us from sinning through choice. Sins against the Holy Spirit are unforgivable in the sense that they remove those things which are a means toward the pardon of sins. Of course, God is still able to bring to repentance a person who has sinned against the Holy Spirit. Normally a sin against the Holy Spirit is the result of many previous sins.

Certain sins are opposed to the gifts of understanding and knowledge. Mental blindness is the complete failure to consider spiritual realities, while dullness of sense is a partial failure to do so. Both are sinful, insofar as they are voluntary. Both sins arise from sins of the flesh, especially gluttony and lust, which in their vehemence fix a person's attention on corporeal things and distract him or her from intelligible things.

In conclusion, Thomas makes a brief reference to the precepts concerning faith, understanding and knowledge which are to be found in the Old Testament. There the only precept bearing upon faith had to do with faith in the one God (Ex 20:2); and the people were encouraged to pursue knowledge and understanding (Dt 4:6; 6:4-9).

Hope (2a2ae.17-22)

Hope is a prominent theme in the Bible. In the Old Testament Yahweh was the hope of Israel. The reason for Israel's hope in Yahweh was that Yahweh is faithful to his promises; and his mighty deeds in the past testified to his power and willingness to help. When the kingdoms of Israel and Judah were destroyed by conquering armies in the eighth and sixth centuries before Christ, the hope of the people suffered a severe blow. The prophets, however, rekindled the hope of the people in a new way. Jeremiah spoke of a new covenant which God would write upon the hearts of his people (31:31; 32:38-41). Ezekiel promised that God would remember his covenant with his people (16:59-63). God would give them a new heart and a new spirit (36:25-28). However, Israel's hope did not extend beyond the grave. Those who go down into the pit do not await God's kindness (Is 38:18); and when a man dies, he is not roused out of his sleep (Jb 14:12). Only at the very end of the period was there a suggestion of personal survival (Ws 5:5; 2 M 12:46).

In the New Testament, the message of hope is developed in the Pauline writings especially. By hope we were saved; the object of hope is not seen, and we must await it with patient endurance (Rm 8:24-25). Hope is the fruit of proved virtue and patient endurance (Rm 5:4). There are in the end three things that last: faith, hope and charity (1 Cor 13:13). Christians hope for glory (Col 1:27) and the resurrection (1 Cor 15:19). The Christian, as opposed to the pagan, is characterized by hope (Ep 2:12). Like a firm anchor, hope extends beyond the veil (Heb 6:19). The believer should be prepared to give an inquirer a reason for his or her hope (1 P 3:15).

According to the Second Vatican Council, hope looks forward to true life with God: "Although the mystery of death utterly beggars the imagination, the Church, taught by divine revelation, teaches that men and women have been created by God in view of a blessed destiny beyond the reach of earthly misery. Moreover, the Christian faith teaches that bodily death, from which human beings would have been immune had they not sinned, will be vanquished when they, who were ruined by their own doing, are restored to wholeness by an almighty and merciful Savior. For God has called men and women and still calls them, so that with their entire being they might be joined to him in sharing forever a divine life free from all corruption. Christ won this victory when he rose to life, for by his death he freed us from death. Hence, to every thoughtful person a solidly established faith provides the answer to his or her anxiety about the future. At the same time, faith gives a person the power to be united in Christ with his or her loved ones, who have already been snatched by death. Faith arouses the hope that they have found true life with God."[6]

Thomas' treatise on hope, the second theological virtue, studies the virtue itself, its psychic seat, the corresponding gift of fear of God, the sins opposed to hope (that is to say, despair and presumption), and finally the divine precepts relating to hope and fear.

Hope is a virtue, which relies upon the power and mercy of God to attain eternal life. We can hope not only for our own salvation, but also for the salvation of another. While we place our hope of eternal life ultimately in God, we can and may hope in other human beings, such as the saints, as the instruments and agents of God's providence. Hope is a theological virtue, because it relies upon God himself to achieve the vision and fruition of God in eternal life. Hope, by which we trust God to attain eternal life, is distinct from faith by which we adhere to God as the source of truth, and from charity by which we adhere to God for his own sake. Faith goes before hope, revealing the object of hope and the means to attain it. Hope leads to charity, in the sense that a person through hoping to be rewarded by God is encouraged to love God and obey his commandments. Of course, when we speak about the priority of the virtues, we have in mind the sequence of their acts; thus, an act of faith necessarily precedes an act of hope; but the virtues themselves are infused simultaneously with sanctifying grace.

Hope resides in the will since it strives for a divine good. Hope, like faith, is voided in heaven, because the object of hope on earth is possessed. The damned in hell have no hope; they know that the vision of God is no longer possible for them. Our hope is certain since it relies upon the omnipotence and mercy of God to bring us to eternal life. Yet, firm as the anchor of hope is, we must still work out our salvation in fear and trembling for we can always sin and come short of the goal.

The gift of fear corresponds to the virtue of hope. God, who is goodness itself, cannot be the object of fear, but we can be afraid of being separated from him; and in this way God can and ought to be feared. Fear is servile if a person adheres to God through fear of punishment; it is filial fear if a person is afraid of offending him who is our loving Father; and it is initial fear if it is something between servile and filial fear. Worldly fear means turning away from God because one is afraid of losing worldly goods; it is always evil. Servile fear or fear of punishment by God is compatible with the love of God; but servile fear differs substantially from filial fear which is afraid of offending God who is loved.

Both servile fear and filial fear constitute the beginning of wisdom, although in different ways: servile fear by keeping a person from sin through fear of punishment, and filial fear by submitting a person to God in all things. Filial fear is a gift of the Holy Spirit and it increases with charity, for the more one loves God the more one fears to offend him and be separated from him. Filial fear, but not servile fear, will continue to exist in heaven in a perfected state. Poverty of spirit (Mt 5:3) is the beatitude corresponding to the gift of fear, for, from the very fact that a person shows reverence and submission to God, he or she is characterized not by a proud spirit, but by poverty of spirit.

The two sins contrary to hope are despair and presumption. Despair is a sin against hope, because the despairing person does not trust God to save him. Despair is not necessarily a sin of unbelief, since a person can believe in God's willingness to forgive sinners while at the same time he thinks that there is no pardon for him. Despair is not the greatest sin; hatred of God and unbelief, which are opposed to charity and faith respectively, are worse; but despair is very dangerous because it encourages one to yield to other sins. Despair arises particularly from sloth since the slothful person is unwilling to grapple with the difficulties of the Christian life; but sometimes despair arises from lust which leads a person to have a distaste for spiritual things.

The sin of presumption means that a person relies on the power and mercy of God in an immoderate way when, for example, a person hopes to obtain pardon without repenting of his sins. Presumption is indeed a sin, but not so serious a sin as despair, for presumption does recognize the divine mercy and forgiveness. Presumption is opposed to hope for both rely on God, but hope ordinately and presumption inordinately. Presumption springs from pride; that is to say, a person has such a high opinion of himself that he does not believe that God would punish him or exclude him from heaven, however much he sin.

Every Biblical promise of reward is an implied precept of hope; but there are other inducements to hope, even by way of warning or command; for example, we read in Psalm 62:9, "Hope in the Lord at all times, O my people." Moreover, it is a matter of precept that we should fear God: "And now, Israel, what does the Lord, your God, ask of you but to fear the Lord, your God?" (Dt 10:12).

Charity (2a2ae.23-46)

Charity is the third and greatest of the theological virtues; and it too is a prominent theme in the Bible. In the Old Testament, love is the sentiment which Yahweh has for Israel (Ho 11:1); it is the band by which he draws his people to himself (Ho 11:4); but he will withdraw his love because of their wicked deeds (Ho 9:15). The selection of the Israelites to be the people of God was a matter of free choice and love on the part of the Lord (Dt 7:6-8). Out of love the Lord led the Israelites out of Egypt (Dt 4:37; 7:8). He will love and bless and multiply them (Dt 7:13). In turn, the Israelites are commanded to love the Lord their God with all their heart and soul and strength (Dt 6:5). They are to love the Lord and heed his statutes, decrees, and commandments (Dt 11:1).

In the Synoptic gospels, Jesus identifies the great commandments of the law as love of God and neighbor (Mt 22:34-40; Mk 12:28-34; Lk 10:25-28). Jesus commands us to love even our enemies (Mt 5:43-48). The love of God must be exclusive, suffering no rival (Mt 6:24; Lk 16:13). One must love Jesus more than his father or mother, son or daughter (Mt 10:37).

According to Paul, the love of God has been poured out in our hearts through the Holy Spirit (Rm 5:5). God has proved his love for us in that Christ died for us, while we were still sinners (Rm

5:8). No trial or creature can separate us from the love of God that comes to us in Christ Jesus (Rm 8:35-39). Husbands are to love their wives, as Christ loved the Church (Ep 5:25). He who loves his neighbor has fulfilled the law (Rm 13:8). Love is the root and foundation of the Christian life (Ep 3:17). Love binds all the virtues together (Col 3:14). Love is the most excellent of the gifts (1 Cor 13:1-13).

There are many references to love in the Johannine writings. The Father has bestowed his love on us in letting us be called his children (1 Jn 3:1). Jesus showed his love for his own to the very end (Jn 13:1). God is love, and he who abides in love abides in God, and God in him (1 Jn 4:16). Love is demonstrated by keeping the commandments of God (Jn 14:15, 21, 23). The new commandment of Jesus is to love one another (Jn 13:34; 15:17). Out of love God sent his Son into the world, so that all who believe in him may have eternal life (Jn 3:16). In these writings, therefore, love is a mutual, all-embracing, and unifying force.

In many passages, the Second Vatican Council drew out the implications of love for the modern world.

Thomas' study of charity or love follows the order that we have come to expect. He considers charity itself, the object of charity (those whom we are to love), its acts, the vices opposed to it, the precepts relating to charity, and the corresponding gift of wisdom, which elevates love to the heights of mystical contemplation.

Thomas identifies charity with the friendship of men and women for God. Friendship between two persons is characterized by mutual benevolence; that is to say, each friend wishes good things to the other. Moreover, friendship springs up between persons who have something in common, something which brings them together. We find this common ground among the members of a family, among students and workers and travelers and artists, and so on. With all this in mind, we may say that charity makes us friends of God in the strictest sense of the word. With charity in our hearts, there is mutual benevolence: God loves us; indeed, his love is the cause of the good that we have; and we in turn love God in whom we see the essence of goodness. The common ground upon which our friendship with God is based is the life of God himself which we share through sanctifying grace. Accordingly, charity is a supernatural virtue affecting the will in the exercise of friendship with God. It is the most excellent virtue of all whose object is God as the supremely lovable being. No true supernatural virtue is possible without charity, for it is through charity that a person's actions are ultimately directed to his or her principal good, which is the last end. Thomas calls charity the form of all other virtues because it makes us do everything out of love for God.

Charity is located in the will, since the object of charity is God as the supreme good in whom our happiness lies. Charity, as a supernatural virtue, is infused by the Holy Spirit (Rm 5:5). The degree of charity infused by the Holy Spirit does not depend upon the recipient in any way, but only upon the Holy Spirit who dispenses his gifts according to his good pleasure (1 Cor 12:11). Charity can increase; the love of God can grow stronger in our hearts; it does so by taking deeper root in the will, as a plant takes deeper root in the soil. Not every act of charity strengthens the virtue of charity, but only an act more fervent than the virtue itself; still, every act of charity does dispose a person to act more readily out of love, and so it leads to a more fervent act eventually. Charity can increase indefinitely as long as we are pilgrims on this earth.

The charity of all is perfect in this life, at least to the extent that those who love God neither think nor desire anything contrary to that love. From another point of view, we can distinguish three degrees of charity: that of beginners, who are particularly concerned with avoiding sin; that of the proficient, who seek to strengthen their charity by good works; and that of the perfect, who seek union with and enjoyment of God. Charity cannot be diminished, let us say, from a strength of 10 to a strength of 9, although venial sins and even the failure to perform good works can lead to its total corruption through mortal sin. Charity can be lost once we have it, because in this life we do not see God face to face, and so we can choose to be separated from him. In the next life, however, we shall see God as he is, and so we shall be unable to choose anything apart from him. Charity is lost through mortal sin which creates an obstacle to the infusion of charity by the Holy Spirit just as a wall creates an obstacle to the entry of light into a room. So much for charity considered as a virtue.

What about the object of charity? Whom are we to love? The love of charity does not stop at God but extends to our neighbor insofar as we find God in him or her. We cannot love animals and other irrational creatures out of charity because they do not have the capacity to share in the life of God which charity supposes; however, we can love them for the good they bring to us. Human beings can love themselves out of charity since they can find God in themselves. They can love their bodies out of charity as something to be used in the service of God and neighbor. Sinners are lovable in respect to their nature but not in respect to their sinful ways. Sinners do not really love themselves because they do not love themselves aright.

We are called to love our enemies (Mt 5:44), not because they seek to harm us, but because they are human beings capable of friendship with God. We must show them the general signs of good will that we show to all men and women; hence, we must pray for them and not exclude them from any benefits that we might confer on the whole community. On the other hand, we are not required to show them the particular favors that we confer on our friends. For example, we do not have to invite an enemy into our homes. We ought to love the angels out of charity since they share with us the life of God and the call to eternal happiness. We cannot love the demons out of charity because we do not share these things with them.

Thomas teaches that we must observe an order in our charity, which means that some have a greater claim upon our love than others. God is to be loved before all others, including ourselves, because he is the common good of all. We must prefer our own spiritual welfare to the spiritual welfare of a neighbor; therefore, we may not sin in order to withdraw another from sin; but we must prefer the spiritual welfare of a neighbor to the welfare of our own bodies. We are to love our neighbors in proportion to their closeness to God and to ourselves. We should wish a greater good, a greater measure of eternal happiness, to one who is closer to God; but we wish good to those who are closer to us with greater affection and intensity even if that good is less significant. Those persons are closest to us, who are united to us by some tie such as citizenship, enrollment in the same school, service in the same military unit, and so on. The strongest tie of all is the tie of blood; hence, it is natural that we love our relatives more intensely than others. We ought to love our parents more than our children since they have given us life; sometimes, however, it is easier to love one's children than one's parents. A man loves his wife more intensely than his parents; but he loves his parents with greater reverence. We ought to love our benefactors for their kindness to us; and, of course, we love those who are the beneficiaries of our kindness. The order of charity, since it is derived from nature, will endure in heaven where nature is not done away with but perfected. So much for the order that we must observe among the persons we love.

Next Thomas has something to say about the principal act of charity which is to love. It is more proper to charity to love than to be loved, since a virtue inclines a person to act. Out of charity we love God for himself, just as we love our parents for themselves. It is true, though, that we are *disposed* to love God for the benefits that he has conferred upon us. In this life we know creatures immediately, and we come to know God through creatures; but in the case of charity the process is reversed: we love God immediately and we come to love creatures because of God. Out of charity we can love God wholly; that is to say, we can love all that pertains to God with all our might, and we can refer all that we have to God. Even so, our love remains a finite response to the infinite goodness of God. Thomas thinks that it is more meritorious to love a friend than an enemy, because a friend is better and more closely united to us through a mutual bond of charity.

Several effects follow upon the principal act of charity which is to love. The first three effects to be considered are interior, and they are joy, peace and mercy. Where there is charity, there is spiritual joy, for charity implies a kind of union with God, the supreme good, even in this life. Still this joy leaves room for a measure of sorrow over anything that hinders our complete union with God such as sin and our distance from God in this life. Our joy cannot be full on this earth, since we do not see God face to face, but it shall be overflowing in heaven when we shall have the full enjoyment of God. Joy is not a virtue distinct from charity, but an act or effect of charity; and it is numbered among the fruits of the Holy Spirit (Gal 5:22).

Peace too is an effect of charity. For Thomas, peace means inner repose and outer harmony. In other words, a person is at peace when he or she is not tormented inwardly by conflicting desires, and when he or she lives in concord with others, their wills consenting to the same thing. All things desire peace; that is to say, every person wishes to achieve his or her objectives with tranquility and without obstacles. When this situation prevails we have true peace which Augustine defined as the "tranquility of order."[7] Peace is the effect of charity which focuses all of one's desires on God and fulfills our neighbor's will as though it were ours. Peace, like joy, is an act and effect of the virtue of charity; it too is a fruit of the Holy Spirit (Gal 5:22). Peace can be perfect only in heaven, where we shall find complete rest in God; peace cannot be perfect on this earth where there are always certain things within and without which disturb the peace.

Mercy is an effect of charity. According to Augustine, mercy "is heartfelt sympathy for another's distress, moving us to help, if we can."[8] We are moved to pity another's distress, either because we love that person, whose distress we regard as our own, or because we realize that the same thing could happen to us. Mercy is a special virtue. Charity, which unites us to God, is greater than mercy, which tries to relieve a neighbor's distress; but of all the virtues which relate to our neighbor, mercy is the greatest, since, as Thomas puts it, it belongs to one who is higher and better to supply the defect of another. In Shakespeare's *Merchant of Venice* we read: "The quality of mercy is not strained. 'Tis mightiest in the mightiest: it becomes the throned monarch better than his crown."[9]

There are also three outward acts or effects of charity, namely, beneficence, almsgiving (which is a part of beneficence), and fraternal correction (which is a kind of alms). Beneficence is an act of charity and friendship, and it simply means doing good to someone. We are bound to do good to all human beings (Gal 6:10) as time and place require. This duty extends particularly to those who are more closely united to us, just as God confers his gifts most plentifully on those creatures nearest to him. Beneficence is not a special virtue; it is an act of charity.

Almsgiving is an act of mercy; but because mercy is an effect of charity, almsgiving is an act of charity through the medium of mercy. The different kinds of almsdeeds are the corporal and spiritual works of mercy. The chief corporal works of mercy are to feed the hungry, give drink to the thirsty, clothe the naked, visit the imprisoned, shelter the homeless, visit the sick and bury the dead. The chief spiritual works of mercy are to instruct the ignorant, counsel the doubtful, comfort the sorrowful, reprove the sinner, forgive injuries, bear with those who trouble and annoy us, and pray for the living and the dead. Of themselves, the spiritual works of mercy are more excellent than the corporal works because a spiritual gift is better than a corporal gift; but in a particular case a corporal work of mercy may be better; for example, it is better to feed a hungry man than instruct him.

We are bound to give alms from our surplus, that is, from what we do not need for ourselves and those in our charge. A person is not obliged to sacrifice what is necessary for his or her state in life in order to supply the ordinary needs of others. To make such a sacrifice is a matter of counsel and not of precept. Alms are to be given out of a donor's own property and not from ill-gotten goods, which belong to their owner. Those who are closest to us have first claim upon our alms. It is praiseworthy to give alms abundantly, for the Bible teaches: "If you have great wealth, give alms out of your abundance; if you have but little, distribute even some of that" (Tb 4:8).

The third outward act or effect of mercy is fraternal correction. Fraternal correction is the reproof of a wrongdoer with a view to his or her amendment. It is obviously an act of charity. Fraternal correction is a matter of precept when it is necessary for a brother's amendment. This precept binds all in high and low places; and one in a low station of life may have to correct someone in a higher station but always in a becoming way with gentleness and respect. Even a sinner may correct another sinner because sin does not deprive a sinner of all right judgment. When correction may have no effect, or an evil effect, it should be omitted. A private admonition of the sinner, aiming at his amendment, while avoiding his disgrace, should precede a public denunciation (Mt 18:15). But even before a public denunciation, there should be a revelation of the brother's sin to a few witnesses for the same purpose (Mt 18:16).

After studying the effects of charity, Thomas takes up the vices opposed to charity: hatred which is opposed to love; sloth and envy which are opposed to the joy of charity; discord, contention, schism, war, strife and sedition which are contrary to peace; and scandal which is opposed to charity and beneficence.

Thomas asks if it is possible for anyone to hate God. He answers that God can be hated by some debased individuals, because he forbids sin and inflicts punishment. Hatred of God is the worst of sins because it means turning away from God directly whereas in other sins, fornication for instance, a person turns away from God indirectly by desiring an inordinate pleasure, to which aversion from God is connected. Hatred of one's neighbor is always a sin; but hatred of one's neighbor does not hurt him or her as much as some outward sins such as theft, murder and adultery. Hatred of God and neighbor is not a capital sin since it is not so much the first, but the last step in the path of sin. Hatred of a neighbor grows out of envy, which is sorrow over a neighbor's good.

Sloth and envy are the two vices opposed to the joy of charity. This joy is either about the divine good, and then the contrary is sloth, or about our neighbor's good, and then its contrary is envy. First, sloth. Sloth is spiritual laziness; it is sadness over the many demands God makes upon us; it is weariness in doing good. If it comes to deliberate dislike, horror and detestation of spiritual things, it becomes a mortal sin. Sloth is a capital sin; that is, it is a reason why men and women commit other sins, for it leads to the neglect of good works that are of grave obligation.

Envy is sorrow over the good things another possesses because these things seem to diminish our own reputation and lessen the esteem in which we are held. The envious person grieves over another's good insofar as this good surpasses his or hers. Such grief is sinful since it is grief over what should make us rejoice, namely, our neighbor's good. Envy can be a mortal sin when it is fully deliberate. Envy is a capital sin because it is a source of hatred, calumny and complacency in another's misfortune.

Next, Thomas considers the sins which are contrary to peace: discord, which is in the heart; contention, which is on the lips; and those things which consist in deeds, namely, schism, war, strife and sedition.

Discord is opposed to charity and peace, which unite individuals. It is the sin of those who wrongfully fail to agree upon what is right and good. If this disagreement is expressed in words, it becomes the sin of contention. Sometimes discord and contention are the fault of one party only, who obstinately resists what is good; sometimes they are the fault of both parties; but sometimes they are not the fault of either, when, for example, both parties seek the good, but disagree as to what it is in a particular instance. The sins of discord and contention arise from pride and vainglory, whereby one clings obstinately to his or her own opinion.

One sins against peace, not only in one's heart and by words, but also by deeds. Schism is such a sinful deed. St. Thomas considers schism to be a sin against charity. Unity is the effect of charity, and schismatics separate themselves from the unity of the Church either by their refusal to submit to the Pope or to associate with those who recognize his leadership; hence, schismatics sin against charity. In itself, schism is a grave sin, but it is not as serious as unbelief, for unbelief is opposed to God himself while schism is opposed to ecclesiastical unity. Schismatics do not lose the power of orders, but only the right to exercise it. They do, however, lose the power of jurisdiction. Schismatics deserve to be excommunicated for their sin.

War is an armed conflict between nations. It is not necessarily sinful. Three conditions are necessary for a just war: (1) it must be declared by the civil authority, which is responsible for the welfare of the state; (2) it must be waged for a just cause: to right very serious wrongs; and (3) even if it is waged for a just cause, it must be fought with a good intention: to foster good and avoid evil, and not just to inflict harm or dominate others or enlarge one's territory. Clearly St. Thomas implies that there are values worth the loss of life. An act evil in itself is never permitted in the name of war.

The Second Vatican Council (1962-65) had much to say about war. Governments, it taught, cannot be denied the right to legitimate defense, once every means of peaceful settlement has been exhausted. Those who devote themselves to military service of their country should regard themselves as agents of security and freedom, and they make a genuine contribution to peace. The horror and perversity of modern warfare are immensely magnified by the addition of scientific weapons. Any act of war, aimed indiscriminately at the destruction of entire cities or extensive areas along with their population, is a crime against God and human beings. The accumulation of a modern arsenal does seem to deter a possible enemy attack, and this maintains a kind of peace, but not a sure and authentic one. The human race must seek to put an end to the arms race and to make a true beginning of disarmament, not unilaterally indeed, but proceeding at an equal pace according to agreement, and backed up by true and workable safeguards.[10]

Along with schisms and unjust warfare, strife is an external sin against charity and peace. Strife means fighting between individuals. It is a kind of private war, one person attacking another, let us say, with his fists. It is a mortal sin in the person who inflicts harm on another unjustly. Strife arises from anger. Sedition is also an external sin against peace. Sedition exists when one segment of the population rises up against another segment. Sedition subverts the unity and peace of a nation.

It remains for us to consider the vice which is opposed to charity and beneficence, namely, scandal. Scandal is a word or deed which is evil or has the appearance of evil and affords another the occasion of sinning. For example, a prominent person who is frequently divorced gives scandal because his or her bad example encourages others to treat marriage lightly. Scandal is opposed to charity and beneficence which bid us seek our neighor's good. Scandal can be a mortal or venial sin, depending upon the intention of the one who gives scandal and upon the gravity of his or her scandalous word or deed. Scandal is taken by those who are weak and unsettled in virtue. Scandal is neither given nor taken by those who are relatively perfect in charity. The "scandal of the Pharisees" tries to make evil out of good, and we ought to treat it with contempt (Mt 15:14). The "scandal of the little ones" or scandal of the weak sees evil where there is none, not by reason of malice, but for lack of understanding and instruction. We should avoid scandal of the weak at considerable inconvenience to ourselves, until we can remove it by further instruction.

The two great precepts of charity were given in the Old Testament (Dt 6:5; Lv 19:18) and reaffirmed by Jesus in the New Testament (Mt 22:36-40): "You shall love the Lord your God with your whole heart, with your whole soul, and with all your mind. This is the first and greatest commandment. The second is like it: You shall love your neighbor as yourself." These two precepts induce us to love God as the one in whom we find our ultimate happiness, and to love our neighbor for the sake of God. We are told to love God with our whole heart to signify that we ought to do all things for God, consenting to nothing that is contrary to his love. We can fulfill this precept perfectly only in heaven; but we can approach the ideal more and more in this life. The command to love our neighbor as ourselves indicates the reason why we ought to love others, that is to say, because they bear the image of God, just as we do; and it also indicates the manner of loving others, that is, as ourselves, not indeed as much as we love ourselves, but for the same reasons.

The gift of the Holy Spirit, which corresponds to the virtue of charity, is wisdom. Wisdom enables us to judge and set in order all things in relation to God, the highest cause and the supreme principle. Inasmuch as it involves a judgment, wisdom resides in the intellect. It contemplates the things of God, but it also directs human activity in accordance with divine rules. Wisdom presupposes charity and cannot exist without it; hence, it is expelled by mortal sin. The seventh beatitude, "Blessed are the peacemakers; they shall be called sons of God" (Mt 5:9), corresponds to the gift of wisdom, for wisdom establishes the tranquility of order, which is peace; and it conforms us to the Son of God, who is wisdom begotten.

The vice opposed to wisdom is folly. The foolish person has a dulled sense of judgment, especially where the things of God are concerned. Dullness of judgment arises from absorption in earthly things and chiefly from lust, which is about the greatest of pleasures; and these absorb the mind more than any others.

Chapter 15

THE CARDINAL VIRTUES OF PRUDENCE AND JUSTICE (2a2ae.47-122)

St. Thomas considers the cardinal virtues after the theological virtues. The cardinal virtues are prudence, justice, fortitude and temperance. They are called the cardinal virtues because of their basic importance. All the moral virtues, many as they are, can be reduced to these four. The cardinal virtues are also distinguished by the importance of their matter. We shall study prudence and justice in this chapter, and fortitude and temperance in the next one.

In connection with the cardinal virtues, Thomas also speaks of what he calls their integral and subjective and potential parts. The integral parts of a cardinal virtue are those things which must come together if the cardinal virtue is to function properly; and these parts may be compared to the walls, roof and foundation of a house. The subjective parts are the virtues which comprise the different species of a cardinal virtue; and they may be compared to an ox and a lion which are the subjective parts of the species of animal. The potential parts are the virtues which have something in common with the cardinal virtue, but differ in some respect; and they may be compared to the vegetative and sensitive powers, which are potential parts of the soul.

For both the Old and New Testaments of the Bible, the fundamental virtue is to seek God with one's whole heart in obedience to the divine will. The fundamental vice is to be disobedient to the divine will, as manifested through Moses in the Old Testament and through Jesus Christ in the New Testament. Still, the Bible knows many other specific virtues and vices. The book of Wisdom, for example, speaks of virtue (4:1; 5:13) and mentions the four cardinal virtues (8:7); it also gives a list of vices (14:22-29). In this respect, Wisdom shows the influence of Greek ethics. Paul, for his part, offers numerous catalogs of virtues (2 Tm 3:10; Col 3:12-14; Ph 4) and vices (Rm 1:29-31; 1 Cor 6:9-10; 2 Cor 12:20). These catalogs reflect both Jewish and Greek influences.

Prudence (2a2ae.47-56)

Speaking of prudence, Thomas discusses the virtue itself, its parts, the gift of the Holy Spirit (counsel) corresponding to it, the vices opposed to it, and the precepts concerning prudence.

The prudent person tries to foresee the future from knowledge of the present and past, and this is the work of reason; hence, prudence resides in the intellect. The work of prudence is to direct our actions to an end; hence, it resides in the practical intellect. The prudent person knows not only the universal principles of reason, but also the contingencies of life. For example, a prudent person knows that he or she may not endanger human life without sufficient reason (a universal principle), and he or she also knows that driving an auto while under the influence of alcohol endangers human life without sufficient reason (a particular situation). Prudence has something in common with the intellectual virtues because it perfects the intellect, and something in common with the moral virtues because it directs our actions. The other moral virtues incline us to act for an end determined by reason, and prudence determines in what manner and by what means the end is to be achieved in accordance with reason. For example, temperance inclines a person to act in accordance with reason despite one's concupiscences, and prudence determines what it means to act temperately in a particular situation.

The chief act of prudence is to command what one has judged appropriate after taking counsel. Prudence is ever careful, watchful, and solicitous that a person's conduct be right. One can exercise prudence in seeking one's own good (personal prudence) or the good of one's family (domestic prudence) or the good of the community and state (political prudence). True and perfect prudence, which takes counsel, judges and commands aright with respect to the true end of human life, is found only in the just, and not in sinners. Whoever has grace has charity and all the other supernatural virtues including prudence. While we have been speaking mainly of supernatural prudence, there is also a natural prudence which is learned especially through experience and time. Prudence is not forgotten but rather is corrupted by the passions.

St. Thomas distinguishes eight integral parts of prudence which must come together if one is to act prudently. To act prudently, one must remember the past, have a right understanding of the principles at stake, be prepared to learn from others, be capable of making comparisons, be an apt reasoner, have foresight, take account of circumstances, and exercise caution.

We have already spoken of three subjective parts or species of prudence: personal, domestic and political. St. Thomas also mentions a fourth: military prudence, which seeks to repel the attack of an enemy.

There are three potential parts of prudence—virtues in their own right: *eubulia* by which a person is led to take counsel; *synesis* by which a person exercises good judgment in practical matters; and *gnome* by which one judges according to the higher principles of human conduct especially in extraordinary affairs.

The gift of the Holy Spirit which corresponds to the virtue of prudence is counsel, because both the virtue and the gift have to do with what has to be done for the sake of an end. Through the gift of counsel, one is advised, as it were, by the Holy Spirit. The gift of counsel remains even in heaven, so that the blessed may help others to achieve the end they have attained. The fifth beatitude, "Blessed are the merciful, for they shall obtain mercy'' (Mt 5:7), corresponds to the gift of counsel for counsel is properly about things useful for an end, and works of mercy are particularly useful for the attainment of our end.

One sins against the virtue of prudence by imprudence. One is sinfully imprudent when he or she acts precipitously, thoughtlessly and inconstantly. All these sins are brought about principally, but not exclusively, by sins of lust which totally absorb the mind. One sins against prudence by negligence, which is a culpable lack of concern for the things of God and one's own salvation. Carnal prudence is the sin of a person who looks upon the care of his body as the whole purpose of his existence. Craftiness is the sin of one who uses illegitimate means to secure a certain end, either good or evil. Guile is the execution of a crafty person's plans either in words or deeds. It is sinful to be solicitous about earthly and temporal goods before all others; rather, we should be solicitous most of all about spiritual goods, hoping that temporal goods also may be granted to us according to our needs, if we do what we ought to do. We should not be solicitous about the future, for the future will bring its own burden of solicitude. All the vices about which we have been speaking arise chiefly from covetousness.

There is no special precept about prudence in the Decalogue; and yet all the precepts of the Decalogue are related to prudence, which directs the virtuous activity prescribed by the Decalogue. The Old Law does forbid the vices opposed to prudence, such as craftiness and the vices allied to it (Lv 19:13; Dt 25:13).

Justice (2a2ae.57-122)

The Bible uses the terms, justice and just, with a variety of meanings. In the Old Testament God is said to be just in the sense that he is faithful to his covenant (Gn 18:25; Is 26:4). The person who holds to God's way is himself just or righteous (Gn 18:19; Jb

17:9). The people did not hold to God's way; hence they abandoned justice (Am 5:7). A just weight is one that is exact (Dt 25:15). Judges should not show partiality, but justice (Lv 19:15). A good king loves justice and hates wickedness (Ps 45:8). Justice is the implementation of the rights of others (Ex 23:6-8). The prophets condemned injustice (Am 5:11-15; Is 5:23; Jr 22:13-18).

According to the New Testament, a just person is one who lives an upright life (Mt 1:19; 5:45; Lk 1:6; 2:25). Jesus himself fulfilled all justice (Mt 3:15) and blessed those who hunger for it (Mt 5:6). The justice or righteousness of Jesus' disciples must exceed that of the scribes and Pharisees (Mt 5:20). Christians must "do justice" (1 Jn 3:7). "The way of justice" means to live according to God's command (2 P 3:13). For Paul, the justice of God works through faith in Jesus Christ for all who believe (Rm 3:22). A person is not justified by observance of the law, but by faith (Rm 3:28). One who has been made just lives a new life (Rm 6:4, 12-14). Christians are the slaves of justice (Rm 6:18). All Scripture is useful for training in justice (2 Tm 3:16). Perfect justice eludes us now, but it remains an object of hope (Gal 5:5).

Thomas does not use the terms, justice and just, with such a variety of meanings. Rather, for him, justice means giving each one what is his or hers by right. It is a social norm in that it guides the actions of people in their dealings with one another. It is in this sense that the Church has used the term justice to enunciate its teaching on social justice.

The Church has had much to say about social justice, especially in the twentieth century. In *Rerum Novarum* (1891), Pope Leo XIII stressed the dignity of workers as human beings and their right to a just wage and decent working conditions. He also defended their right to organize labor unions to protect themselves. In *Quadragesimo Anno* (1931), Pius XI reaffirmed the dignity of workers and the responsibility of the state to promote the welfare of every member of society. In his *Mater et Magistra* (1961) John XXIII emphasized the global aspect of justice, the right of all to share in the fruits of society, and the need to correct economic imbalances. In *Pacem in Terris* (1963), the same Pope listed the rights and duties flowing from the dignity of personhood. In *Gaudium et Spes* (1965), the Second Vatican Council spoke of the Church's unique contribution to the establishment of justice; but it also recognized the contribution of other agencies to this enterprise.

Two years later, Paul VI's *Populorum Progressio* (1967) called upon advanced nations to assist developing nations not only by economic aid, but also by establishing a more just economic order. His *Octogesima Adveniens* (1971) spoke of many new problems in which justice is a factor: urbanization, youth, the role of women, the victims of change and discrimination, the environment, and unemployment. In the same year, the Synod of Bishops in their document, *Justice in the World* (1971), said that action on behalf of justice and participation in the transformation of the world are a constitutive dimension of the preaching of the gospel. Finally, John Paul II, in his encyclical, *Redemptor Hominis* (1979), explained the social implications of the incarnation and redemption.

Thomas treats the virtue of justice and its parts at greater length than any other virtue. The subjective or essential parts of justice are the virtues of distributive and commutative justice. The quasi-integral parts of justice are to do good and refrain from evil. The potential parts of justice include the virtues of religion, piety or filial respect, observance, gratitude, vengeance or vindication, truthfulness, friendliness and liberality. The treatise on justice ends with an exposition of the gift of piety, the corresponding gift of the Holy Spirit and with a review of the divine precepts which regulate justice.

Justice establishes a kind of equality between two persons, for example, between a buyer and a seller. The former gives the equivalent in money to the seller for his merchandise. Justice is concerned with the right or the just, which is the good work that establishes this equality. What the right or the just is in a particular instance, is determined in two ways: first, by its very nature, as in the case of a buyer who gives so much that he or she may receive equal value in return; and, secondly, by public or private agreement, as in the case of a legislature which decrees what is right and just here and now. In the first case, we have natural right or what is naturally just; and in the second case, we have positive right or what is just by decree or agreement. Justice establishes equality between two distinct persons; so Thomas holds that in a domestic group we cannot speak of the right or the just in a strict sense, because in a sense all the members of the group are one.

Justice may be defined as the virtue whereby a person renders what is due to another by a constant and perpetual will. Justice is located in the will and not in the intellect, for we are not said to be just through knowing something aright, but through doing something aright. Thomas distinguishes legal justice from particular justice. Legal justice is the virtue of the legislator primarily, inasmuch as he or she directs the activity of citizens so as to secure the common good; but secondarily and administratively, legal justice belongs to citizens too. Particular justice governs the activity of one individual in relation to another. Aristotle said that particular justice has its application in matters that belong to social life. Hence, justice is not concerned with passions, as temperance and fortitude are, but with actions which have reference to others. The mean of justice is an external fact; it is a real mean; it is achieved when equality is established between the external thing and the external person, when, for example, the worker receives the wages he or she is entitled to. The act of justice is to render each one his or her own (*unicuique suum*). Justice stands foremost among the moral virtues, because it is located in the will and not in the sensitive appetite, and because it includes the good of another.

Injustice is a special vice opposed to justice. Injustice is twofold; illegal injustice is opposed to legal justice and contemns the common good; particular injustice is opposed to particular justice and contemns the good of individuals. To do what is unjust intentionally and by full choice is the mark of an unjust person, a person with the vice of injustice. Injustice is to be found only in what is suffered against one's will. Injustice is either a mortal sin or a venial sin according to the matter involved.

Judgment is an act of the virtue of justice; it is the act of a judge; it is a decision or determination of what is just. Judgment is an act of justice insofar as justice inclines a judge to judge aright; but it is an act of prudence insofar as prudence determines what is right and just. It is lawful to judge when the judge seeks to act justly, when he or she has authority to judge, and when he or she passes judgment on sufficient grounds. A judge ought to deem a person good unless there are evident reasons to the contrary. Judgment must be rendered according to written laws which embody either natural or positive right, of which we spoke earlier.

Having spoken of the virtue itself, Thomas now takes up the parts of justice. First, he considers the subjective parts or species of justice. There are two species of justice, commutative and distributive. Commutative justice is concerned with the mutual dealings between two individuals, particularly in matters of buying and selling. Distributive justice has to do with the distribution of rewards, honors and burdens among the members of a community. The equality demanded by commutative justice is absolute and arithmetical; for example, if I owe someone five dollars, commutative justice is satisfied when I repay five dollars, no more, no less. On the other hand, the equality demanded by distributive justice is proportional or geometrical, in the sense that rewards are granted to, and burdens are imposed upon, individuals in accordance with their position, prominence and capability in the community; for example, a just legislature will impose higher taxes upon those who have more resources.

The outstanding act of commutative justice is called restitution. It means to restore what belongs to another; and it is occasioned by one person's having what belongs to another, either with his consent, for instance on loan or deposit, or against his consent, as in robbery or theft. One who makes restitution must restore the full value of what he took. In no case may a thief keep stolen goods; he or she must return them to the owner or, if the owner cannot be found, give them to pious causes. Those who cooperate in a theft by giving assistance to the thieves are bound to restitution. Restitution is to be made as soon as possible, so that the owner may not be deprived of the use of the property.

Next Thomas discusses the vices opposed to distributive and commutative justice. Respect of, or partiality to, persons is a sin opposed to distributive justice. It means the conferring of favors without regard to the merits of the person rewarded. For example, to promote a relative to a position of prominence and responsibility in the community to the exclusion of another person who is better qualified is a sin of partiality. The sin is also committed by showing honor to unworthy individuals or for unjust reasons. A judge can be guilty of the sin of partiality by failing to administer justice evenhandedly.

Murder is a sin against commutative justice. Plants and animals may be deprived of life to serve as food for humans, because the lower exists for the higher. Thomas allows the execution of criminals for the good of the community, just as he allows the amputation of a diseased arm or leg for the good of the body. Suicide is sinful because it is contrary to the natural law and to charity, and because it violates the rights of God and the community. Needless to say, a mentally disturbed person, who takes his or her own life, is not guilty of suicide. The direct killing of an innocent person is never lawful. One may take the life of an unjust aggressor if taking his life is necessary to save one's own life. The term, unjust aggressor, refers to what the aggressor is actually doing and not to his innocence or guilt in the eyes of God. In this sense, an insane person, who attacks another with a knife, is an unjust aggressor.

Just as society may take the life of a criminal for certain heinous crimes, so it may inflict the lesser punishment of mutilation. A parent may lawfully spank a child so that instruction may be reinforced by correction. It is lawful to imprison a criminal.

Theft and robbery are sins against commutative justice in that they injure a neighbor in his or her property. Thomas believes in private property. Private property is necessary for the good order of society, because there is greater care, less confusion, and fewer quarrels when property is owned by individuals than when it is held in common. Theft consists in taking secretly what belongs to another, whereas robbery consists in taking it violently. Both are opposed to justice and charity. Theft is a mortal sin or venial sin depending upon the amount stolen. Robbery is more serious than theft. When a person's need is manifest and urgent, he or she may take from another without sin.

Judicial Proceedings. One can sin against commutative justice in the course of judicial proceedings. Obviously a *judge* can justly judge only those who are subject to his jurisdiction. He must pass sentence only on the basis of the evidence presented to him and not on the basis of personal knowledge. In criminal cases a judge must decide between an accuser and a defendant; and he may not condemn a defendant who has not been confronted by his or her accuser. A lower judge cannot remit the punishment imposed on a guilty person by the laws of the community.

An *accuser* aims at the punishment of a criminal for the good of the community, whose calm is insured by the punishment of evil-doers. In the case of a crime that seriously affects the welfare of a community, a person is bound to accuse the criminal, provided he or she can offer sufficient proof of the crime. An accusation should be made in writing, so that the judge may be sure of the details. A false accusation is always unjust to the defendant and harmful to the community. One who accuses another falsely should himself be punished.

An accused person or *defendant* is bound to tell the truth which a judge exacts of him according to the law; but the accused person may defend himself by withholding the truth he is not bound by law to reveal. In any case, an accused person may not defend himself by lying. When his cause is just, an accused person may appeal the sentence of a judge to a higher authority. A person justly condemned to death may not resist his executioners; but a person unjustly condemned to death may defend himself even with violence against the agents of the state.

A *witness* must testify in a trial if the witness is subpoenaed or if his or her evidence is necessary to save a defendant from harm. The evidence of two or three witnesses is sufficient for a judge or jury to render a verdict. The evidence of a witness may be rejected for several reasons without any fault on the part of the witness; for example, the evidence offered by an enemy or relative of the defendant may be rejected on the suspicion of bias without any fault on the part of the witness. A false witness commits a mortal sin of perjury and injustice.

A *lawyer* is bound to defend a poor person only when the poor person has no other person to turn to here and now. St. Thomas does not permit a lawyer to defend an unjust cause or a guilty client, because no one is allowed to cooperate in evil. We must add, however, that a lawyer may defend a guilty party, so that the defendant is not punished beyond measure. A lawyer may take a reasonable fee for services rendered.

While the principles enunciated by St. Thomas in these matters are universally valid, they will be applied somewhat differently according to the procedure established in different places.

One can sin against commutative justice by words not only in judicial proceedings, but also in other circumstances. One can sin in this way by reviling, backbiting, talebearing, derision and cursing. To revile is to subject a person to verbal abuse. To backbite is to say mean or spiteful things about another behind his or her back. Modern theologians distinguish between true and false backbiting, calling the first detraction, and the second calumny; but St. Thomas makes no distinction. Talebearing means spreading gossip, scandal, or idle rumors, which has the effect of stirring up others against the victim. One who derides or mocks another intends to shame that person. To curse is to bring down evil upon another by way of command or wish. To curse irrational creatures, such as a stone or mosquito, is idle and vain and consequently unlawful. To curse a man or woman is sinful. To curse God is blasphemy; it is always a mortal sin, except for lack of reflection and consent. The other sins are either mortal or venial according to the gravity of the evil that is intended or caused.

One can sin against commutative justice in buying and selling. To sell an object for more than it is worth or to buy it for less than it is worth is in itself unjust. A seller may not charge a higher price for something just because the buyer has great need of it; but the seller may charge for any damage that he or she suffers by the sale. A seller sins by selling defective merchandise. On the other hand, a buyer sins when he or she buys at a lower price merchandise, whose value the seller does not recognize. A seller is bound to call the attention of the buyer to hidden defects in his merchandise. A merchant may sell his merchandise for more than he bought it as payment for his labor.

Thomas regarded the taking of interest on money lent to a borrower as a sin against commutative justice. To ask for interest was to ask the borrower for more than he received in the first place and to destroy the equality of justice. On the other hand, Thomas did allow someone to invest his money with a merchant or craftsman in a business venture and demand part of the profits derived from the use of his money. And with these remarks Thomas concludes his discussion of the subjective or essential parts of justice, which are the virtues of distributive and commutative justice.

Thomas' discussion of the quasi-integral parts of justice is quite brief. The quasi-integral parts of justice are required for a perfect act of justice. There are two such parts: one, to establish the equality of justice by doing good, that is, by rendering another what is due, and, two, to decline from evil, that is, by inflicting no injury on one's neighbor so as to disrupt the equality of justice. Transgression violates the rule of avoiding evil, while omission violates the rule of doing good insofar as this is due to someone. Simply and absolutely speaking, transgression is a graver sin than omission.

The potential parts of justice are virtues in their own right. In common with justice they have to do with another person; but they fall short of the perfection of justice because in some cases the note of equality is lacking, and in other cases, the note of debt. The potential parts of justice are religion, piety or filial respect, observance, gratitude, vengeance or vindication, truthfulness, friendliness and liberality.

Religion. The virtue of religion has to do with the worship of God. Religion pays the honor that is due to God as the first principle and the last end of all things. Religion is not a theological virtue, like faith, hope and charity, whose object is God; rather, it is a moral virtue which has to do with such things as prayer and sacrifice, by which God is honored. Religion excels the other moral virtues because of its close relationship to God. Religion gives rise to both internal and external acts of worship, the latter expressing and intensifying the former.

The first and fundamental act of religion is the act of devotion. Devotion is an act of the will by which a person surrenders himself or herself to God through worship. The cause of devotion is meditation upon the goodness and kindness of God and upon our own defects and insufficiencies. The effect of devotion is joy which is caused by the remembrance of God's goodness.

Prayer, like devotion, is an internal act of the virtue of religion. Here Thomas uses the word, prayer, in the restricted sense of petition, exclusive of contemplation, adoration, thanksgiving and reparation. Since prayer proposes to obtain something from God, it is a kind of setting things in order and is, therefore, an act of the practical reason, a step towards getting something done. We pray, not that we may change God, but that we may seek that which God has disposed to be fulfilled by our prayers. Prayer is an act of religion because it shows reverence to God, subjecting us to him and recognizing him as the source of all good. We pray to the saints, whether angels or men and women, not that they may inform God about our prayers, but that our prayers may be effective through their prayers and merits. We may pray for definite things, including temporal favors, insofar as these things are conducive to our eternal salvation. Charity requires that we pray for others. We may not exclude our enemies from the general prayers we offer up for others. Human beings on earth, the angels and blessed in heaven, and the souls in purgatory are able to pray; but the divine persons and dumb animals do not pray.

Prayer is common or individual. Common prayer is that which is offered to God by the ministers of the Church, representing the body of the faithful. Such prayer should be vocal, so that it may come to the knowledge of all for whom it is offered. Individual prayer is that which is offered by an individual for oneself or others. Such prayer need not be vocal; yet it is good to employ the voice for three reasons: to arouse interior devotion, to pray with one's whole person, that is to say , with soul and body, and, finally, to reflect the sentiments of the soul by a kind of overflow from the soul into the body. In the course of vocal prayer we can attend either to the words themselves or to the sense of the words or to the end of prayer, namely, God himself. Involuntary distractions do not detract from the merit or effectiveness of prayer, but they do diminish the spiritual refreshment of the mind, which is an effect of prayer. Prayer should be continued as long as it does not cause weariness and continues to arouse fervor. This principle applies to both public and private prayer. Prayer is meritorious when it proceeds from charity as its root. No prayer is left unanswered, although we do not always obtain the precise thing we ask for because this is not expedient. We always obtain what we ask for when we ask for ourselves what is conducive to salvation in a pious and persevering manner. Out of pure mercy God hears the prayers of sinners when they ask for what is conducive to their salvation.

Devotion and prayer are the interior and principal acts of religion. In due sequence, Thomas takes up the external acts of religion of which the first is adoration, whereby one uses one's body to worship God. Adoration is an act of religion, because it is proper to both adoration and religion to show honor to God. We distinguish latria, the honor to God; hyperdulia, the honor due to Mary as the mother of God; and dulia, the honor due to the saints. In English we speak of adoration only in connection with God; we do not speak of adoring the saints. As Thomas uses the term, adoration includes both a spiritual adoration of the mind and an exterior humbling of the body, such as a genuflection before a crucifix.

A second external act of the virtue of religion is the offering of sacrifice. The natural law dictates that a person should offer certain sensible things to God as a sign of subjection and honor; and if these sensible things are changed in some way, as animals were slain and burnt under the Old Law, then we have a sacrifice properly speaking. If something is offered to God without changing it in any way, something like money or bread, then we have what is called an oblation. Offering sacrifice to God implies that he is the beginning and end of all things, and so sacrifice may be offered to God alone. It is an act of the virtue of religion, which offers due honor to God.

A third external act of the virtue of religion is to take a vow. By a vow we promise something to God with the intention of binding ourselves. A vow concerns a greater good which we are not already bound to do; for example, one might vow to contribute a sum of money to a charitable cause or to adopt a certain state of life. It is useful to take a vow, because it fixes our resolve immovably on that which it is expedient to do. A vow is an act of religion or divine worship. A vow adds to a good act the merit of the virtue of religion. A vow is solemnized by the reception of holy orders or the profession of a religious rule, such as that of Francis or Dominic. A person who is subject to another person is hindered from taking a vow; such a person cannot freely dispose of his or her own life. Competent ecclesiastical authority can dispense from, or commute, all vows.

A fourth external act of the virtue of religion is the administration and reception of the sacraments; however, Thomas reserves his study of the sacraments for the third part of the *Summa*.

A fifth external act of the virtue of religion is the taking of an oath. An oath may call upon God to witness and confirm one's intention to do something in the future; and in this case we have a promissory oath, such as a civil official takes upon taking office. An oath is lawful in important matters, because it recognizes the knowledge and truthfulness of God and seeks to avoid or end litigation. A rash oath lacks judgment, because it is taken frivolously; a false oath lacks truth; and a wicked oath lacks justice, because one swears to do what is unlawful. Oaths are not to be taken frequently. Sometimes human beings swear by creatures, such as the gospel or the saints, since these reflect the divine truthfulness. An oath has binding force out of reverence for God. An oath admits of dispensation and can be voided by certain conditions of person and time.

A sixth external act of the virtue of religion is adjuration. To adjure a person is to put him or her under oath, that is, to require or seek an oath from that person. One recalls how the high priest adjured Christ before the Sanhedrin (Mt 26:63). A superior can require an oath from an inferior; an inferior can beseech his superior to take an oath. We may repulse the demons themselves by aduring them through the power of God's name, lest they do harm to soul or body.

A seventh act of the virtue of religion is to praise God with our lips. To praise God in this way is most fitting, not to make our thoughts known to him, but to stimulate our own devotion and the devotion of others. The use of music in divine worship serves the same purpose.

Next Thomas considers the vices that are opposed to the virtue of religion. Superstition is a vice opposed to the virtue of religion by excess, not because it offers too much worship, but because it offers divine worship either to whom it ought not, or in a manner it ought not. There are various kinds of superstition: undue worship of God, idolatry, divination and superstitious observances. The worship of God is undue when it signifies something false; for example, to worship God by the rites of the Old Law, which speak of Christ as still to come, is to give undue worship to God. Idolatry is to give divine worship to creatures. Divination means consulting creatures, like demons and stars, in order to learn the future which is known to God alone. Superstitious observances are the outward expression of the belief that divine powers are found in certain creatures, like rabbit's feet or horse shoes. The use of medals and relics by the Church reminds us of God and the saints and expresses confidence in their willingness to help us.

A number of vices are opposed to the virtue of religion, because they deny to God the reverence that is due to him out of justice. These vices come under the general heading of irreligion. The sins of irreligion express contempt or irreverence for God and holy things. The sins of irreligion are tempting God, that is to say, putting him to the test, perjury, sacrilege and simony.

To put God to the test, to tempt him, is to try to find out if God is truly wise, powerful and willing to help us. For example, to place ourselves in a dangerous situation without good reason, in order to find out if God will help us, is to tempt God. To tempt God usually involves a doubt about God's knowledge and power; and it is a sin against religion. Superstition, however, is a more serious sin than tempting God.

Perjury is a lie confirmed by an oath. It is a sin against religion, because it calls upon God to witness to a falsehood. By its very nature, perjury is a mortal sin.

Whatever pertains to irreverence for sacred things is an injury to God and comes under the head of sacrilege. A sacrilege may be committed against a sacred person, place or thing. For example, profanation of the Holy Eucharist, which is the body and blood of Christ, is a sacrilege.

Simony is the sin of trying to buy or sell something spiritual. The name is derived from Simon the magician, who tried to buy a spiritual power from the apostles (Ac 8:18-19). Simony is irreverence for God and for spiritual things: for God, who gives his spiritual gifts gratuitously, and for spiritual things, which cannot be appraised at any earthly price. It is always unlawful to give money for the administration and reception of the sacraments; but it is lawful to give or receive something for the support of the ministers of the Church, in accordance with the statutes of the Church and approved customs. To grant something spiritual as a remuneration for a service is simony; and whoever acquires spiritual things in return for a remuneration cannot lawfully retain or use them.

Piety. A second potential part of justice is the virtue of piety. Here piety does not mean religious devotion; rather, it means to revere one's parents and country, which are the principles of our life and nurture. Our parents have given us life and reared us; our country has provided the broader social context in which a full and complete human life is possible. Modern authors speak of reverence for our country as the virtue of patriotism. Piety leads dutiful sons and daughters to honor, obey, thank and help their parents. It leads them to provide for sick and poor parents. We may not omit the duties of piety toward our parents for the sake of religion. Our Lord rebuked the Pharisees for hindering children from supporting needy parents (Mt 15:3-6). There can be no real conflict between the claims of religion and piety, since no virtue is opposed to another virtue. Patriotism leads good citizens to obey the laws of their country, honor its leaders, vote, participate in public affairs, and serve in the armed forces, if necessary.

Observance. A third potential part of justice is the virtue of observance, whereby we pay honor and reverence to persons in positions of dignity. It is the respect that we should have for pastors, teachers, employers and all those who direct our lives in some way. We have to manifest honor and reverence for others by external signs; otherwise, our sentiments would remain hidden from them. The external signs of honor and reverence include greeting those whom we wish to honor in a respectful manner, complying with their wishes, expressing our sentiments in words, giving them places of honor, and presenting gifts. The external honor due to men and women above us is called by the Greek name of *dulia*. It is to be distinguished from the honor due to God, which is called *latria*.

Obedience is connected with observance, and it is a virtue in its own right. A person obeys when he or she does what a superior commands. Obedience is required by both the natural and divine law. The virtue of obedience, whereby we forsake our own will for God's sake, is more praiseworthy than the other moral virtues, whereby we forsake other earthly goods for the sake of God. God is to be obeyed always and in all things. A subject is bound to obey a superior within the sphere of his or her authority, but not when the superior commands what is sinful. Faith in Christ and evangelical freedom by no means excuse the faithful from the obligation of obeying civil laws. In the social order obedience to law is absolutely necessary; society cannot survive without it.

To disobey the commandments of God is sinful; such disobedience is contrary to the love of God, which requires us to obey his commandments. Moreover, the commandments of God oblige us to obey superiors, so that disobedience to superiors is sinful. The gravity of the sin of disobedience depends upon the gravity of the thing commanded, upon the person who issues the command, whether it be God or a human being, and upon the degree of contempt for the lawgiver behind the disobedience.

Gratitude. A fourth potential part of justice is the virtue of gratitude. Gratitude inclines us to give thanks to a benefactor, who has placed us in his or her debt by a gift. The gift of a benefactor may not be ignored. The steps involved in gratitude include acceptance of the gift as a sign of the benefactor's love, an expression of thanks, and, ultimately, the return of a gift for the gift received.

Gratitude always inclines us, as far as possible, to give back even more than we have received. In this way, a benefactor and a grateful recipient are bound together by an endless chain of favors. In estimating a debt of gratitude, we must take into consideration the disposition of the giver even more than the value of the gift. The simple gift of a child to a parent means so much more in virtue of the child's love.

According to Thomas, the reception of a favor creates a debt of gratitude, and the failure to repay this debt is a special sin. A person is guilty of ingratitude by failing either to return a favor or express thanks for it. The height of ingratitude is to scorn a favor or to treat kindness as though it were unkindness. Usually ingratitude is a venial sin. A benefactor has the joy of acting like God, who showers his benefits upon the grateful and ungrateful alike.

Vengeance or Vindication. A fifth potential part of justice is the virtue of vengeance or vindication. Here vengeance means punishing an evil-doer. To punish an evil-doer simply to harm him or her is tantamount to hatred, which is contrary to charity; but to punish a guilty party, so that he or she may amend his or her life and leave others in peace, is lawful. Vengeance is a virtue in the circumstances described, because it seeks to remove evil. An evil-doer may be punished by executing him or imprisoning or fining him in proportion to the evil he has done. Sometimes a person who has done evil involuntarily is punished to preserve him or her from such a thing in the future.

Truthfulness. A sixth potential part of justice is truthfulness by which one is accustomed to say what conforms to the facts. Truthfulness is connected with justice: both in life and in speech the truthful person shows others what he or she is; still, truthfulness falls short of justice, because it is not concerned with a debt in the proper sense. A truthful person is reluctant to speak about himself or herself, lest he or she exaggerate and give others the wrong opinion.

Lying is a vice opposed to truthfulness. A person lies when he or she intends to say what is false with the intention of deceiving another; however, when a person says what is false, thinking it to be true, he or she does not lie in the strict sense. Lies are called officious, jocose, or mischievous, according as they are told to help someone, or for fun, or out of malice for the purpose of hurting someone. Every lie is a sin, because the liar signifies by his words something that is not in his mind and so deceives others. A mischievous lie can be a mortal sin, if it causes great harm; but jocose and officious lies are usually venial sins. A jocose lie may not be a sin at all, because it is not a serious statement.

Dissimulation is to hide under a false appearance; it is a kind of lie, perpetrated not by words, but by deeds. For example, a person who pretends to be poor, when in reality he is not, is guilty of dissimulation. Hypocrisy is a kind of dissimulation; it is the sin of one who simulates another person, as in the case of a sinner who simulates the person of a just man. Boasting is opposed to truthfulness by way of excess, for the boaster exaggerates his good qualities. To belittle oneself is opposed to truthfulness: it is to ascribe falsely to oneself something mean or to deny falsely to oneself something great. All these things are distinct sins against truthfulness and alienate a person from the company of other human beings.

Friendliness. A seventh potential part of justice is the virtue of friendliness or affability. The friendly or affable person behaves in a pleasant manner toward others both in word and deed. Friendliness is related to justice because, like justice, it governs our relations with others; but it falls short of the strict notion of justice, because it lacks the full aspect of debt. Flattery and quarreling are the vices opposed to friendliness. Flattery is opposed by way of excess. To flatter someone is to praise that person for good qualities he or she does not possess or for base qualities which ought rather to be condemned. Flattery is usually a venial sin. Quarreling erupts in words and is the vice of the contentious person, who is opposed to everything. It is more serious than flattery, for quarreling tries to displease, while flattery tries to please.

Liberality. An eighth potential part of justice is the virtue of liberality. The liberal person uses money well by parting with it, especially by using it for others rather than for oneself. Liberality is allied to justice in that it gives money to others; however, it gives not what is due, but what is its own. Opposed to liberality are the vices of avarice and prodigality. Avarice is the sin of the greedy person; it is the inordinate love of money, of getting and possessing it. Avarice is not necessarily a mortal sin. It is considered to be a spiritual sin and not a carnal sin, because it is consummated in the mind and not in the flesh, as sexual sins are. Avarice is a capital sin because it gives rise to other sins which facilitate the acquisition and retention of money. The sins which can be inspired by avarice are treachery, fraud, falsehood, perjury, dissatisfaction, violence and insensibility. Opposed to liberality by way of excess is the sin of prodigality or extravagance. The prodigal person throws money away. Prodigality is not as serious as avarice, because the prodigal person, as opposed to the avaricious person, does some good with his or her money.

Epikeia. In the last place, Thomas speaks of the virtue of epikeia, which he regards as a subjective part of justice and not a potential part. Epikeia is the virtue which is concerned with what is just in a particular case, when the application of the general law would work an injustice. To use Thomas' example, the general law requires something deposited with another to be returned, because this is just in the majority of cases. Yet, the return of a deposit is sometimes injurious, as in the case of a madman who deposits his sword with another and demands its return while he is still mad. In this and similar cases, it is bad to follow the law; and it is good to follow the dictates of justice and the common good. It is epikeia which governs such cases.

Having dealt with the parts of justice, Thomas now speaks of the gift of the Holy Spirit, which corresponds to the virtue of justice, namely, the gift of piety. Piety, which is a gift of the Holy Spirit, pays duty and worship to God as our heavenly Father, while piety, which is a moral virtue, pays reverence to one's earthly father and mother. The second beatitude, "Blessed are the meek" (Mt 5:5), corresponds to the gift of piety, inasmuch as it removes obstacles to acts of piety.

Finally, Thomas considers the precepts of justice. The precepts or demands of justice are formulated in the Decalogue, which governs our relationship with others. The first three precepts of the Decalogue are about acts of religion, which is the chief part of justice. Religion, of course, pays worship to God. The fourth precept of the Decalogue has to do with acts of piety, which is the second part of justice. The virtue of piety leads us to revere our parents and our country. The six remaining precepts of the Decalogue are about justice too: they govern our relationship with others as one equal to another.

Chapter 16

THE CARDINAL VIRTUES OF FORTITUDE AND TEMPERANCE (2a2ae.123-170)

In this chapter we continue our study of the cardinal virtues by considering fortitude and temperance.

Fortitude (2a2ae.123-140)

In his study of the cardinal virtue of fortitude, Thomas considers the virtue itself, its parts, the gift of the Holy Spirit corresponding to the virtue, and the precepts pertaining to it.

Thomas thinks of fortitude or courage as the virtue which prevents us from doing what is unreasonable or sinful through fear of bodily injury and death. It is the virtue of the soldier and of all those who face death in a just cause, like a nurse who attends the victims of a plague or like an astronaut who undertakes a hazardous space voyage. Sometimes a courageous person is called upon to take aggressive action against an evil that threatens him, as in the case of a soldier who defends his country against an enemy. Sometimes, however, a courageous person is called upon to stand firmly in the face of danger, endure it, and bear up under it, as in the case of a martyr who suffers for the cause of Christ. The latter is the principal and more difficult act of courage. The brave person intends to act courageously, but his or her ultimate reason for acting courageously is to achieve happiness with God. The brave person takes pleasure in a courageous act and in the reason for it, but at the same time he or she has cause for sorrow in the thought of losing one's life and of bodily pain. Fortitude meets danger as it comes, often suddenly and without warning. The brave person is moved by a moderate anger in the face of an impending evil. Fortitude is a cardinal virtue, because it has a foremost claim to what belongs to the virtues in common, namely, to act steadfastly, and this even in the face of death. Fortitude ranks below the theological virtues and the moral virtues of prudence and justice.

The supreme act of fortitude is martyrdom, whereby a person suffers death in order to cling to truth and justice. Martyrdom is the greatest proof of the perfection of charity: a person is prepared to sacrifice even life itself out of love for God and virtue. The perfect notion of martyrdom requires that a person suffer death and not only physical torment for Christ's sake. The virgin who dies in defense of her purity, the priest who dies while ministering during a plague, a Christian mother who will not allow the destruction of her unborn child as a means of preserving her own life, all these are martyrs.

There are three vices opposed to fortitude, namely, fear, insensibility and foolhardiness. Fear is a sin against fortitude when it leads us to shun bodily injury and death against the dictate of reason. Of course, fear is not a sin when it leads us to shun what ought to be shunned. If, however, a person does what is forbidden or omits what is commanded by divine law through fear of death or of any other temporal evil, such fear is sinful. Fear diminishes a person's responsibility somewhat, because it hampers freedom of choice; nevertheless, even when a person is fearful, he or she can still commit a sin.

If a person does not love what he ought to love, namely, life and all that fosters it, and if that person fears death and other temporal evils less than he ought, then that person is guilty of insensibility. Insensibility can proceed from a lack of love for the right things or from overconfidence in oneself or from stupidity. Insensibility is a deficiency of reasonable fear.

Foolhardiness is another vice opposed to fortitude. Fools rush in where angels fear to tread. The foolhardy person is reckless and bold, without judgment.

At this point, Thomas takes up the parts of fortitude. As a special virtue, fortitude does not have subjective or essential parts; that is to say, it is not divided into several specifically distinct virtues, since it is about very special matter.

Fortitude does have quasi-integral parts which are required, if one is to act courageously. The quasi-integral parts of fortitude are magnanimity, magnificence, patience and perseverance. For example, a courageous person is sometimes called up to take aggressive action in the face of death, as in the case of a nurse ministering to the victims of a plague; and for this he or she needs magnanimity (or self-confidence, as Thomas understands the term here) and magnificence (by which Thomas means execution with greatness of purpose). Sometimes, however, a courageous person is called upon to endure bodily torment and death, as in the case of a martyr; and for this he or she needs patience and perseverance.

Fortitude also has potential parts, which have the same names as the quasi-integral parts, namely, magnanimity, magnificence, patience and perseverance. The potential parts of fortitude are virtues in their own right, but they are concerned with lesser hardships than the dangers of death. St. Thomas examines each of these potential parts in turn.

Magnanimity. The magnanimous person is the one with a great soul. He or she is the one who attempts great and difficult things, which bring honor in their train. Magnanimity is the virtue of the statesman, humanitarian, reformer and all those who initiate and head great enterprises. The virtue enables them to deal reasonably with the honors that come their way, neither exaggerating their significance nor deprecating them. Magnanimity agrees with fortitude in enabling a person to act reasonably in a difficult matter:

fortitude, in the face of death; and magnanimity, in the matter of honor; but magnanimity falls short of fortitude in that it is concerned with a less arduous difficulty. The magnanimous person is a confident and secure person. Magnanimity regards two things: honor as its matter, and the accomplishment of something great as its end. Goods of fortune are conducive to both these ends.

Several sins are opposed to magnanimity by way of excess, namely, presumption, ambition and vainglory. Presumption is the sin of one who attempts what is beyond his or her powers. Ambition (as Thomas uses the term here) is an inordinate desire for honor, for example, by seeking and accepting honor for a quality one does not possess. Vainglory consists in glorying in things that are not worthy of glory or in the testimony of individuals whose testimony is not worth much. Vainglory is a capital sin giving rise to disobedience, boasting, hypocrisy, contention, obstinacy, discord, and the love of novelties. Faintheartedness or pusillanimity is opposed to magnanimity by way of defect; it is the failure to measure up to one's capabilities. Just as the magnanimous person tends to great things out of greatness of soul, so the pusillanimous person shrinks from great things out of littleness of soul.

Magnificence. This virtue has to do with the expenditure of great sums of money in order to accomplish some great work. It is the virtue of the philanthropist and others who are in a position to spend great sums of money. Unlike liberality, magnificence does not belong to all uses of money, but only to larger expenditures. Like fortitude, magnificence tends to do something arduous and difficult; but magnificence falls short of fortitude, the latter deriving its difficulty from life-threatening dangers, whereas the former derives its difficulty from the dispossession of one's property. Meanness is opposed to magnificence. The mean person undertakes great things without spending the necessary funds. At the other end is a vice that might be called waste or consumption. It is willing to pay out huge sums for what is insignificant. A mean person spends less than the undertaking is worth; a wasteful or prodigal person spends more than the work deserves.

Patience. The moral virtues safeguard the good of reason against the impulse of the passions. Patience is a moral virtue which supports a person against sorrow, lest reason give way to sorrow. A patient person bears the sorrows of life with equanimity, so that he or she does not abandon that which is truly good. Patience endures evil, not to do evil, but rather that evil might not be done. Patience, as a virtue, comes from charity, which loves God above all things and is prepared to bear anything to preserve this love. Patience, of course, is related to fortitude as a potential part, fortitude enduring the dangers of death, patience enduring other kinds of evil.

Perseverance. This is the virtue which persists even for a long time in doing good, until it is accomplished. It is the virtue which puts up with delays in accomplishing the good, insofar as this is necessary. Perseverance is allied to fortitude because it, like fortitude, stands firm in the face of difficulty. Thomas distinguishes perseverance and constancy: the former makes a person persist in doing good in the face of the difficulty that arises from the very continuance of the act, whereas constancy makes a person persist in doing good in the face of difficulties arising from external hindrances. Opposed to perseverance is the vice of softness, which departs from the way of virtue even when the stress is slight. Also opposed to perseverance is pertinacity. The hard, stubborn, pertinacious person does not know when to yield, or knowing, refuses to yield. So much for the potential parts of fortitude.

Following the usual order of things, Thomas takes up the gift of the Holy Spirit corresponding to the virtue of fortitude. This is the gift of fortitude. Fortitude as a virtue perfects the mind in the endurance of all perils whatever, but it does not go so far as to give confidence of overcoming all danger; this belongs to the fortitude which is a gift of the Holy Spirit. The gift gives a person confident hope of eternal life at the last. The gift makes the exercise of the virtue easier, richer, and more confident.

The fourth beatitude, "Blessed are they who hunger and thirst for justice" (Mt 5:6), corresponds to the gift of fortitude. The correspondence exists because, as Thomas explains, fortitude is about difficult things. Now it is very difficult, not merely to do virtuous deeds which may be called works of justice in general, but furthermore to do them with an insatiable desire, which may be signified by hunger and thirst for justice.

St. Thomas notes that precepts about the practice of fortitude are to be found in both the Old and New Laws, for example, in Dt 20:3-4 and Mt 10:28, so that God's people might not be withdrawn from their allegiance to God out of fear of corporal dangers. The divine law also contains precepts about the practice of patience and perseverance on account of the very nature of these virtues.

Temperance (2a2ae.141-170)

St. Thomas approaches the virtue of temperance as he approaches the other cardinal virtues. First, he considers the virtue itself and the vices opposed to it; then he takes up the integral, subjective and potential parts of the virtue, and, finally, the precepts connected with it.

The very name, temperance, suggests that it is a virtue, for to act temperately is to act reasonably or virtuously. As a special virtue, temperance has to do with the pleasures connected with the use of food, drink and sex. There is a pleasure necessarily and naturally connected wih the use of these things, which are required for the preservation of the individual and the species. Temperance does not touch that pleasure; but it enables one to use the restraint which reason dictates in these matters. The reasonable use of food, drink and sex is determined by the needs of the present life. Temperance is a cardinal virtue because it is particularly praiseworthy for the moderation it shows in such a difficult matter. In point of excellence, temperance comes after the other cardinal virtues.

Opposed to temperance is the vice of insensibility, a word that we have used before in a different context. Here insensibility means the rejection of pleasure to such an extent that one gives up eating and drinking and sexual activity to the detriment of life and nature. Sometimes, however, it is good and even necessary for a person to abstain from the pleasures which result from such activity, as in the case of sick persons. Such abstinence does not pertain to the vice of insensibility, because it is in accord with right reason. At the other extreme is the childish sin of intemperance, which overindulges itself in bodily pleasures, just as children overindulge themselves in sweets. Intemperance is the most disgraceful of sins, because it lowers us to the level of animals.

Next Thomas takes up the parts of temperance, and first the integral parts. These must concur if one is to act temperately. The integral parts of temperance are what Thomas calls shamefacedness and honesty. Shamefacedness recoils from the disgrace which accompanies an evil deed. It is not strictly a virtue; rather, it is a passion or a reaction to something apprehended as evil, namely, shame or disgrace. A person is more likely to be ashamed of disgraceful actions in the presence of his family and friends than in the presence of strangers. Old people and virtuous people are not greatly fearful of shame and disgrace, because they regard these things as impossible to themselves or as easy to avoid. Of course, they would be ashamed if there were cause.

The other integral part of temperance is called honesty. In this case, honesty signifies a kind of spiritual beauty which consists in virtuous action, that is to say, action governed by reason. The spiritual beauty of a human person understood in this sense is particularly disfigured by yielding to what is most disgraceful and unbecoming to human beings, namely, animal lusts. Because temperance maintains the good of reason by repelling animal lusts, Thomas connects honesty with temperance as an integral part of it.

After the integral parts, Thomas considers the subjective parts of temperance. The subjective parts of a virtue are its species; and the species of a virtue have to be differentiated according to the difference of matter or object. The subjective parts of temperance are abstinence and sobriety, which have to do with the pleasures of eating and drinking, and chastity and purity, which have to do with sexual pleasures.

Abstinence is a virtue which keeps our use of food within reasonable limits. It is not easy to eat in a reasonable way, since we find food so attractive, as countless dieters will attest. Abstinence leads us to eat with due regard for others and our own health. Fasting is an act of the virtue of abstinence. To fast is to eat sparingly or to abstain from food altogether for a time. Fasting is a virtuous act, because it is a reasonable act: it tempers the desires of the flesh, it frees the mind for the contemplation of heavenly things, and it makes satisfaction for sin. For the reasons given, fasting is prescribed by the natural law, but the Church determines when and how the law is to be fulfilled by the members of the Church. According to the revised Code of Canon Law (1983), all those over fourteen years of age are to abstain from meat every Friday of the year and on Ash Wednesday, and all those who range in age from eighteen to fifty-nine are to fast on Ash Wednesday and Good Friday (cc. 1251-52). In general, those who fast eat only one full meal a day.

The vice opposed to abstinence is gluttony. The sin of gluttony is committed by one who knowingly eats too much simply because of the pleasure involved in eating. Gluttony is ordinarily a venial sin. It is not the greatest sin; but it is a capital sin giving rise to other sins which Thomas names as unseemly joy, scurrility, uncleanness, loquaciousness, and dullness of mind.

Sobriety is also a subjective part of temperance and a special virtue itself. It has to do with moderation in the use of intoxicating drink. To drink wine in moderation is not wrong. Scripture says, "That which goes into the mouth does not defile a person" (Mt 15:11). Sobriety is most necessary for young people, lest they fan the flames of passion, and for those in authority who need all their faculties to meet their responsibilities.

Drunkenness is the vice opposed to sobriety. As it is understood here, drunkenness is a mortal sin, because thereby a person knowingly and willingly deprives himself of the use of reason, whereby he performs virtuous deeds and avoids sin. Drunkenness, which Thomas regards as a carnal sin, is not so bad as spiritual sins. Involuntary drunkenness excuses from any sinful actions that may follow, but voluntary drunkenness does not entirely excuse from the sinful actions one may commit as a result.

Chastity is also a species of temperance; it regulates the use of sex in a reasonable way. Chastity, which is about the pleasures of sex, is a virtue distinct from abstinence and sobriety, which regulate the pleasures of eating and drinking. A person is *unchaste*, if he or she indulges in unlawful sexual union; a person is *impure*, if he or she indulges unlawfully in the actions that attend sexual union, such as impure looks, kisses and touches. St. Thomas says that purity is directed to chastity, not as a distinct virtue, but as something expressing a circumstance of chastity.

In connection with chastity, Thomas considers the virtue of virginity. Virginity is the virtue by which a person intends to abstain perpetually from the pleasures of sex. Virginity abstains from venereal pleasure, such as is found in marriage, to give oneself more freely to divine contemplation. As Paul states the matter, "The virgin—indeed, any unmarried woman—is concerned with the things of the Lord, in pursuit of holiness in body and spirit. The married woman, on the other hand, has the cares of this world to absorb her and is concerned with pleasing her husband" (1 Cor 7:34). As a virtue, virginity is related to chastity, as magnificence is related to liberality. Sacred as marriage is, virginity is superior to it for the reasons given by Paul. Virginity is not the greatest of the virtues; the theological virtues, for example, are greater.

Lust is the vice opposed to chastity, and it means indulgence in unlawful sexual pleasure. Venereal acts are without sin, if they are performed in the proper manner and order, in keeping with the end of human procreation. Lust consists essentially in violating the order and mode of reason in the matter of venereal acts. Lust is indeed a capital vice, giving rise to mental blindness, thoughtlessness, inconstancy, rashness, self-love, hatred of God, love of this world, and abhorrence or despair of a future world.

There are various species of lust. Fornication is a species of lust, and it is, of course, the union of an unmarried man with an unmarried woman. It is a mortal sin, because it is opposed to the good of children for whom married parents and a home are required. Lustful kisses and touches are also mortal sins in the case of those who seek venereal pleasure outside of marriage. Nocturnal pollution is not a sin, except perhaps in cause, since a person is not responsible for what happens while he or she sleeps. Adultery is a species of lust; it is a mortal sin against both chastity and justice. Incest is sexual intercourse with a woman related by consanguinity or affinity; it too is a species of lust. Lust takes on the added deformity of sacrilege, when it involves sacred persons, places and things. Unnatural vice is any lustful perversion of the normal and natural processes for procuring sexual pleasure. Unnatural vice includes masturbation, bestiality and homosexuality. Unnatural vice is the worst of all sins of lust.

Next, the potential parts of temperance. *Continence* is a kind of embryonic virtue by which a person resists unreasonable and vehement desires for the pleasures connected with eating and drinking and sexual activity. There is a difference between the temperate and continent person. The temperate person does not experience unruly and vehement passions in the sensitive appetite, because he or she has them under control; but the continent person does experience such passions and resists them unsuccessfully. It follows that continence resides in the will and not in the sensitive appetite. Continence stands to temperance as imperfect to perfect.

Incontinence is the vice directly opposed to continence. The incontinent person is not an ignorant or malicious person, but a weak one. He or she fails to resist the vehement passions, which can and should be resisted. Incontinence is a sin, because it means yielding to shameful pleasures. Incontinence is not so bad as intemperance, because the intemperate person sins out of habit and rejoices in his or her sin; but the incontinent person sins out of passion and is humiliated and saddened by his or her weakness.

Meekness and Clemency. These two virtues work hand in hand. Meekness keeps anger within bounds, and clemency represses the tendency to punish the guilty too harshly. Clemency is the virtue exercised by a superior, such as a parent, teacher, employer and judge. Both meekness and clemency are virtues, because they lead a person to act reasonably in the matter of internal anger and external punishment. Both meekness and clemency are potential parts of temperance because both, like temperance, suppose a certain restraint; meekness restraining anger, and clemency moderating the punishment of the wrong-doer. Meekness and clemency are not the greatest virtues, because they only withdraw a person from evil, while other virtues, like prudence and justice, direct one to the good.

The vice which is opposed to meekness is *unlawful* anger. Anger, as we know, is a passion of the irascible appetite, and it must be regulated by reason if it is to be lawful. Lawful anger seeks to right injustice and punish wrong-doers in a reasonable way; but unlawful anger seeks to punish an innocent person or go beyond the bounds of reason in punishing the guilty. It is the latter which is opposed to the virtue of meekness. Unlawful anger is not the most grievous sin, nor is it always a mortal sin. Unlawful anger is a capital sin, giving rise to such sins as indignation, injurious speech, contumely, quarreling and blasphemy. A person who is incapable of anger is defective in some way; he or she is unable to resent evil.

Cruelty is the vice which is opposed to clemency. As Seneca put it, "They are called cruel who have reason for punishing, but lack moderation in punishing."[1] Cruelty differs from brutality or savagery, which is indifferent to guilt or innocence and hurts purely for the purpose of hurting.

Modesty. This virtue too is allied to temperance as a potential part; but it differs from temperance in this, that temperance governs the concupiscible appetite in those matters where restraint is most difficult, while modesty governs the appetite in those matters that present less difficulty. There are various species of modesty, namely, humility, studiousness, modesty in words and deeds, and modesty in dress.

Humility. This virtue is a species of modesty. Humility presupposes a knowledge of self; humility itself resides in the irascible appetite and moderates the passion of hope, so that a person does not aspire to things beyond his or her capacity. Truth is rather the rule of humility than humility itself. Humility has the effect of subjecting us to God and to others because of what they have from God. Pride is the vice opposed to the virtue of humility. It means aspiring to things beyond one's capacity. In this way, it is opposed to right reason and is sinful. Pride is to be found not only in the irascible appetite, but also in the will, since it aspires inordinately not only to sensible goods, but also to spiritual things. Hence, pride is to be found in demons too. St. Gregory the Great (540-604) distinguishes four species of pride: "There are four marks by which every kind of pride of the arrogant betrays itself: either when they think that their good is from themselves; or when they believe it to be from above, yet they think that it is due to their own merits; or when they boast of having what they have not; or when they despise others and wish to appear the exclusive possessors of what they have."[2] Those who sin by pride in these ways aspire inordinately to an excellence and superiority which have not been appointed to them by God. In a sense pride is the most grievous of sins because aversion from God, which is consequent upon other sins, belongs to pride by its very nature. Pride may be described as the queen and mother of all vices because of its general influence upon them.

The sin of the first man was a sin of pride insofar as he coveted a spiritual good above his measure. He sinned because he wished to be like God, determining for himself what was good and what was evil. As a result of his sin, Adam suffered the rebellion of his lower nature against his spiritual nature and, consequently, death, sickness and all defects of the body. Scripture recounts other punishments for the sin of Adam and Eve: expulsion from the Garden of Eden, fatiguing toil, the pains of childbirth, the reluctance of the earth to yield its fruits and others too. God permitted Adam and Eve to be tempted by the devil in accordance with the condition of human beings whereby other creatures are a help or a hindrance to them. The devil appealed to both the intellectual and sensitive natures of Adam and Eve, when he tempted them.

Studiousness. This virtue is a potential part of temperance and a species of modesty. Studiousness disposes a person to acquire and extend one's knowledge; but it also has the effect of restraining an individual from seeking knowledge and experience that would be useless or harmful. Studiousness is not directly about knowledge itself, but about the desire for knowledge and about study in the pursuit of knowledge. The vice of curiosity is opposed to studiousness. The sinfully curious person seeks knowledge in a certain area to the neglect of what he or she should study. For example, a candidate for the priesthood who studies literature, when he should be studying theology, is sinfully curious. Moreover, a person who for no good reason seeks sense experience which is potentially harmful, let us say, by taking drugs, is sinfully curious.

Modesty in Words and Deeds. This virtue includes taste and good manners. It means acting in accordance with what befits the person and the situation. The person who acts his age, the religious sister who is ever mindful of her consecration in dealing with others, the civil official who shows respect for his office, all these are examples of those who practice modesty in words and deeds. Modesty in words and deeds carries over into recreation. Just as one needs rest to refresh a weary body, so one needs recreation to refresh a weary soul. A soul is wearied particularly by intellectual and spiritual work, such as that of the student, scientist, philosopher and contemplative. A weary soul recovers its energy by innocent amusement and recreation. The virtuous person takes as much recreation as he or she needs, no more and no less, although the right amount cannot be measured too accurately. If it is lawful to recreate moderately, then it is lawful for others to provide the recreation people need.

Modesty in Dress. One is modest in dress by wearing what good people wear in similar circumstances. St. Thomas believes that a person can sin in dress by open violation of custom or by sloppiness and raggedness. Cosmetics may be used according to the customs of the good people among whom one lives.

To conclude his treatise on temperance, Thomas asks if we find any precepts in the Scripture relating to temperance. He notes that the Decalogue forbids adultery both in thought and deeds; and adultery is, of course, a sin opposed to temperance. Thomas also notes that the Decalogue forbids certain actions which may be the result of the vices opposed to the virtues allied to temperance. Thus, the Decalogue forbids murder, which may be the result of unlawful anger, a vice opposed to meekness.

Chapter 17

SPECIAL GIFTS AND STATES (2a2ae.171-189)

After he has considered the virtues and vices that have a bearing upon the lives of all men and women, Thomas takes up certain matters that pertain to particular individuals especially. These matters include special gifts or *gratiae gratis datae*, the active and contemplative lives, and certain states of men and women.

Special Gifts (2a2ae.171-178)

From time to time God gives men and women special gifts, *gratiae gratis datae*, which are intended primarily for the sanctification of others and not for the personal sanctification of the recipient. These gifts can also be called the apostolic graces. One of these gifts or graces is *prophecy*. The apostolic grace of prophecy enables a person to know infallibly and predict with certainty what is unknowable to anyone but God, that is to say, future contingent things such as the free acts of human beings. Generally the prophet is able to confirm the divine origin of his or her prophecy by appealing to miracles. Prophecy is not a habit in the sense that a virtue is a habit, because the prophetic insight is not a permanent reality. A prophet does not know all that can possibly be prophesied; each prophet knows only what God chooses to reveal to him or her. In some cases, the prophet clearly recognizes an express revelation from God; but in other cases, the prophet cannot always distinguish what is of God and what is of his or her own spirit. In any event, nothing false can contaminate a prophetic utterance.

The knowledge of the prophet is from God; it is revealed knowledge. Angels convey prophetic knowledge to the prophet since God is wont to act upon lower creatures through higher ones. God chooses as prophets those whom he will, sometimes even those who are not in the state of grace. One who proclaims knowledge acquired from demons may be called a prophet in a restricted sense; and such a false prophet may speak some truth, since evil spirits have knowledge.

Prophetic vision is not the same as the vision of God; the prophet remains a wayfarer even after his or her vision. Prophetic knowledge may be conveyed by the direct infusion of new ideas or by new insight into ideas already possessed or by the presentation of sensible images to the senses and imagination. The prophet may not always fully understand what he or she foretells.

Needless to say, St. Thomas emphasizes the role of the prophet as seer. We know, however, that the role of the Biblical prophet was much more extensive. The Biblical prophet contributed to the development of revealed religion, denounced idolatry, defended the moral law, and counseled kings and private citizens.

The apostolic grace of *rapture* is a kind of divine violence, whereby a person is withdrawn from his or her senses by the Holy Spirit and lifted up to a supernatural experience. Thomas has in mind the rapture of Ezekiel (8:3) and Paul (2 Cor 12:2). Rapture is primarily a cognitive experience, a vision of truth, although delight is a necessary consequence. It seems that Paul in his rapture did see the essence of God in a transitory manner. While he was raptured, Paul was withdrawn from his senses, but his soul was not wholly separated from his body.

By the gift of *tongues* Christ's first disciples spoke and understood the languages of the peoples to whom they were sent. The gift of prophecy is a greater gift than the gift of tongues, since it is better to have knowledge than to have the words to express one's knowledge.

The gift of tongues enables speaker and hearer to understand each other, while the gift of *conviction*, a grace that attaches to words, enables the speaker to convince and convert his listeners. Thomas did not think that it was becoming for women to teach publicly in the Church, and he pointed to Paul's words (1 Cor 14:34; 1 Tm 2:12) to substantiate his position.

God gives certain persons the gift of *miracles* to confirm the preaching of his messengers and to demonstrate the sanctity of a holy person, whom he wishes to propose as a model of virtue. In these cases, God is the principal cause of miracles and human beings are his instruments.

The Active and Contemplative Lives (2a2ae.179-182)

Some men and women devote themselves especially to the contemplation of truth, and they lead what Thomas calls a contemplative life. Others devote themselves especially to external activity, and they lead what Thomas calls an active life. Every person living in a human way is primarily a thinker or a doer. Those who give themselves over to a life of pleasure lead the life of a beast, as Aristotle said; and they do not lead active or contemplative lives, as Thomas uses the terms here.

The contemplative life consists essentially in the consideration of truth, but it begins in love, endures in love, and intensifies in love. The contemplative must possess the moral virtues, which dispose the soul for contemplation by quieting the passions and reducing the tumult of the external world. The contemplative considers not only God himself, but also his effects, which show the way to God. Unless one is raptured as Paul was, the contemplative cannot achieve the vision of God in this life. To contemplate we have to listen, read, pray, meditate and ponder the divine truths. Since contemplation is an act of the highest human faculty, the intellect, and since it is directed to an infinitely lovable object, namely, God himself, contemplation affords great delight. One thinks of the delight a mother experiences in contemplating her child. The contemplative life will continue unabated even after death; the contemplative is already busy at the work of heaven.

The active life is given to works rather than to the consideration of truth. Prudence and the moral virtues are supremely important for the active life. A teacher contemplates the truth, but teaching belongs to the active life. It is a kind of intellectual hod-carrying. The life of external actions ends with this world.

In itself, the contemplative life is more excellent and meritorious than the active life, because the contemplative life has to do primarily with God and not with his creatures. Of course, human existence could not be sustained on this planet if everyone chose the contemplative life; but there is no danger of such a universal choice. Evidently, the active life can hinder contemplation, although in some cases the active life furthers contemplation by quelling disorderly passions. In point of time, the active life generally precedes the contemplative life as a kind of disposition for it.

States of Life (2a2ae.183-189)

St. Thomas begins by saying that a state of life is a permanent condition of a human person with regard to freedom or servitude in spiritual or civil matters. In other words, there are two general states: the state of freedom and the state of slavery. Immediately, one thinks of the ancient distinction between free persons and slaves. One thinks too of the states of grace and sin, which are states of freedom and slavery in their own way. Here, however, Thomas is particularly concerned with what he calls the state of perfection, which belongs to bishops and religious alone.

Christian perfection consists essentially in charity, in the exercise of love and in conformity to the divine will. Secondarily and instrumentally, perfection consists in binding oneself in perpetuity and with a certain solemnity to those things that pertain to perfection. It is in the latter sense that religious and bishops are in a state of perfection. Religious bind themselves by vow to the observance of the evangelical counsels, which facilitate the act of charity, when, in virtue of their consecration, they commit themselves to perfect others. Thomas does not think that priests and deacons are in a state of perfection; rather, they have an *office* pertaining to perfection. In any event, as Thomas notes, bishops and religious are not necessarily as firmly grounded in charity as some of those who are not in these states of perfection.

Paul wrote that if a man desires the office of bishop, he desires a good work (1 Tm 3:1). The work of the bishop is necessary and precious, wholly indispensable. However, to desire the office of bishop for its authority and temporal advantages is unlawful. It would be wrong for a qualified man to refuse the episcopal office in opposition to the appointment of his superior. The man chosen to be a bishop should not necessarily be the holiest person, but one who is able to instruct, defend and govern the faithful in peace. A bishop may withdraw his bodily presence from his flock for the sake of some advantage to the Church or on account of some danger to himself, provided he can care for his flock through another person. It is perfectly lawful for a bishop to have property of his own. Bishops should use the goods of the Church for the benefit of the poor, the decency of divine worship, and other worthy causes. A religious, who is raised to the episcopacy, retains those duties of his religious profession, which are compatible with his episcopal responsibilities.

The religious state is a state of perfection, because religious give themselves completely to Christ, in whom human perfection is to be found. Religious must observe such counsels as bind them by vow, and they must follow faithfully the rule they have professed.

The vows of poverty, continence, and obedience confer an immobility or permanence upon the religious state; and they are essential to it. The vows remove a person's attachment to worldly goods, reduce concupiscence and curb self-will. Obedience is the greatest of the three vows, because it sacrifices what is greater, namely one's will. A religious does not always sin mortally by transgressing the rule. A sin committed by one in religious life is more deplorable than the same sin committed by one who is not in that state.

It is lawful and suitable for those in the religious state to teach and, if they are authorized, to preach. It is not lawful for those in religious life to carry on secular business for motives of gain; yet, out of charity religious may, with due moderation, occupy themselves with business affairs. Religious are not bound to manual labor any more than other people are bound to it. It is certainly lawful for religious to live on alms and even beg for them. It is suitable for religious to use common and coarse attire, for such apparel befits those who do penance and look down on worldly glory.

Religious communities are distinguished by the works of charity to which they are devoted and by the religious practices which they adopt. Some communities give themselves to the contemplative life; others, to the active life, which ministers to the needs of one's neighbor. A military order may be established to maintain divine worship and public safety and to defend the poor and the oppressed. A community may be founded to preach, hear confessions and study. A contemplative community is more excellent than one devoted to the active life. Religious life is not hampered by the possession of a reasonable amount of worldly goods in common. Thomas notes that Jesus and his apostles had a purse in common (Jn 12:16). Religious living in community are a help to one another in striving for perfection.

The religious life is a school of perfection and even those who are not practiced in keeping the commandments may enter that school to advance in virtue. It is praiseworthy to *vow* to enter a religious community, and such a vow binds in conscience. A person may vow to enter a religious community and then conclude, after a trial, that he or she is not called to religious life. Even children can be received into a community for the purpose of training. When parents need their support, children may not enter a religious community. Parish priests may surrender their parochial duties to enter the religious state. For a serious reason a religious may pass from one community to another. A person who feels called to the religious life does not have to deliberate a long time and consult many persons before entering.

The Third Part of the SUMMA THEOLOGIAE (3a)

In a brief prologue to this part, St. Thomas writes: "By saving his people from their sins, as the angel announced (Mt 1:21), Our Savior, the Lord Jesus Christ, manifested to us in his own person the way of truth, which we must travel in order to attain the joy of eternal life by resurrection. Hence, if we are to complete the work of theology, after considering the ultimate end of human life and virtues and vices, we must consider the Savior of all and the benefits he conferred on the human race. Therefore, we shall take up (1) the Savior himself, (2) the sacraments by which we attain our salvation, and (3) everlasting life to which we rise by the resurrection."

Chapter 18

THE SAVIOR (3a.1-26)

In this chapter we shall review St. Thomas' teaching about the mystery of the incarnation and in the next chapter his teaching about the life, death and glorification of the Savior of all.

Our understanding of the person of the Lord Jesus Christ is derived chiefly from the New Testament. According to the apostolic preaching which is recorded in the Acts of the Apostles, Jesus is both Lord and Messiah, that is to say, the divine Son of God and the fulfillment of Jewish messianic hopes (Ac 2:36). Jesus is the servant of God (Ac 3:13), the holy and just one (Ac 3:14), the author of life (Ac 3:15), a prophet like Moses (Ac 3:22), the judge of the living and the dead (Ac 10:42; 17:30), and Savior (Ac 5:31).

The same conception of Jesus recurs in the Synoptic gospels. The gospel of Matthew revolves around the idea that Jesus is the expected messiah-king of Israel. The gospel of Mark focuses on the two titles of Jesus, "Christ" or "Messiah" and "Son of God" (Mk 1:1). The gospel of Luke calls Jesus a Savior (Lk 2:11) and portrays his concern for all of humanity and his identification with the poor, the outcast, and the criminal. In all the Synoptic gospels, Jesus refers to himself as the "son of man" in two cases especially—in his role as judge and as the suffering servant of God (e.g., Mt 24:30; Mk 8:31). The title is probably borrowed from Daniel 7:13.

In the Pauline writings, one finds the famous Christological hymn which speaks of the preexistent Christ, his self-effacement in the incarnation, his obedience to the Father even to death on a cross, and his exaltation by God, so that every tongue must proclaim him as Lord (Ph 2:5-11). For Paul, Jesus is Lord (1 Th 1:6; Ph 1:2; etc.), the Messiah of the Jews (Rm 9:5; 10:4; etc.), the Son of God (1 Th 1:10; 1 Cor 1:9; etc.), the image of God (2 Cor 4:4), the firstborn before all creatures (Col 1:15-16), the Savior (Ph 3:20; Ep 5:23), the head of the Church (Col 1:18; Ep 1:22), the last Adam (1 Cor 15:45), and, in equivalent terms, God (Ph 2:6; Col 1:15; 2:9).

To a large extent, the Synoptic and Pauline titles of Jesus are also found in the Johannine literature. In this literature, Jesus is the Messiah (Jn 20:31; Rv 11:15), the Son of God (Jn 20:31; 1 Jn 1:3; etc.), Lord (Jn 20:2; 21:7), son of man (Jn 1:51; 13:31), son of Joseph (Jn 1:46; 6:42), the prophet (Jn 6:14), the king of Israel (Jn 1:49), the Savior (Jn 4:42), the lamb of God (Jn 1:29, 36), and the Word of God (Jn 1:1-18), because he reveals the Father. The "I am" statements in the gospel (Jn 8:24; 13:19; etc.) are an expression of Jesus' divinity.

Subsequently, the official teaching of the Church about the incarnate Son of God was formulated by the first ecumenical councils. The Council of Nicea (325), the first ecumenical council, taught that Jesus Christ is true God. He was born of the Father and is of one substance with the Father. There never was a time when he was not.[1] The Council of Ephesus (431), the third ecumenical council, taught that there is only one person in Christ, the person of the Word.[2] The Council of Chalcedon (451), the fourth ecumenical council, recognized two distinct natures in the one person of Christ. He is perfect in divinity and perfect in humanity, being true God and true man.[3] The Third Council of Constantinople (680-681), the sixth ecumenical council, defined the existence of two active principles and two wills in Christ, a divine will and a human will. The human will is perfectly subject to the divine will and without sin.[4]

In the *Summa* St. Thomas does not study the incarnation until he has treated exhaustively of God and man—and with good reason. It is only by knowing something of God and something of man that we can appreciate the splendor of the union of the two in the incarnate Word. In this chapter we shall discuss three subjects: the suitability of the incarnation, the union of the two natures in the incarnate Word, and the consequences of this union.

The Suitability of the Incarnation (3a.1)

The suitability and necessity of the incarnation are questions introduced into Scholastic theology by Anselm of Canterbury (1033-1109). The mystery of the incarnation is known only because God has revealed it; but once known, we can try to gain some little understanding of it. The New Testament proclaims Jesus to be the natural Son of God, even while he displays all the characteristics of a human being. Hence, Jesus is both God and man.

Was it fitting that God should become man? Yes, Thomas replies. It is essential to goodness to communicate itself to others. One thinks how parents share good things with their children. Hence, it is fitting that Infinite Goodness should communicate itself in the most perfect manner, and it does so by joining human nature to itself in a personal union. As Thomas understands the Bible, God became incarnate to redeem the human race and destroy sin. Had the human race not sinned, God would not have become incarnate. Still, the incarnation was not absolutely necessary for human salvation, since God could have restored sinful human beings to his friendship in other ways. But the incarnation was a most noble, effective, and admirable way to reconcile God and his rebellious children. God became incarnate to take away all sins, that is to say, actual sins and especially original sin. God did not become incarnate immediately after the first sin, so that the human race might come to understand its need of redemption;

however, the incarnation was not delayed until the end of the world, so that things might not get too bad.

The Union of the Incarnate Word (3a.2-15)

To begin with, Thomas inquires about the union between God and man in the incarnation. Thomas makes a distinction between nature and person. A person is one who is the subject of, and responsible for, his or her actions, while a nature is the essential principle by which this agent acts. This distinction is clarified, when we apply it to the incarnate Word, Jesus Christ. In virtue of his divine nature, Jesus Christ is equal to his Father and acts as God acts, creating, sustaining the universe, and glorifying his rational creatures. In virtue of his human nature, Jesus Christ is like us in all things, being born of Mary, growing up, suffering and dying. However, it is the one divine person, the Son of God, the second person of the Blessed Trinity, who is the subject of, and responsible for, the actions of both natures. Thus, thinking of Jesus Christ, we may say with equal justification that God cured the sick and read the hearts of men and women (and this in virtue of his divine nature), and that God was born of Mary, suffered, and died on the cross (and this in virtue of his human nature). The union of the incarnation is a personal, substantial union, in which the person is not caused by the union, but rather exists prior to it. We call the union of the two natures in the one divine person the hypostatic union. The person of Christ, a divine person, subsists in two natures, human and divine.

Since Christ is true man as well as true God, there is a union of soul and body in Christ, as there is in any other man. The union of the two natures in Christ or the hypostatic union is the work or creation of God and took place in time. We must say that God assumed human nature; we may not say that man assumed a divine nature. It is correct to say that the hypostatic union took place by grace, if by grace we mean not habitual or sanctifying grace, but simply a gratuitous act of God. No one could merit the incarnation condignly, although the holy people of the Old Testament could merit it congruously by desiring it and beseeching God for it. Grace, whether it be understood as the grace of the hypostatic union or sanctifying grace, was natural to the man Christ inasmuch as he had them from his nativity, since from the beginning of his conception the human nature was united to the divine person and his soul was filled with sanctifying grace.

Having considered the manner in which the two natures are united in the one person of Christ, St. Thomas now considers the union from the standpoint of the divine nature assuming the human nature. A divine person is said to have assumed a human nature in the sense that a divine person took a human nature to itself in a personal union. Since all works of God's power are common to the three persons of the Blessed Trinity, the three persons caused the human nature to be united to the one person of the Son. Had it been the will of God, the Father or the Holy Spirit could have become incarnate. Indeed, the three divine persons could have assumed one and the same human nature. Moreover, Thomas believes, the Son could have assumed two distinct human natures. In any case, it was most fitting that the Son, rather than the Father or the Holy Spirit, should have become incarnate, so that through the natural Son of God men and women might become adopted sons and daughters of God.

Next Thomas considers the union of the incarnation from the standpoint of the human nature assumed by the Word of God. It was most fitting that the Word of God should assume a human nature rather than an angelic or irrational nature because of the dignity of human nature and its need for redemption. The human nature, which the Word assumed, was taken from the line of Adam, so that the nature, whereby we had sinned, might make satisfaction for human sinfulness. The Son of God assumed a human nature; therefore, he assumed a human body with flesh and bones, and a human soul with intellect and will. He assumed body and soul simultaneously and not one before the other. Sanctifying grace was not the bond or cement of the union between the divine person and his human nature; it was rather the effect.

There was sanctifying grace in the human soul of Christ. As a fire warms objects close to it, so the divine person of the Word sanctified the human soul joined to it in so close a union. In virtue of sanctifying grace, the powers of Christ's soul were perfected by the infused virtues. However, Christ had neither faith nor hope. As Thomas shall make clear later on, Christ saw God's essence fully from the first moment of his conception; and such a vision excludes faith, which has to do with things not seen, and hope, which has to do with things not possessed. All the gifts of the Holy Spirit were present in the soul of Christ in a most excellent manner. Even the gift of fear, filial fear, was present. In his capacity as the first and chief teacher of spiritual doctrine and faith, Christ had all the special gifts, the *gratiae gratis datae*, such as miracles, prophecy and tongues. United to the Word of God in a personal union, the soul of Christ was full of habitual grace to the highest possible degree and with the greatest possible effect. Still, this grace remained finite, since it vivified the soul of Christ, which was created. The grace of Christ could not be increased during his lifetime because of its fullness even at the moment of his conception. The union of the human nature with the divine person preceded the habitual grace of Christ not in point of time, but by nature and in thought; for the grace of union was the cause of habitual grace in Christ's soul.

The habitual grace of Christ's soul was significant, not only for himself, but for others, since all have received grace on account of his grace (Jn 1:16). Christ's grace, as the source of grace for others, is called capital grace. By reason of his capital grace, Christ is the head of the Church, influencing the other members of the Church somewhat as the head influences the other members of the physical body. As a matter of fact, the whole humanity of Christ, body and soul, influences other human beings in body and soul by reason of his grace; therefore, Christ is the head of men and women and not merely the head of souls. With the exception of those who are in hell, Christ is the head of all men and women and especially of those who are united to him by grace and glory. Christ as man is the head of the angels, since they too are subject to his influence. Christ alone is the head of the Church; the Pope is his vicar on earth. The devil is the head of all the wicked. Antichrist is the head of the wicked in the sense that he is the worst of all who are influenced by the devil.

Having discussed the grace of Christ, Thomas inquires about Christ's knowledge. As God, Christ had divine knowledge, a knowledge which Thomas studied in the first part of the *Summa*. As man, Christ had human knowledge of which there are three kinds: the knowledge which the blessed have in heaven through the direct vision of God, infused knowledge, and acquired knowledge. Thomas looks at each of these three kinds of human knowledge in the soul of Christ.

Beatific Knowledge. Thomas argues for the existence of this type of knowledge in the soul of Christ by saying that men and women achieve beatitude only through Christ (Heb 2:10). Hence, the beatific knowledge, which consists in the vision of God, belonged preeminently to Christ, since the cause ought always to be more efficacious than the effect. As a creature, the human soul of Christ does not comprehend the divine essence, that is to say, know it as perfectly as God knows it. However, the soul of Christ does know all that in any way whatsoever is, will be, or was done, said or thought, by whomsoever and at any time; for in the beatific vision one sees whatever pertains to oneself, and all these things pertain to Christ as king and judge. Because the human soul of Christ is united to the Word in person, it beholds the divine essence more clearly than any other creature in heaven.

Infused Knowledge. This is the type of knowledge given to the angels when they were created, a type of knowledge deemed necessary by Thomas for the perfection of Christ's passive intellect. This knowledge too had a kind of universality. The soul of Christ could use this knowledge without turning to the sense-images called phantasms. The infused knowledge of Christ was greater than that of the angels. The knowledge infused into the human soul of Christ was habitual knowledge, a stable possession, to be used when he pleased.

Acquired Knowledge. This is the type of knowledge gained by human beings through the senses and abstracted from sense-images or phantasms by the active intellect. In this life human beings normally gain their knowledge in this way, and Christ was no exception to the rule. With his acquired knowledge Christ knew whatever can be humanly known by the action of the active intellect. There was real growth in this knowledge as Christ matured (Lk 2:52). Curiously, St. Thomas said that it was beneath the dignity of Christ, as the head of the Church and its chief teacher, to be taught by any other creature human or angelic.

Next Thomas inquires about the power of Christ's soul. Was the soul of Christ omnipotent? No, Thomas replies, because the soul of Christ was a creature and therefore finite in its power. It follows that the soul of Christ could in no way create or be the instrument of creation. Still, the soul of Christ, as the instrument of divinity, could work all miracles conducive to the end of the incarnation; and so we read in the gospels that Christ drove out devils, forgave sins, healed lepers and raised the dead. With respect to his body, Christ's soul had no greater power than we exercise over our bodies. It is true that by its own power the soul of Christ could do all that it willed, but this was simply because Christ was too wise to will what could not be done.

While grace, knowledge and power pertain to the perfection of Christ's nature, Thomas holds that it was also appropriate for him to assume a body that was subject to human infirmities and defects, such as death, hunger, thirst and the like; and this for three reasons: to satisfy for sins, to demonstrate the truth of the incarnation and to offer an example of patience. The Son of God did not have to assume a body with such deficiencies, but he did so of his own will. Christ as man did not have the defects that conflict with his perfect knowledge, grace and dignity, such defects as ignorance and proneness to evil. Nor did Christ suffer from any defects which do not flow from the whole of human nature on account of Adam's sin, but are caused in some individuals by certain particular causes as leprosy, epilepsy and the like.

Was the soul of Christ subject to any defects, as his body was? There was no sin in Christ. Jesus himself asked, "Which of you shall convict me of sin?" (Jn 8:46). One cannot stand next to fire and shiver; the soul of Christ could not be united to the Word and sin. The capacity to sin would have contributed nothing to our redemption. Neither was the inclination to sin to be found in Christ; this too had no redemptive value. Our Lord did suffer sorrow of soul and pain of body. He experienced fear at the prospect of his approaching passion, for fear is a natural shrinking from pain. Christ was capable of wonder. Wonder is caused by what is new and unusual. The new and unusual could be an element of Christ's acquired knowledge and a source of wonder. The New Testament tells us that Christ was angry at times; anger is zeal for the triumph of justice. Christ was human, and the passions are a part of human nature; but, of course, Christ's passions were balanced. Thomas concludes that Christ was at once a wayfarer and a comprehensor prior to his passion and death. He was a comprehensor in the sense that his soul was blessed by the direct vision of God; and he was a wayfarer in the sense that his soul and body could and did suffer.

The Consequences of the Incarnational Union (3a.16-26)

Lastly, St. Thomas considers the consequences of the hypostatic union, and these with respect to Christ himself, his relationship to the Father and his relationship to us.

One consequence of the incarnation is our manner of speaking about it. In this case, both a human nature and a divine nature, with their distinctive properties, belong to one and the same person. All that is true of God and all that is true of man is true of this divine person. Hence, it is true to say that God is man, that man is God, because the concrete terms, God and man, signify the second person of the Blessed Trinity. However, it is not true to say that in Christ humanity is divinity, because these two terms signify the two natures which are not the same. It is true to say that by the incarnation God was made man, because a thing is said to be made that which is predicated of it for the first time. It is correct to say that Christ as man is a creature, that Christ as God is eternal. It is wrong to say that Christ as man is God, that Christ as man is a person. In these cases, the qualifying phrases, as man, as God, refer to the natures and determine the sense of the statements.

Christ is one person, a divine person; yet, he has two natures, a divine nature and a human nature, and so it follows that he has two wills, a divine will and a human will. Because Christ had a perfect human nature, he also had a sensual appetite with the corresponding passions. Having a human will, Christ had freedom of choice. Such freedom does not mean that Christ could sin, for sin is an abuse of freedom; and, as someone has noted, the abuse of freedom no more enters into its definition than monstrosities enter into the definition of a human being. It is true to say that in one sense the human will of Christ recoiled from what is evil in itself, such as suffering and death; still, the human will of Christ accepted these things in conformity to the divine will for the salvation of the human race. Therefore, Christ was able to say in the garden of Gethsemane, "Not my will, but your will be done" (Mt 26:39). Throughout his whole voluntary life the rational will of Christ was in complete conformity with the divine will.

St. Thomas also distinguishes two operations in Christ, one of the divine nature and one of the human nature. Both the divine and human natures did what was proper to each, but in union with the other. In this case, the divine nature made use of the operation of the human nature, as a principal agent makes use of the operation of an instrument. We call such a joint operation, involving the collaboration of both natures, a theandric operation, the operation of a God-man. Thus, when Jesus healed the leper with a touch, when he walked and taught, when he did anything for our salvation, these were theandric operations. St. Thomas holds that there was such a perfect unity in the operations of the God-man that even the operations of his sensitive and nutritive parts were subject to his human will. In virtue of his human operation, Christ was able to merit, not the grace of union or the habitual grace which he had from the beginning, but rather the glorification of his body and whatever pertained to his outward excellence, such as his ascension, veneration, and other things of this nature. Of course, Christ was able to merit, not only for himself, but also for others, who form one mystical person with him.

What are the consequences of the hypostatic union with respect to the relationship between Christ and his heavenly Father? Christ is the Son of God, equal to his Father and one with him in essence and nature. However, Christ is also man, and as man he is subject to the Father. Christ in his human nature is subject to himself in his divine nature.

As a consequence of the hypostatic union, Christ as man was able to pray to his Father in heaven. Prayer is nothing more than the unfolding of our will to God, that he may fulfill it. Because Christ had a human will, he was able to pray. Christ prayed for himself when, for example, he prayed for the glory of his resurrection (Jn 17:1). When Christ prayed for himself, he gave us an example of prayer, and he acknowledged that his Father was the source of all the good that he possessed in his human nature. Every prayer of Christ was answered; every absolute will-act of Christ as man was fulfilled, because he willed nothing but what he knew God to will.

As a consequence of the hypostatic union, Christ ministered, and continues to minister to his Father as a priest. For Thomas who cites the letter to the Hebrews (5:1), a priest is a mediator between God and the people, transmitting the things of God to the people and offering prayers and satisfaction to God in the name of the people. Christ as man was a priest, for he brought the gifts of God to the human race (2 P 1:4) and reconciled sinful mankind to its heavenly Father (Col 1:19). As mediator, the chief act of a priest is to offer sacrifice to God. Christ offered sacrifice to God throughout his life and especially on Calvary, where he was both priest and victim for the sins of others. It was he who offered the sacrifice, bringing truth, love, grace and even God himself to us. His gift to God on our behalf was full satisfaction for sin. Christ himself was not the beneficiary of his priesthood; rather, we are the ones who benefit. The priesthood of Christ endures forever in the sense that the effects of his sacrifice have an everlasting significance. Christ is said to be a priest "according to the order of Melchizedek" (Ps 110:4) because of the excellence of his priesthood in relation to the priesthood of the Old Law. As Thomas explains, the excellence of Christ's priesthood was foreshadowed in the priesthood of Melchizedek, who received tithes from Abraham (Gn 14:18-20), in whose loins the priesthood of the Old Law was tithed.

Even after the incarnation, we may *not* speak of Christ as an adopted son of God. God is said to adopt sons and daughters inasmuch as he admits men and women to the inheritance of beatitude. As a matter of fact, it is the three divine persons, and not the Father alone, who adopt us as children, since the production of any effect in creatures is common to the whole Trinity. Only rational creatures, that is to say, angels and human beings, and, indeed, only those who have charity are adopted sons and daughters of God. Our Lord himself is not an adopted son of God, even in virtue of his human nature. Adoption belongs to the person, not to the nature; and the second person of the Blessed Trinity is the natural Son of God, not an adopted son.

The union of natures in the person of Christ was predestined from all eternity. Therefore, it is true to say that Christ as man was predestined to be the Son of God. The predestination of Christ according to his human nature was the model of our predestination for two reasons: first, he was predestined to be the natural Son of God, whereas we are predestined to be adopted sons and daughters, who bear a resemblance to his natural sonship; and, second, both the human nature of Christ and ourselves achieved their exalted status by grace without any antecedent merits. Indeed, the predestination of Christ was the cause of our predestination, for God so decreed our salvation, that it should be achieved through Jesus Christ.

What are the consequences of the hypostatic union with respect to us? For one thing, we offer Christ one adoration, the adoration of latria, which is the worship proper to God, since he is one divine person at whom our worship terminates. Even the humanity of Christ is adored with the adoration of latria, because it is the humanity of a person who is God. We worship an image of Christ with the adoration of latria, since this worship is really given to Christ. Thus, we genuflect before the crucifix on Good Friday. We do not offer the Mother of God the worship of latria, because she is only a creature; but we offer her the veneration of hyperdulia, which is a veneration greater than that given to any other creature. We honor the relics of the saints with a true veneration that is directed to the saints themselves; and in honoring the saints we honor Christ whose members they are.

At the conclusion of his treatise on the person of the incarnate Word, Thomas speaks about Christ as mediator. Christ is the mediator between God and the human race because he brought them together, reconciling the human race to God by his death (2 Cor 5:19). However, others too may be called mediators in some sense, insofar as they unite men and women to God dispositively or ministerially. Christ is the mediator between God and the human race in virtue of his humanity, which enables him to stand, so to speak, between God and his rational creatures.

Chapter 19

WHAT JESUS DID AND SUFFERED (3a.27-59)

Once St. Thomas has treated of the person of the Incarnate Word, it remains for him to consider what Jesus did and suffered. Under this heading, Thomas discusses four main topics: the coming of Jesus into the world, his public life, his passion and death, and his exaltation including his resurrection, ascension and sitting at the right hand of his Father.

The Coming of Jesus into the World (3a.27-39)

Speaking of the conception of Jesus, Thomas develops his teaching on Mary, the Mother of God. Mary was sanctified before her birth from the womb. She, who was the Mother of God, was no less privileged than certain other persons, such as Jeremiah (Jr 1:5) and John the Baptist (Lk 1:15), who were sanctified in the womb. Thomas teaches that Mary did incur the stain of original sin at her conception and only later was sanctified. Had this not been the case, Thomas argues, Mary would not have been redeemed by her divine Son, who must be acknowledged as the Savior of all. In this opinion, however, Thomas erred. It was the Franciscan theologian, Duns Scotus (1265-1308), who taught that Mary was preserved from all stain of original sin through the merits of her Son. She was not liberated, but preserved, from the stain of original sin.

Subsequently, the doctrine of Mary's immaculate conception was solemnly defined by Pope Pius IX in 1854.[1] By reason of her abundant grace Mary experienced no rebellion of the lower powers against her reason. Thomas holds that Mary committed no actual sin, mortal or venial. Had she committed any sin, she would not have been the worthy Mother of God, which she actually was. When she was sanctified in the womb, Mary received the fullness of grace, for she was closer to the source of grace than anyone else.

The mother of Christ conceived her divine Son in a virginal manner through the overshadowing of the Holy Spirit; hence, Jesus had no human father. Mary remained a virgin even when she gave birth to her Son, for, Thomas holds, it was not fitting that he who came to take away our corruption should corrupt his mother's virginity at his birth. Both the conception of Jesus and his birth were flatly miraculous. Mary remained a virgin even after the birth of her divine Son, since she could not be otherwise than content with such a Son. Thomas believes that Mary's words to the angel, "I know not man" (Lk 1:34), indicate that Mary had taken a vow of virginity; but Mary's vow could be kept only with the consent of her husband Joseph, who also vowed virginity. When Thomas speaks of virginity, he means abstention from all voluntary venereal pleasure, whether lawful or unlawful; and in Mary's case he includes physical integrity. Thomas' teaching about the perpetual virginity of Mary reflects a very old tradition of the Church that Mary was a virgin "before, during, and after the birth" of her Son.

The marriage of Mary and Joseph was a true marriage in the sense that they were united to each other by a bond of mutual affection that could not be sundered. While their marriage was not consummated, it was dedicated to the upbringing of Mary's child. The marriage of Joseph and Mary served a useful purpose: it forestalled the charge that the birth of Jesus was illegitimate; it enabled Joseph to assist Mary; and it honored both virginity and wedlock.

What is to be said about the annunciation? It was right that

Mary should be told about the incarnation beforehand, so that she might cooperate more fully in that great mystery of the Christian religion. The ministry of an angel to Mary was appropriate, since in God's providence divine things are communicated to human beings in this way. It was fitting that the angel of the annunciation should appear to Mary in a bodily form, because he was sent to announce the incarnation of the invisible God. Gabriel instructed Mary about the mystery and won her consent.

Christ assumed flesh derived from Adam that he might heal human nature by the assumption. Christ is said to be the son of Abraham and David particularly, because the promises made to the two patriarchs were fulfilled especially in him. Christ took flesh of a woman, so that both sexes might have a role in the redemption.

The whole Trinity of divine persons effected the conception of our Lord's body; but the conception is attributed to the Holy Spirit in a special way, because it was a work of love. It is not correct to say that Christ in his humanity is the son of the Holy Spirit, for Christ is the Son of the Father by eternal generation. Beyond her consent, Mary cooperated in the conception of Christ to the extent that she supplied the matter of Christ's body upon which the Holy Spirit acted. As soon as the angel gained Mary's consent, the Holy Spirit acted, and the Word became flesh. At the moment in which Christ was conceived, his body was animated by a rational and spiritual soul, and soul and body were assumed by the Word. Our Lord's conception, although natural in a certain respect, should be described as miraculous and supernatural on the part of the Holy Spirit. In the first instant of Christ's conception, as a consequence of the union between humanity and divinity in the person of the Word, the humanity of Christ had the fullness of sanctifying grace, the beatifying vision of God, the use of free will, and the capacity to merit.

Next, Thomas turns his attention from the conception of Christ to his nativity. The nativity of Christ was the birth of the Son of God as subsisting in human nature. Christ had a twofold nativity: one by which he was born of the Father from all eternity, and one by which he was born of Mary in time. Mary is truly Christ's mother; Christ is truly God; therefore, Mary is truly the Mother of God. Our Lord was born of Mary without suffering on her part, for he passed miraculously from her womb. It was fitting that our Lord, the seed of David, should be born in Bethlehem, the city of David. We know that Christ was born at a suitable time, for he chose the time, and he is the all-wise God.

Thomas goes on to examine the circumstances of Christ's birth. The birth of Christ was made known, not to all, but to some, through whom it could be made known to others. God is not wont to bestow his gifts and secrets on all equally, but only to some immediately, through whom they are made known to others. Since salvation, which was to be accomplished by Christ, concerns all, Christ manifested his birth to male and female, to Jew and Gentile, in the persons of the Jewish shepherds, the Gentile magi, and Simeon and Anna. Christ made his birth known to the Jewish shepherds through angels, because the Jews were accustomed to divine communications through angels; and he made his birth known to the Gentile magi through a star, because the Gentiles, especially astrologers, were wont to observe the course of the stars. The order in which the birth of Christ was revealed—first, to Jewish shepherds, then to the Gentile magi, and finally to the fullness of the Jews in the persons of Simeon and Anna—reflects the order in which the gospel was preached and will be accepted. Thomas believed that the star of the nativity was a newly created heavenly body near the earth, and its movements varied according to the will of God.

Eight days after his birth, the child was circumcised for a variety of reasons, among them, to demonstrate the reality of his human nature and his Jewish heritage. Our Lord was called Jesus, that is Savior, by divine command (Lk 1:31), because he was to save his people from their sins. Jesus was presented to God in the temple in accordance with the Old Law (Lk 2:22), so that he might give an example of obedience and humility. Out of obedience and humility Mary, too, went to the temple to be purified.

A few decades later, Christ was baptized with the baptism of John in the Jordan River. The baptism given by John prepared the people for the baptism given by Jesus. God sent John to baptize, but John's baptism effected nothing that a human being could not accomplish. The baptism of John was a preparation for grace, but it did not give grace, which comes through Jesus Christ (Jn 1:17). John did not cease to baptize even after he had baptized Christ, because, as Thomas said, the baptism given by John prepared the way for others to approach Christ's baptism. Of course, those who were baptized by John needed to be baptized again with Christian baptism in order to receive grace and the baptismal character. Scripture tells us that the apostles administered the sacrament of baptism to those who had already received the baptism of John (Ac 19:1-5).

Christ was baptized, the Fathers say, to sanctify the natural element of water for its use in Christian baptism and to show his approval of the rite of baptism. Our Lord was baptized at the age of thirty (Lk 3:21-23) to inaugurate in a formal way, as it were, his mission of teaching and preaching. It was fitting that Christ should be baptized in the Jordan River through which the Israelites entered the promised land, for baptism is the entrance to the kingdom of God, which is signified by the land of promise. At Christ's baptism the heavens were opened (Lk 3:21) to show that the way to heaven is open to the baptized. The Holy Spirit, taking the form of a dove, descended upon Christ at his baptism (Lk 3:22) to show that all those who are baptized with the baptism of Christ receive the Holy Spirit. The dove that came upon Christ was a real bird directly created for the purpose, since an imaginary bird would have been unworthy of the Holy Spirit, the Spirit of truth. The Father's voice was heard when Christ was baptized (Mt 3:17) to signify that the faithful are baptized in the name of the Father, Son and Holy Spirit, all of whom were represented at Christ's baptism.

The Public Life (3a.40-45)

Under this heading, Thomas is concerned with Christ's manner of life, his temptation, his preaching and his miracles.

Christ did not lead a solitary life; rather, in accordance with the purpose of the incarnation, he associated freely with men and women. He conformed to their manner of living, eating and drinking as they did (Mt 11:19). Still, Christ led a life of poverty (Mt 8:20) so that he might give himself completely to his ministry without the burden of temporal possessions. Christ observed the precepts of the Old Law to show that he had come to fulfill the Law and not abolish it (Mt 5:17).

Christ allowed himself to be tempted by the devil (Mt 4:1) to teach us how to act when we are tempted. Christ was tempted in the desert because the devil prefers to assail a person who is alone. By fasting before his temptation, Christ showed us the need for fasting to equip ourselves against temptation. The first temptation of the devil had to do with the food necessary to sustain the body; then the devil appealed to ostentation and vain glory; and finally he appealed to riches and the glory of the world.

Thomas notes that Christ himself preached only to the Jews and not to the Gentiles (Mt 15:24). In this way he showed that by his coming he fulfilled the promises that were made to the Jews of old and not to the Gentiles. Sometimes Christ offended the leaders of the people by his preaching, for they hated the truth; but he had to risk offending them for the sake of the people. Christ spoke openly to the people, although he used parables to convey his message, parables which he explained more fully to his disciples. Our Lord wrote nothing; he left the task to writers inspired by God. As the most excellent of teachers, Christ imprinted his words on the heart and not on books.

Our Lord worked miracles to confirm the truth of his preaching and reveal the presence of God in his person. The miracles were worked by divine power, for they outstripped the powers of nature;

but the human was the instrument of the divine. Christ worked no miracles until he worked his first miracle in Cana at the beginning of his public life (Jn 2:11). Up to that point there had been no need to confirm the truth of his preaching. The miracles of Christ proved his divinity, because he adduced them in support of his claim to be God.

After considering Christ's miracles in general, Thomas takes a closer look at specific miracles. Christ miraculously expelled demons from others, so that the demons could not keep their victim from believing in him. Our Lord worked miracles among the heavenly bodies—by an eclipse of the sun, for example (Lk 23:44), to prove that he is God, who alone controls the course of those bodies. Christ worked miracles for the benefit of men and women, curing them in a wonderful way, to show that he is the universal and spiritual Savior of all. Our Lord worked miracles on irrational creatures to show that he is God, to whom every creature is subject.

Thomas devotes particular attention to the miracle of the transfiguration. Our Lord was transfigured in the presence of three of his disciples (Mt 17:2) so that they might bear persecution bravely in anticipation of the glory that awaited them. The brilliance of Christ's transfigured body was essentially the same brilliance that is a permanent quality of resurrected bodies. Moses and Elijah were present in the name of all who had gone before; Peter, James and John, in the name of all who were to come after. The Father testified to the natural sonship of Jesus both at his baptism and at his transfiguration (Mt 17:5) to show the connection between the grace of baptism and heavenly glory by which God's adopted sons and daughters are conformed to his divine Son.

The Passion and Death (3a.46-52)

Under this heading, Thomas considers all that relates to Christ's leaving this world, namely, his passion, death, burial and descent into hell.

The passion of Christ was necessary in the sense that it was the means chosen by God for the redemption of the human race. Yet God could have willed to redeem the human race in some other way. Indeed, God could simply have forgiven his repentant sons and daughters. However, the passion of Christ was the most suitable means of delivering the human race for several reasons: for example, the passion of Christ showed us how much God loves us, for God did not spare his only Son for our sake; by his passion Christ gave us an example of obedience, humility and constancy; and by his passion Christ delivered us from sin and merited grace and glory for us.

For many good reasons Christ chose to die on a cross; for example, by his execrable death on a cross, he showed that no kind of death should trouble an upright person. In a sense Jesus endured every kind of human suffering that can be inflicted by an extrinsic agent. His suffering was of greater intensity than any other the world has seen. However, even in the midst of his suffering, Christ continued to enjoy the vision of God, although not in a physical way. Both the time and place of Christ's suffering were divinely arranged. Christ was crucified between two thieves to show that he suffered as a guilty one among the guilty for our salvation. It was the divine person in his human nature who suffered and died.

The efficient cause of Christ's suffering and death was, directly and actively, his human executioners; still, Christ laid down his life voluntarily, since he could have prevented his passion and death. Christ died out of obedience to God, so that by the obedience of one man, many might be made just, just as by the disobedience of one man, many were made sinners (Rm 5:19). It is accurate to say that God the Father delivered up Christ to his passion and death (Rm 8:32). It was fitting that the Jews should hand Christ over to the Gentiles to signify that Christ's passion wrought its effect first of all among the Jews (Ac 2:41; 4:4) and then among the Gentiles. The leaders of the people knew whom they were persecuting in the person of Christ; but the common folk lacked full understanding.

Obviously, the gravity of their sin depended upon the extent of their knowledge.

Next, Thomas inquires about the effects of Christ's passion; but before he considers the effects themselves, he asks *how* the effects were brought about. First of all, by his passion Christ merited salvation for the members of his mystical body. Secondly, by his passion Christ atoned for the sins of the human race, offering superabundant satisfaction for them (1 Jn 2:2). Thirdly, the passion of Christ was a sacrifice acceptable to God, offered to appease him and manifest his supreme dominion over all things (Ep 5:2). Fourthly, the passion of Christ was a redemptive work, releasing men and women from the bondage of sin and the debt of punishment due to it (1 P 1:18). The principal efficient cause of our salvation was the triune God; and the humanity of Christ was the instrument of God in working out our salvation.

What, then, were the effects of Christ's passion? We can describe them quite succinctly in the light of what we have just said. The effects of Christ's passion were freedom from sin (Rv 1:5), liberation from the power of the devil (Jn 12:31), release from the punishment due to sin (Is 54:4), reconciliation with God (Rm 5:10), opening of the gates of heaven (Heb 10:19), and the exaltation of the God-man Christ (Ph 2:8).

The death of Christ followed upon his passion. Christ underwent death for several reasons; for example, to take upon himself the penalty we deserved for our sins and to demonstrate the reality of his flesh. When Christ died, his divinity was not separated either from his soul or his body, although Christ's soul was separated from his body in death. It is not correct to say that Christ was a man during the period of his death, since a man means a living man with soul and body united, and Christ truly died. Christ's body was identically the same body living and dead. The one death of Christ in the body destroyed in us both the death of the soul caused by sin (Rm 4:25) and the death of the body consisting in the separation of the soul (1 Cor 15:54).

After his death, Christ was buried. Christ's burial established the certainty of his death and gave us hope of rising from the grave through him. Thomas believed that Christ's body did not deteriorate in any way while it lay in the tomb. The sacred body was in the tomb one day and two nights. The two nights signify the twofold death from which Christ delivered us, namely, the death of the soul and of the body. The day signifies the charity that motivated Christ during his passion and death.

While his body lay in the tomb, the soul of Christ descended into hell. In this case hell refers to limbo, the place and state of those who were awaiting the redemption. Christ did not descend locally into the hell of lost souls and demons. The whole Christ was in limbo, because the whole person of Christ was there by reason of the soul united with him. It seems that Christ's soul was in limbo from the moment of his death on the cross to the moment of resurrection. Christ liberated the righteous of the Old Testament from limbo, where they were held until the gates of heaven were opened by Christ's passion and death. Christ's descent into limbo meant no deliverance of any soul from the hell of the lost. The infants held in limbo by reason of original sin were not released by Christ's descent, because they were without charity; but they suffered no distress or pain. Christ's descent into limbo did not liberate souls from purgatory, since Christ's passion had no greater efficacy then than it has now.

The Exaltation of Christ (3a.53-59)

The exaltation of Christ refers to his resurrection, ascension, sitting at the right hand of his Father, and judiciary power.

It behooved Christ to rise from the dead for several reasons; for example, to confirm our belief in his divinity and to encourage our hope of rising from the grave. Christ remained in the tomb for a short time to certify his death; but he rose shortly thereafter, without waiting until the end of the world, to ground our faith in him. Christ was the first to rise from the dead (1 Cor 15:20) without the need of dying again. All those who had been miraculously restored to life before him had to die again. It is correct to say that Christ himself was the cause of his resurrection.

Christ retained his own true body after his resurrection. Had this not been a true body, but only an imaginary one, or had it not been the body in which Christ had died, the resurrection would not have been real. The same body that had been laid in the tomb by others came forth by itself in a glorified condition. Christ's resurrection with a glorified body is the exemplar and cause of our resurrection with a glorified body (1 Cor 15:43). Though Christ's body was a spiritualized body, he asked the disciples for something to eat, not because he needed food, but to demonstrate the nature of his risen body. It was a complete and perfect body. Our Lord kept the scars of wounds in his glorified body as a sign of victory.

After his resurrection Christ manifested himself to witnesses preordained by God (Ac 10:40). These witnesses were to make the resurrection known to others in accordance with God's plan whereby he reveals divine things through higher persons. No human eye was privileged to see our Lord in the first moment of his resurrection. An angel was the herald of his rising. Christ did not live continuously with his disciples after his resurrection to show that he did not rise to the same life as before. After the resurrection Christ revealed himself in his own shape to some who were well disposed to believe in him and in another shape to some who had grown weak in their faith, as in the case of the two disciples on the road to Emmaus (Lk 24:21). Christ proved the truth of his resurrection not by intellectual argumentation, but by many sensible signs (Ac 1:3). In appearing to the apostles, Christ made two points: the truth of the resurrecton and the glory of his risen body.

Christ's resurrection is the cause of the resurrection of our bodies. The Word of God first bestows immortal life upon that body which is naturally united with himself, and through it works the resurrection in all other bodies. The passion of Christ and his resurrection are the cause of the resurrection of our souls from the death of sin.

Forty days after his resurrection, Christ ascended into heaven. It was fitting that Christ, who had entered upon an immortal and incorruptible life, should pass from the place of corruption to the place of incorruption. Christ's ascension belonged to him according to his human nature, which was limited by place and could be the subject of motion. Christ ascended primarily by his divine power and secondarily by the power of his glorified soul moving his body at will. Paul wrote that Christ ascended above all the heavens (Ep 4:10) and above every spiritual creature (Ep 1:21). Christ's ascension fosters our salvation by encouraging faith, hope, charity and reverence on our part; moreover, by his ascension Christ has gone to prepare a place for us (Jn 14:2), and in heaven he continues to make intercession for us (Heb 7:25).

In Mark's gospel we read that Jesus, after being taken up to heaven, now sits at the right hand of God (Mk 16:19). To sit at the right hand of God means to abide in the Father's glory, reign with him, and have judiciary power from him. Both as God and as man, Christ sits at the right hand of the Father: as God, in the sense that he reigns equally with the Father; and as man, in the sense that his humanity is favored with the Father's gifts beyond all other creatures. It follows that sitting at the right hand of the Father belongs to no one else, angel or human, but to Christ alone.

Finally, Thomas considers Christ's judiciary power. The whole Trinity is the judge of the living and the dead; but judgment is attributed especially to Christ as the Wisdom of God, for wisdom is the soul of judgment. Judiciary power belongs to Christ even as man in his capacity as head of the Church. Judiciary power also belongs to Christ because he merited it. The sweep of Christ's judgment staggers the mind. Christ will judge all persons for every detail of their lives. After the judgment that takes place in the present time, there remains yet another general judgment. The reason is that men and women live on even after they die by reason of the effects of their actions; and so there will be a general judgment at the last day, in which everything concerning every person in every respect shall be perfectly and publicly judged. Christ's judiciary power extends even to angels and demons, for they too are subject to him.

Chapter 20

THE SACRAMENTS (I) (3a.60-83)

After considering those things which pertain to the incarnate Word, Thomas takes up the sacraments of the Church, which derive their efficacy from the incarnate Word. In this chapter we shall see what Thomas had to say about the sacraments in general and about baptism, confirmation and the Holy Eucharist. In the next chapter we shall see what he had to say about the remaining sacraments.

The Sacraments in General (3a.60-65)

With the help of Thomas' *Summa*, the Council of Trent solemnly formulated the Church's teaching on the sacraments in general in 1547. According to the council, there are seven sacraments, all of which were instituted by Jesus Christ.[1] These sacraments are necessary for salvation.[2] The sacraments confer grace *ex opere operato* upon those who receive them.[3] Three sacraments imprint an indelible character upon the soul, namely, baptism, confirmation and holy orders.[4] Not all Christians have the power to administer all the sacraments.[5] Even an unworthy minister can confer the sacraments validly, provided he observes what is essential.[6]

For Thomas, a sacrament means, first of all, a sign of something sacred insofar as this sacred thing makes people holy. A sacrament is a sign signifying three things: the passion of Christ which he underwent in the past, the grace which is the effect of his passion in the present, and eternal glory to which Christ's passion and grace bring us in the future. A sacramental sign is something sensible, which is aptly used to signify spiritual things. It is God who determines the nature of the sensible signs by which we are sanctified. Words are essential to determine the ultimate significance of the sensible sign. For example, we may wash a person for several reasons, let us say, to remove dirt or cool him. If, however, a minister says, "I baptize you," as he or she washes the person, it is clear that the minister is conferring a sacrament. Any words added or omitted, so as to change the essential meaning of the sacramental formula, would invalidate the sacrament itself.

Sacraments are necessary in the sense that human beings need corporeal and sensible things to lead them to spiritual and intelligible things. In the state of innocence there were no sacraments, because Adam and Eve did not need to be perfected in knowledge or grace by anything corporeal. After Adam and Eve had sinned, however, there was need of sacraments, so that sinners might profess their faith in Jesus Christ, through whom is the remission of sins. Of course, the sacraments of the New Law, that signify Christ in relation to the past, necessarily differ from those of the Old Law, that foreshadowed the future.

The principal effect of the sacraments is grace. God is the principal cause of grace; sacraments are instrumental causes. To show how the sacraments cause grace Thomas cites the letter of Paul to Titus: "He saved us through the baptism of new birth" (3:5). The grace conferred by the sacraments is essentially sanctifying grace. However, each sacrament administers to a different human need; and so, some commentators on the *Summa* say, sacramental grace is habitual or sanctifying grace which confers a right to the actual graces necessary to attain the end of each sacrament. Grace is in the sacraments of the New Law as a transient instrumental power. The humanity of Christ is the conjoined instrument of sacramental grace. This means that Christ's Godhead causes grace through his humanity, which is united to him in person, by means of the sacraments. The sacraments of the New Law derive their efficacy especially from the passion of Christ. The sacraments of the Old Law could not of themselves cause grace; they could only signify the faith by which men and women were justified through grace.

A second effect of some sacraments is an indelible mark or character. The sacramental character is an instrumental power of the soul by which we are rendered capable either of conferring or receiving things pertaining to the worship of God, according as that power is an active or passive one. The sacramental character is the character or mark of Christ insofar as it is a participation in Christ's eternal priesthood. The sacramental character resides in the power of the soul and not in its essence. The character cannot be removed from the soul, because it is a participation in Christ's priesthood, which is eternal (Ps 110:4). Only baptism, confirmation and holy orders imprint a character on the soul.

God is the principal cause, and the human minister is the instrumental cause of the grace and character effected by the sacraments. Of course, God and the human minister work through the sacramental rites to produce these effects. Only God can institute a sacrament, since only God can produce the grace and character of the sacraments as the principal cause. Christ produces the inward sacramental effect, both as God and man, but not in the same way. For, as God, he works in the sacraments by authority; but, as man, he is the chief minister of the sacraments, his humanity being the conjoined instrument of his divinity. The sacraments can be conferred by evil ministers, that is, by those who are not in the state of grace; but wicked ministers sin when they administer the sacraments. Angels cannot administer the sacraments, although God could communicate this power to them. The intention of the minister is required for the confection of a sacrament to specify even more particularly the meaning of the rite. Even though a minister should lack faith, he can validly administer a sacrament, provided he has the intention of doing what the Church does. A minister who intends to confect a sacrament for an evil purpose, let us say, to take advantage of someone, does not necessarily act invalidly; but he sins grievously in having such an intention.

It is a matter of faith that there are seven sacraments. The sacraments of the Church were instituted for a twofold purpose, namely, to worship God and to be a remedy against sin. In either case, Thomas finds a need for seven sacraments. One must read the text of the *Summa* for his explanation. The sacraments greet a person coming from the womb and accompany a person to the grave. The seven sacraments are baptism, confirmation, Holy Eucharist, penance or the sacrament of reconciliation, extreme unction or anointing of the sick, holy orders and matrimony. This enumeration mentions first those sacraments which pertain to the good of the individual, and then those sacraments which pertain to the good of the community. The Eucharist is the greatest of all the sacraments, because it contains Christ himself, whereas all the other sacraments are simply instruments of his power. Baptism is the one absolutely necessary sacrament; penance is necessary in the case of mortal sin committed after baptism; and holy orders is necessary for the community. The other sacraments complete the work of these sacraments.

Baptism (3a.66-71)

According to the New Testament, John the Baptist was baptizing in the Jordan before Jesus began his public ministry; but the baptism of John was not the Christian sacrament (Mk 1:8; Ac 11:16). Jesus himself was baptized by John. Jesus stated the necessity of baptism: "No one can enter into God's kingdom unless he is born again of water and Spirit" (Jn 3:5). Jesus commanded his disciples to baptize in the name of the Father, Son and Holy Spirit (Mt 28:19). For Paul, baptism means experience of the passion, death and resurrection of Jesus (Rm 6:3-5). Those who have been baptized have been washed, consecrated and justified in the name of our Lord Jesus Christ (1 Cor 6:11). Through baptism we are reborn and regenerated by the Holy Spirit (Tt 3:5). Baptism makes us members of the body of Christ (1 Cor 12:13). Baptism saves us as the ark saved Noah and his family (1 P 3:20-21).

In 1547 the Council of Trent drew up certain canons, which are of decisive importance for the Catholic doctrine of baptism. According to the council, true and natural water is necessary for the administration of baptism.[7] Heretics can baptize validly.[8] Baptism is necessary for salvation.[9] One can lose the grace of baptism through sin.[10] A baptized person is bound to observe the precepts of the Church.[11] Infants should be baptized.[12]

The Second Vatican Council (1962-65) taught that the laity are called upon to expend all their energy for the growth of the Church and its continuous sanctification. The laity are commissioned to this apostolate by our Lord himself through their baptism and confirmation.[13] The council also noted the ecumenical significance of baptism, which is a bond of unity uniting all separated Christians who have received it.[14]

In treating of the sacrament, Thomas speaks of the sacrament itself, its minister, those who receive it, and its effects.

The sacrament of baptism is the washing of the body with water accompanied by the recitation of the prescribed words. Thomas holds that the sacrament was instituted when Christ was baptized by John in the Jordan, but its reception was imposed only after Christ's passion and resurrection. Water is the proper matter of the sacrament, and no other liquid may be used to wash the body. What is called the form of the sacrament is the words: "I baptize you in the name of the Father, and of the Son, and of the Holy Spirit." This baptismal form mentions both the principal cause, the Trinity of divine persons, and the instrumental cause, the human minister, of the effects of the sacrament. One must baptize in the name of the whole Trinity and not in the name of Christ only. Baptism means a washing, and one may be washed by either immersion or sprinkling or pouring the water. A single immersion or sprinkling suffices for the validity of the sacrament. Baptism can be received only once. The Church has surrounded the reception of baptism with suitable ceremonies and prayers to arouse the devotion of the faithful and instruct them about the significance of the sacrament. Thomas distinguishes three kinds of baptism: of water, blood and the Spirit. We have been speaking about baptism of water, while baptism of blood means the shedding of one's blood for Christ's sake, and baptism of the Spirit means believing in and loving God and repenting of one's sins. Each of these produces the grace of baptism; hence, each one is given the name of baptism; but only baptism of water produces the character and the capacity to receive the other sacraments. Baptism of blood is the most excellent of the three kinds of baptism.

The minister is the one who confects or confers the sacrament. Today the ordinary minister of baptism is a bishop, priest or deacon.[15] In case of necessity, however, anyone can baptize, including a lay person, a woman, and even a non-baptized person. Two people cannot act together in baptizing, one saying the words of the form and another applying the matter; for just as there is one Christ, so should there be just one minister to represent Christ. A sponsor is to instruct and guide the baptized person in the Christian walk. The sponsor is said to "raise the baptized person from the sacred font."

All are bound to receive baptism, because baptism incorporates a person in Christ, outside of whom there is no salvation (Rm 5:18). To be saved a person must have at least baptism of desire, that is to say, the wish to be baptized along with faith and charity.[16] Infants should be baptized promptly, lest they die without the sacrament. An adult should undergo a period of instruction before baptism, so that he or she may know how to live as a Christian. An adult sinner, who is not repentant, is not to be baptized, for baptism cannot incorporate an unrepentant sinner into Christ. No kind of penance or work of satisfaction is to be imposed on an adult who is baptized, for baptism takes away all sin and all punishment due to sin. An adult who is to be baptized must have sorrow for sins, but he or she is not required to confess them to a priest. An adult must have the intention of being baptized. One who is baptized in a non-Catholic Church community can receive both the grace and character of baptism.

Infants are to be baptized, because they have incurred the stain of original sin and need the redemption of Christ. The children of non-Christians are not to be baptized without the consent of their parents, since by natural justice young children are under the rule and control of their parents. Insane persons and imbeciles are to be baptized like infants; but a person who, during his normal life, manifested no desire to be baptized, is not to be baptized if he becomes insane.

What are the effects of baptism? Baptism takes away all sin, original and actual. It cancels completely the debt of punishment due to sin. Even though baptism does not remove all the penalties of sin, such as death, suffering, hunger and the like, in this life, it will remove them from the just in the resurrection. Baptism confers grace and the infused virtues on the recipient. Through baptism a person is incorporated in Christ, enlightened by him, and made fruitful in good works. Baptized infants receive grace and the virtues, even though their immaturity prevents the exercise of these gifts. Baptism opens the gates of heaven, in the sense that it removes the guilt of sin and the debt of punishment, which are obstacles to one's entrance into heaven. The degree of sanctifying grace received by baptized infants is the same in every case, for they are equally disposed to receive the sacrament; in adults, however, the degree of grace varies according to the disposition of the recipient. A person can receive the baptismal character without receiving the grace of the sacrament, if, for example, he intends to receive the sacrament without repenting of his sins. However, as soon as such a person repents, baptism produces its normal effect of grace.

Circumcision was a preparation for, and a figure of, baptism; for, like baptism, circumcision was a profession of faith in Christ. Circumcision was instituted in the person of Abraham. Grace was conferred when a child was circumcised, not in virtue of the rite itself, but in virtue of faith in Christ, of which circumcision was a sign.

Before one is baptized, he or she must be instructed in the faith, because baptism is a profession of the Christian faith. A candidate for baptism should be exorcised beforehand, so that demons do not impede the effects of the sacrament. It is fitting that deacons should cooperate with the priest in the administration of this sacrament.

Confirmation (3a.72)

Confirmation is the second of the seven sacraments. It is the sacrament by which a baptized person receives the Holy Spirit in greater measure to bear witness to Christ. The gospel of John records the promise of Christ to send another comforter (Jn 14:16) who would bear witness to Christ and enable the disciples to bear witness to him (Jn 15:26). The prototype of Christian confirmation is the descent of the Holy Spirit upon the apostles at Pentecost (Ac 2:2-4). According to Acts 8:14-17, Peter and John imposed hands on some Samaritans who had been previously baptized, and they received the Holy Spirit. In the primitive Church, the rite of conferring the Holy Spirit was closely connected with the baptismal rite and was separated from it only later.

The Council of Trent affirmed the sacramental character of confirmation and its institution by Christ.[17] The Second Vatican Council taught that the faithful are bound more intimately to the Church by the sacrament of confirmation, that they are endowed by the Holy Spirit with a special strength through the sacrament and that, as a consequence, they are more strictly obliged to spread and defend the faith and bear witness to Christ.[18]

For Thomas, confirmation is the sacrament of Christian maturity; it brings a person who has been reborn in baptism to adulthood in the spiritual order through the grace of the Holy Spirit. The sacrament is conferred by anointing the forehead with chrism, a mixture of olive oil and balm. This anointing includes an imposition of the hand of the minister and is accompanied by the recitation of the words prescribed in the approved liturgical books.[19] The oil signifies the grace of the Holy Spirit. Confirmation imprints a character on the soul; hence, confirmation can be received only once. Confirmation supposes the reception of baptism for validity. In confirmation, the Holy Spirit is given to the baptized for strength, just as he was given to the apostles on the day of Pentecost; moreover, the Holy Spirit is not given except with sanctifying grace. All should receive this sacrament to bring all to spiritual maturity. St. Thomas notes that the soul, to which spiritual birth and perfect spiritual age belong, is immortal; and just as it can in old age attain to spiritual birth, so it can attain to perfect spiritual age in youth or childhood.

The person confirmed is anointed on the forehead to show that he or she is a Christian. A sponsor is needed to see that the confirmed person acts as a true witness to Christ and faithfully fulfills the obligations connected with this sacrament. It is desirable that the one who undertook the role of sponsor at baptism be sponsor for confirmation.[20] The ordinary minister of confirmation is the bishop, who completes in confirmation the work of generation begun in baptism. In special cases, however, an authorized priest may also confirm.[21]

The Holy Eucharist (3a.73-83)

The Holy Eucharist is the sacrament of our Lord's body and blood. The institution of the Holy Eucharist is described in Mt

26:26-29; Mk 14:22-25; Lk 22:15-20; and 1 Cor 11:23-25. The bread is the body of Christ; the cup is his blood, the blood of the covenant, to be poured out on behalf of many for the forgiveness of sins (Mt 26:26-29). The Eucharist is the memorial and proclamation of the death of Christ (Lk 22:19; 1 Cor 11:24-26). It is a sacrificial banquet (1 Cor 10:14-22) and an effective sign of Christian unity (1 Cor 10:17). The Eucharist looks forward to the messianic banquet in the kingdom of heaven. The institution of the Eucharist is not related in the gospel of John, but he clearly knows it. For John, the Eucharist is primarily the food which nourishes one to eternal life (Jn 6:53-58).

In 1551, the Council of Trent taught that the Holy Eucharist contains the body and blood together with the soul and divinity of our Lord Jesus Christ truly, really and substantially.[22] The whole substance of the bread is changed into the body of Christ, and the whole substance of the wine is changed into his blood, only the appearances of bread and wine remaining. This change is aptly called transubstantiation.[23] In 1562, the same council formulated its teaching on the holy sacrifice of the Mass. According to the council, a true and real sacrifice is offered to God in the Mass.[24] By the words, "Do this in commemoration of me," Christ made the apostles priests and ordained that they and other priests should offer his body and blood.[25] The sacrifice of the Mass is a propitiatory sacrifice and not just a commemoration of the sacrifice consummated on the cross.[26]

For the Second Vatican Council (1962-65), the Holy Eucharist is a meal of brotherly solidarity and a foretaste of the heavenly banquet.[27] The Holy Eucharist is the basis and center of the Christian community.[28] For other sacraments, as well as every ministry and apostolate of the Church, are directed toward it.[29] The Eucharist is the sacrament by which the unity of the Church is both signified and effected.[30]

Considering the Holy Eucharist, Thomas treats of the sacrament itself, its matter, form, effects, recipient, minister and rite.

The Holy Eucharist is the sacrament which nourishes and preserves the spiritual life received in baptism. The Eucharist is just one sacrament, because the consecrated bread and wine are just one spiritual meal. Just as one can receive the grace of baptism by desiring it, so one can receive the grace of the Eucharist by desiring it. The Church knows the sacrament by various names: it is called a sacrifice, because it commemorates the Lord's sacrificial passion and death; it is called communion or synaxis, because it effects the union of the faithful with Christ and one another; it is called viaticum (from the Latin *via* or way), because it takes us along the way to heaven; and finally it is called Eucharist or "good grace," because, as Thomas understands the matter, it contains Christ, who is full of grace. Our Lord instituted this sacrament at the Last Supper as a memorial of himself, when the apostles were particularly receptive to his words and actions. There were many figures of the Eucharist in the Old Testament, but the chief figure was the paschal lamb.

The matter of the sacrament is bread and wine. This was the ordinary nourishment of the people of Christ's time. No determinate amount of bread and wine is required for this sacrament; the priest must consecrate as much as is needed for the people. Christ is believed to have employed wheaten bread for this sacrament, and the bread was unleavened. The Latin Church uses unleavened bread for the Eucharist, while the Greek Church uses leavened bread. True wine of the grape is the proper matter of this sacrament. Water is mingled with the wine, but it is not necessary for the validity of the sacrament. Only a little water is used, lest a large amount vitiate the nature of the wine.

The true body and blood of Christ are present in the Eucharist; this is a truth of faith. While the sacrifices of the Old Law only prefigured Christ crucified, the sacrifice of the New Law contains Christ crucified in reality. By the consecration the substance of the bread and the substance of the wine cease to exist. The substance of the bread is changed into the substance of the body of Christ, and the substance of the wine into his blood. This change is called transubstantiation. The accidents of the bread and wine, such as size, color, shape and taste, remain after the change; otherwise, as St. Thomas notes, it would be horrible for us to eat human flesh and drink blood. Transubstantiation takes place in an instant. Because of this change, it is true to say that the body of Christ comes from bread.

The Catholic faith constrains us to believe that the whole Christ, body and blood, soul and divinity, is contained in the Holy Eucharist. There is a natural union among all these realities, so that where one is, the others must be also. The whole Christ is contained under each species, that is to say, under the appearance of bread and under the appearance of wine, and indeed under every part and every quantity of each species. How can the quantity of Christ's body be contained in a wafer? The quantity of Christ's body is present in the Holy Eucharist, not according to its proper manner by which it is extended in space, but after the manner of a substance, whose nature is for the whole to be in the whole, and the whole in every part. (Evidently, Thomas thinks that the nature of quantity is even more fundamental than extension in space.) Christ's body is present in the tabernacle, because it is present under the appearances of bread and wine, which are in the tabernacle. The body of Christ in the Blessed Sacrament cannot be seen even by a glorified eye, such as we will have in heaven. When, by apparition, flesh and blood are seen in the sacred host, these are not the actual flesh and blood of Christ.

After the consecration, the accidents or appearances of bread and wine remain in this sacrament without inhering in any substance. The other accidents inhere in the quantity of the bread and wine, which is itself an accident; and the accident of quantity is sustained by divine power without a subject in which it inheres. The accidents of bread and wine can affect other bodies. The appearances of bread and wine can be corrupted, and other things can be generated when they do; but Christ ceases to be present when the appearances or species corrupt. The sacred species are capable of nourishing those who receive them. The breaking of the species is not a division of Christ; rather, it is a division of the quantity of the species. Any liquid added to the chalice, that would make it other than the consecrated wine, would corrupt the species. The addition of a tiny amount of an alien liquid would not have this effect.

The form of the Holy Eucharist is the words employed by our Lord at the Last Supper: "This is my body" and "This is the cup of my blood, the blood of the new and everlasting covenant. It will be shed for you and for all, so that sins may be forgiven." The words, "This is my body" and "This is the cup of my blood" are essential; but the other words pertain to the integrity of the form and may not be omitted. The words of consecration actually change the bread and wine into the body and blood of Christ. They derive their instrumental power to effect this change from Christ. The form of the sacrament is not said as the words of a narrative, but with the intention of effecting the change of bread and wine. The words of consecration, including the words over the bread, are effective the instant they are pronounced.

What are the effects of the Holy Eucharist? The Holy Eucharist confers grace because it contains the body and blood of Christ and signifies his passion and death, both of which are the causes of grace. Another effect of the sacrament is heavenly glory, for Christ said, "Whoever eats of this bread will live forever" (Jn 6:52). The Holy Eucharist was not instituted to forgive mortal sins; as spiritual food, it was intended only for those who are spiritually alive. This sacrament effects the forgiveness of venial sins through the acts of charity which it stimulates. The Holy Eucharist effects the partial, but not the full remission of, the temporal punishment due to sin, and this in accordance with the devotion and fervor of the recipient. This sacrament preserves a person from sin by strengthening one's spiritual life and repelling the assaults of demons. This sacrament benefits others insofar as it is a sacrifice offered on their behalf.

Venial sins that *accompany* the reception of the Eucharist partially hinder the effects of the sacrament.

The Holy Eucharist is received sacramentally by one who actually consumes the sacred species, and spiritually by one who desires to receive it sacramentally. Even a sinner can receive the Holy Eucharist sacramentally; but he sins grievously in doing so. Still, to approach this sacrament with consciousness of sin is not the gravest of sins; unbelief and blasphemy, for example, are worse. A public sinner should be refused Holy Communion. An involuntary nocturnal pollution does not necessarily impede one from the reception of Holy Communion. St. Thomas does not think that infants and insane people should receive this sacrament because they are incapable of devotion toward it. One may receive Holy Communion every day, provided he or she has the proper dispositions. Our Lord commanded the reception of his body and blood (Jn 6:54), but by the precept of the Church there are fixed times for fulfilling Christ's command. The whole Christ, is of course, present under each species; and sometimes the Church permits the reception of the body only, lest the blood be spilled.

Christ instituted the Holy Eucharist at the Last Supper, and he received this sacrament himself. It seems that Judas too received the Eucharist at the hands of Christ, because at that moment he was not known publicly as a sinner. What Christ gave to the apostles at the Last Supper was his body as it was then, that is to say, a passible body not yet glorified. If the Blessed Sacrament had been reserved in a pyx at the time of Christ's death, he would have died in the Blessed Sacrament, as he died on the cross.

The consecration of the Eucharist is reserved to the priest who acts in the person of Christ. It is possible for several priests to consecrate one and the same host. In St. Thomas' day only the priest distributed Holy Communion; but today the laity may assist the priest in the distribution of Holy Communion, when their assistance is needed and other ministers are lacking.[31] The priest who consecrates must also receive the Eucharist; otherwise the sacrifice would be incomplete. Even a priest in serious sin can consecrate the Eucharist; and his Mass is of equal value with that of a good priest because the same sacrifice is offered by both. If a duly ordained priest should become a heretic, schismatic or be excommunicated, he would still have the *power* to consecrate, but not the *right*. It is not lawful to assist at the Mass of the aforesaid priests or to receive the Eucharist from their hands. A priest ought to say Mass several times a year at least, even if he does not have the care of souls, for no one may neglect the grace entrusted to him.

The celebration of this sacrament is called a sacrifice because it is a renewal and representation of the sacrifice of the cross and makes us partakers of Christ's passion and death. The Church determines the time for celebrating the Eucharist. Mass is celebrated in a suitable place with vessels blessed or consecrated for this purpose. The Church has surrounded the consecration of the Eucharistic elements with suitable words and actions to prepare and instruct the people, to arouse devotion and reverence and to represent Christ's passion.

So, then, "at the Last Supper, on the night when he was betrayed, our Savior instituted the Eucharistic sacrifice of his body and blood. He did this in order to perpetuate the sacrifice of the cross throughout the ages, until he should come again, and so to entrust to his beloved spouse, the Church, a memorial of his death and resurrection: a sacrament of love, a sign of unity, a bond of charity, a holy banquet in which Christ is consumed, the mind is filled with grace, and a pledge of future glory is given to us."[32]

Chapter 21

THE SACRAMENTS (II) (3a.84; Suppl.1-68)

In this chapter we shall see what St. Thomas had to say about the remaining four sacraments, namely, penance or the sacrament of reconciliation, extreme unction or anointing of the sick, holy orders and matrimony.

Penance (3a.84-90; Suppl.1-28)

Penance is the sacrament by which the sins committed after baptism are forgiven.

The God of the Old Testament was a forgiving God (Ex 34:7; Pss 99:8; 103:3; Mi 7:18-20). Hosea (14:3) mentions the conditions for forgiveness, and they are confession of sin, conversion from sin, and prayer for forgiveness. In some cases, God will forgive a guilty group because of the righteousness of some members of the group (Gn 18:26-32; Jr 5:1). Forgiveness means restoration to former favor (Ex 33:15). Forgiveness of sins is one of the features of the messianic future (Is 33:24; Jr 31:34).

In the New Testament Jesus himself claimed and exercised the power to forgive sins in the case of a paralytic (Mt 9:2-7; Mk 2:5-12; Lk 5:20-25). One needs faith (Ac 10:43; 26:18), love (Lk 7:47), and repentance (Lk 24:47; Ac 2:38; etc.) to obtain forgiveness. The forgiveness of sins is a work of God's patience (Rm

3:25). The forgiveness of sins comes through Christ (Ac 13:38; Ep 1:7; Col 1:14; 1 Jn 2:12). One obtains forgiveness through Christ not only by his own personal forgiveness, as in the case of the paralytic, but also through his redeeming death (Mt 26:28). Confession of sins is a step toward forgiveness (Ac 19:18; Jn 5:16; 1 Jn 1:9). Jesus conferred the power to forgive sins upon the apostles (Jn 20:21-23).

In 1551, the Council of Trent formulated the Church's teaching about the sacrament of penance. Penance is a sacrament instituted by Christ for reconciling the faithful to God, as often as they fall into sin after baptism.[1] Baptism and penance are distinct sacraments.[2] The words of the Lord, "Receive the Holy Spirit. Whose sins you shall forgive, they are forgiven; and whose sins you shall retain, they are retained" (Jn 20:22-23), refer to the sacrament of penance.[3] On the part of the penitent, contrition, confession and satisfaction are required for the remission of sins.[4] One must confess each and every mortal sin and also the circumstances that change the nature of the sin.[5] The absolution of the priest is a judicial act and more than a mere declaration that one's sins have been forgiven.[6] Only priests and not the laity can absolve.[7] Even after sins have been forgiven, some satisfaction on the part of the penitent is often required.[8]

The Second Vatican Council said that those who approach the sacrament of penance obtain pardon for offenses committed against God, and at the same time they are reconciled with the Church, which they have wounded by their sins.[9]

Speaking of the sacrament of penance, St. Thomas considers the sacrament itself, its effect, its parts, those who receive it, the power of the keys exercised by the ministers of the sacrament and the rite of the sacrament.

Penance is a sacrament, because it signifies and confers the remission of sins. The remote matter of the sacrament is the sins over which a person grieves, which he or she confesses, and for which he or she satisfies. The form of the sacrament is the absolution of the priest. No imposition of hands is required for this sacrament. The sacrament of penance is necessary for salvation, just as bodily medicine is necessary for a person who has contracted a dangerous disease. St. Jerome (340-420) called this sacrament "a second plank after shipwreck."[10] It is the means of regaining what was lost through sin. A person ought always to have internal sorrow for his or her past offenses against God, even after they have been forgiven. Penance is a sacrament that can be received many times, for it is always possible to lose charity through grievous sin and penance is the means of recovering it.

The *virtue* of penance is distinct from the *sacrament* of penance. As a virtue, penance is a good habit, by which one grieves for past sins and intends to make amends. It is a species of justice with respect to God; by penance we offer compensation to God for our offenses to the extent we can. The virtue of penance resides in the will. The act of penance results from acts of faith, hope and charity.

Next Thomas turns from the virtue of penance to the effect of the sacrament of penance, which is the remission of mortal sins. In this life every sin, no matter how terrible it is, can be blotted out by the sacrament of penance. However, mortal sin cannot be blotted out without the repentance of the sinner. One mortal sin cannot be pardoned unless all of one's mortal sins are pardoned at the same time. The debt of punishment due to sin is either eternal or temporal. When the guilt of mortal sin is taken away, that is to say, when mortal sin is forgiven, the debt of eternal punishment in hell is taken away; yet, the debt of temporal punishment due to sin may not be taken away entirely. One can make satisfaction for the temporal punishment due to sin either in this life or in purgatory. Even when mortal sin is forgiven, the disposition to sin may remain. The forgiveness of sin is the effect of penance as a virtue, but still more of penance as a sacrament.

What about the forgiveness of venial sins? No sin, including venial sin, is forgiven outside the sacrament of penance by an act of the will directed toward God and away from those sins. Such an act of the will is either implicit or explicit in the reception of any sacrament, in the recitation of the "I confess" at the beginning of Mass, in the pious use of holy water and blessed articles, and so on. A person who is guilty of both mortal and venial sins cannot obtain the remission of venial sins while mortal sins remain.

A sin once forgiven does not return through a subsequent sin. In other words, a person may commit another sin like the one forgiven, but he or she does not reincur the forgiven sin. A person who is pardoned but returns to sins like those pardoned shows base ingratitude to the forgiving God; and this ingratitude may or may not be a special sin. The more numerous or the greater the sins previously pardoned, the greater must be the debt of punishment incurred by any subsequent mortal sin.

Another effect of the sacrament of penance is the recovery of sanctifying grace and the infused virtues. Sometimes a penitent rises to the same degree of grace and virtue he or she possessed, sometimes to a greater degree, sometimes to a lesser degree, and all this according to the disposition of the penitent. Through the sacrament a person becomes a son or daughter of God once more. A person who sins mortally loses the merit of his or her previous good works; but that merit is restored by the worthy reception of the sacrament of penance. However, good works done in the state of mortal sin are not meritorious at any time.

In general, the parts of the sacrament of penance are the acts of the penitent who approaches the sacrament, namely, contrition, confession and satisfaction. By contrition the sinner wills to atone for an offense; by confession the sinner subjects his or her offense to the judgment of the priest standing in God's place; and by satisfaction the sinner atones for an offense according to the decision of God's minister. The three acts of the penitent are called integral parts of the sacrament. Considering penance as a virtue for a moment, we can distinguish three types or varieties of it: penance for sins that precede baptism, penance for mortal sins committed after baptism, and penance for venial sins which impede a more fervent manner of life.

* * * * *

> It was at this point in the composition of the *Summa* that St. Thomas died in 1274. An old manuscript of the third part of the *Summa*, preserved in the Charter Library of Toledo, Spain (Cod. 19-13), concludes with these words: *Hic moritur Thomas, ecclesiae lumen, orbis decus, theologorum gemma* ("Here dies Thomas, the light of the Church, the ornament of the world, the jewel of theologians.") The remainder of the *Summa* known as the Supplement was probably compiled by Reginald of Piperno, O.P., the companion and friend of Thomas, from Thomas' commentary on the *Fourth Book of Sentences* of Peter Lombard. We begin to consider the material of the Supplement at this point.

* * * * *

Having mentioned the integral parts of the sacrament of penance in a general way, St. Thomas takes a closer look at each one of them. The first integral part of the sacrament is the penitent's act of contrition. Contrition is sorrow for sins with a view to confessing them and making satisfaction for them. Contrition is an act of the virtue of penance. Attrition, which is sorrow for sin out of fear of punishment, necessarily differs from contrition, which is sorrow for sin because it is an offense against God; but both are salutary.

One has contrition for personal sins, but not for original sin. Contrition does not look to future sins; yet it disposes a person to be on guard against them. One cannot have contrition for the sins of others, but only for his or her own sins. A person must have contrition for each mortal sin that he or she has committed.

Sin is the greatest of evils, because it turns us away from God; therefore, contrition, which grieves over sin, surpasses all other sorrow. However, this sorrow is an act of the will; and so it may not be felt so keenly in the sensitive part of an individual as, let us say, the hurt of a wound. In the sensitive part of an individual, sorrow for sin could be excessive and harm one's physical well-being; but true contrition is in the will, and here it cannot be too great. One sin is worse than another; hence, the sorrow for one sin may be greater than the sorrow for another.

We ought to grieve for our sins throughout the course of our lives because they have impeded our progress towards God. Indeed, sorrow for sin ought to be continuous insofar as this is compatible with one's other responsibilities. The time or season of contrition ends with this life: the souls in heaven can only rejoice; the souls in purgatory grieve for their sins, but their sorrow is not contrition because it lacks the efficacy of contrition; and the souls in hell are confirmed in their sins.

As part of the sacrament of penance, contrition operates instrumentally for the forgiveness of sin; but contrition can be so perfect that it blots out sin and the punishment due to sin, even before the penitent receives the sacrament. The want of sensible sorrow is no hindrance to the perfection of contrition.

The second integral part of the sacrament of penance is the penitent's confession of sins. The confession of sins is necessary for the reception of the sacrament which, in turn, is necessary for the forgiveness of sins. It was Christ who established the necessity of confessing one's sins. Anyone who has committed a mortal sin after being baptized is bound to confession. To confess a sin that one did not commit is wrong; the penitent thereby deceives the priest about his or her state of soul. One who has committed a mortal sin should confess it as soon as he or she reasonably can. No one can be dispensed from the duty of confessing mortal sins.

St. Augustine defined confession as an act which lays bare a hidden disease with the hope of pardon.[11] Since confession is a manifestation of conscience in which the heart and lips agree, it is an act of virtue, the virtue of penance.

Confession must be made to a duly authorized priest, and none but a priest is the minister of this sacrament. In case of necessity and in the absence of a priest, an individual may confess his or her sins to a layman; and although the latter cannot absolve the penitent, still this defect is remedied by Christ himself. Confession of venial sins to a layman is a sacramental and has a natural aptitude to remit them, just as the beating of one's breast or the sprinkling of holy water. Over and above his sacerdotal character, a priest must have jurisdiction over the penitent in order to forgive his or her sins. A penitent who is at the point of death can be absolved from all sins and censures by any priest whatsoever, for necessity knows no law. A confessor must impose a penance upon the penitent in accordance with the gravity of the penitent's sins and the need to provide a suitable remedy.

Confession of sins is to be made with true sorrow and sincerity of heart. One must confess all mortal sins in kind and number, so that the confessor can know the condition of the penitent and prescribe the proper remedy. Confession is to be made by the penitent in person, and not by proxy or letter.

As part of the sacrament of penance, confession remits the guilt of sin, the eternal punishment due to it, and also the temporal punishment due to sin in greater or lesser measure. Confession opens the gates of paradise because it takes away the obstacles, namely, the guilt of sin and the punishment due to it, which prevent a person from entering paradise. Obviously, confession gives renewed hope of salvation. Confession blots out even those mortal sins which one has forgotten.

Just as God conceals the sins of those who confess to him, so the confessor must conceal the sins confessed to him. This obligation to secrecy is called the seal of confession. The confessor is also bound to conceal anything that might lead to the discovery of the sinner and his or her sin. One who overhears a penitent accusing himself is seriously bound to secrecy. With the permission of the penitent, the confessor may speak about his or her confession; nevertheless, the confessor should beware of giving scandal by revealing the sin, lest he seem to have broken the seal. What a priest knows from a source other than confession does not come under the seal.

The third integral part of the sacrament of penance is the penitent's satisfaction for sin. Satisfaction is something done to make up for the evil of an offense against God. Satisfaction is an act of justice, for justice demands equality in things, an order and balance; and satisfaction seeks to restore such order and balance. Human beings cannot offer equivalent satisfaction for sin, but they can do what they are capable of. One person can make satisfaction for another's sin insofar as satisfaction is the payment of a debt, for one person can pay the debt of another. However, insofar as satisfaction is medicinal, one person cannot satisfy for another's sin, for the flesh of one person is not tamed by another's fast.

It is impossible for a person to make satisfaction for one sin while holding to another, since such a person is still not a friend of God. Such a person's works would have no value as satisfaction, even if they were offered for old and forgiven sins. Nor do works of satisfaction, which were performed in the state of mortal sin, come to life, when the sinner is restored to grace. Works done without charity are not condignly meritorious of any good from God, either eternal or temporal. Good works done in the state of mortal sin diminish the pains of hell in the sense that they withdraw a person from other sins.

Satisfaction seeks to make up for past offenses and to preserve one from future sins. For both purposes, penal works, those involving some pain, are useful. To submit patiently to the trials of life is a satisfactory work. The works of satisfaction may be classified in general as prayer, fasting and almsgiving.

Having discussed the penitent's acts of contrition, confession and satisfaction, Thomas devotes one more question to the recipient of the sacrament of penance. Those who have not sinned mortally have the infused virtue of penance, although they cannot exercise it. The virtue of penance will remain in heaven; but it will not be actualized by regret for one's past sins, but rather by thanksgiving to God for his mercy in pardoning one's sins. The angels cannot have the virtue of penance, for they have not committed any sins; nor can the demons have the virtue or act of penance, for their wills are confirmed in evil.

Next Thomas turns to the power of the keys exercised by the minister of the sacrament of penance. The "power of the keys" is a figure of speech which refers to the power of the priest to forgive sins. By means of the keys, the priest binds and looses, admitting the worthy to the kingdom of heaven and excluding the unworthy. There are only two keys, the first of which regards the judgment about the worthiness of the person to be absolved, while the other regards the absolution.

The power of the keys remits the guilt of sin, the eternal punishment due to it, and at least a part of the temporal punishment. The priest exercises the binding power of the keys, when he judges that absolution must not be given and when he imposes a penance. The priest must exercise the power of the keys according to the mandate of God and not arbitrarily.

The priesthood of the Old Law did not have the power of the keys, as the letter to the Hebrews seems to imply (9:11-12). Our Lord had the power of the keys before all others. Priests alone, as ministers of Christ, have the power of the keys. Even priests in the state of mortal sin have the power of the keys. Schismatic, heretical and excommunicated priests retain the power of the keys, but they cannot use the power, since the Church deprives them of jurisdiction.

Each priest, in virtue of his ordination, has the power to remit all sins; however, the use of this power requires jurisdiction over penitents, a jurisdiction which inferiors derive from their superiors. Hence, a priest exercises the power of the keys in favor of those over whom he has been given jurisdiction. Thus, a priest might receive jurisdiction to hear confessions only in a particular diocese or those of men only. A bishop might reserve to himself the right to absolve from certain sins, which are especially heinous. One cannot use the power of the keys in favor of himself; but any priest, even the youngest, can absolve the highest prelate, provided he has the necessary jurisdiction.

At this point, St. Thomas takes up the subject of excommunication, which is also connected with the power of the keys. In St. Thomas' day, excommunication meant exclusion from the reception of the sacraments and, indeed, from all social intercourse with the faithful. Such a penalty was intended to punish a person for a grave crime and secure his amendment. Today the Church continues to employ the penalty of excommunication for the same reasons. While the modern penalty of excommunication excludes a person from the reception of the sacraments, the discharge of ecclesiastical offices and other privileges, it does not exclude the excommunicated person from all social intercourse with the faithful.[12] Today excommunication is imposed and removed by ecclesiastical authority in accordance with the provisions of the *Code of Canon Law*.

St. Thomas also considers the subject of indulgences in connection with the power of the keys. An indulgence is the remission in whole or in part of the temporal punishment due to sin. It is possible for one person to make satisfaction for the temporal punishment due to another's sin; and an indulgence is the application of the superabundant satisfaction of Christ, Mary and the saints to the temporal punishment of another. This application is made according to the judgment of the head of the Church. To gain an indulgence a person must be in the state of grace, act out of a motive of piety, and fulfill the conditions laid down by the Church. The Church attaches indulgences to the performance of certain good works, such as the recitation of a specific prayer, almsgiving and pilgrimages. We find a similar teaching about indulgences in the *Code of Canon Law*.[13]

Finally, St. Thomas had a word to say about the public and solemn rite of penance. In his day and, indeed, long before it, the Church sometimes imposed a public and solemn penance upon sinners who committed certain notorious crimes. In this way the sinner made up for the scandal he or she had given. St. Thomas believed that such a solemn penitential rite should not be repeated lest it lose its significance; however, the sinner was never precluded from doing penance privately.

Extreme Unction (Suppl.29-33)

For this sacrament, St. Thomas employs the name "extreme unction," whereas the more modern name is "anointing of the sick." The minister confers the sacrament upon those who are dangerously sick by anointing them with oil and reciting the prescribed words, so that they may be relieved and saved.[14]

In Biblical times the uses of oil were many and one of its uses was medicinal (Is 1:6; Lk 10:34). In Mark 6:13 we are told that the Twelve, having been sent by Jesus, expelled many demons, anointed the sick with oil and worked many cures. Then, in James 5:14-15 we read: "Is anyone sick among you? Let him call in the presbyters of the Church, and let them pray over him, anointing him with oil in the name of the Lord; and the prayer of faith will save the sick man, and the Lord will raise him up; and if he be in sins, they shall be forgiven him."

In 1551, the Council of Trent declared the sacred anointing of the sick to be a sacrament instituted by Christ and promulgated by the blessed apostle James.[15] According to the Second Vatican Council, by the sacred anointing of the sick and the prayer of her priests, the whole Church commends those who are ill to the suffering and glorified Lord, asking that he may lighten their suffering and save them.[16]

Discussing the sacrament of extreme unction or anointing of

the sick, Thomas treats of its essence and institution, its effect, minister, recipient and repetition.

Extreme unction is a sensible rite, which takes away the disease of sin, as the apostle James explains (Jm 5:14-15); therefore, it is a sacrament. The several unctions, which are parts of the sacrament, constitute only one sacrament; they are the application of the remedy to the various sources of the wounds of sin. Christ instituted this sacrament, although it was promulgated by the apostle James. The matter of the sacrament is olive oil, which is soothing and penetrating. The oil is blessed by a bishop or, in special circumstances, by a priest. The form of the sacrament, that is to say, the words prescribed in the liturgical books, gives the anointings their sacramental significance. In the Roman Church, the form is expressed as a prayer in accordance with the direction of the apostle James.

The principal effect of this sacrament is to remove what Thomas calls the remains of sin. The remains of sins are the spiritual weakness and languor which are the result in us of actual and original sin. However, the sacrament also takes away mortal or venial sin, if these happen to be present, provided, of course, that the sick person is repentant. The latter situation could arise in the case of a person who is unconscious and unable to confess. Bodily healing is an effect of this sacrament, when it is helpful to the soul. This sacrament is intended as a remedy, and it does not depute a person to do or receive something; hence, it does not imprint a character.

The minister of this sacrament is a priest and not a lay person. The reason is that this sacrament confers the remission of sins, and the office of forgiving sins is proper to Christ's priesthood.

The recipient of this sacrament is a sick person who is in danger of death from sickness or old age; therefore, this sacrament should not be given in every case of sickness. This sacrament should not be given to insane persons and children who are incapable of sin, since the sacrament is intended principally to remove the remnants of sin and even sin itself. In Thomas' day, the ministers anointed the five senses, which symbolize the sources of sin. Today, in the Roman Church, the minister anoints the forehead and hands of the sick person. Deformity in the bodily organ to be anointed is no bar to anointing.

Extreme unction can be repeated, because the health of soul and body, which is the effect of this sacrament, can be lost. A person can be anointed again in the same sickness, if, after recovering somewhat, he or she falls into a new danger of death.

Holy Orders (Suppl.34-40)

Whereas the first five sacraments we have considered look to the good of the individual, the last two sacraments, holy orders and matrimony, look to the good of the community. The sacrament of holy orders has to do with the leadership of the Christian community and the power to consecrate the Eucharist and forgive sins. Holy orders are conferred by an imposition of hands and the consecratory prayers prescribed in the liturgical books. Those consecrated by holy orders are bishops, priests and deacons.

Perhaps we can reconstruct the development of holy orders in this way: the leaders of the early Christian communities were known sometimes as bishops, sometimes as presbyters or elders. These administered the community under the direction of the founding apostle. When he died, it is likely that one of the bishops or elders was elected to succeed him. This bishop functioned as the sole, supreme religious leader of the community, that is to say, as a monarchical bishop. The title, bishop, was reserved to him. Some Churches, it seems, were always led by monarchical bishops; and, in any event, the office very early prevailed throughout Christendom. The presbyters and deacons were associated with the bishop in the direction of the community. As the leader of the community, the bishop presided at the Eucharist and regulated the penance of sinners. The bishop shared this responsibility with the presbyters, who represented the bishop in those places where he could not be present. The presbyters came to be known as priests, because they offered the Eucharistic sacrifice as the representative of the bishop. Bishops, priests and deacons were commissioned by laying hands on them, a Biblical rite signifying, in this case, appointment to an office together with the communication of power and authority.

In 1563, the Council of Trent solemnly taught that the priesthood of the New Testament has the power to consecrate the body and blood of Christ and to forgive and retain sins, that sacred ordination is a sacrament instituted by Christ, that ordination imparts the Holy Spirit and imprints a character. The council went on to teach that there is a hierarchy in the Catholic Church constituted by divine authority. This hierarchy consists of bishops, priests and ministers; bishops are superior to priests; bishops do not need the consent of the people to ordain other ministers; and the only lawful ministers are those ordained and sent by ecclesiastical authority.[17]

Reflecting the teaching of the Second Vatican Council, the *Code of Canon Law* observes that by divine institution some of the faithful are constituted sacred ministers by the sacrament of orders and are marked by an indelible character. Each minister, as the representative of Christ and in accordance with his rank, is deputed to teaching, sanctifying and governing the people of God. The sacred orders are the episcopacy, presbyterate and diaconate.[18]

St. Thomas discusses the sacrament of orders in general, the difference of orders, the minister of the sacrament, the impediments to the reception of orders and things connected with orders.

God is wont to communicate his gifts to creatures through other creatures, and so he grants the sacraments to his people through ordained ministers. Peter Lombard defined the sacrament of orders as "a seal of the Church, whereby spiritual power is conferred on the person ordained."[19] Ordination signifies and confers an interior grace; therefore, it is a sacrament. The matter of the sacrament is the imposition of the hands of the bishop, and the form of the sacrament is the consecratory prayers prescribed in the liturgical books.

Just as one needs grace to receive the sacrament worthily, so one needs grace to dispense the sacraments worthily; consequently, the sacrament of orders confers grace. Each order sets a man above the people in some degree of authority directed to the dispensation of the sacraments; hence each order imprints a character upon the soul. The character of orders presupposes the baptismal character, but not necessarily the character of confirmation, although the latter is most suitable.

A man who receives the sacrament of orders is appointed to lead others in divine things; therefore, he should be a man of holy and exemplary life; however, holiness of life is required for the lawful, but not the valid, reception of the sacrament. A candidate for orders should have the knowledge requisite for the proper discharge of his duties. A man does not advance to a higher order by the mere merit of his life. A prelate who knowingly advances an unworthy candidate to orders commits a grave sin. A man in orders, who exercises his office while he is in the state of sin, commits another grave sin.

A multiplicity of orders exists in the Church, so that one individual might not be excessively burdened with all those things pertaining to the divine mysteries. St. Thomas derives the distinction of orders from their relationship to the Eucharist—either to the consecration of the Eucharist itself or to a ministry connected with it. In St. Thomas' day and until recent times, there were seven orders; that is to say, in addition to bishops, priests and deacons, there were acolytes, exorcists, readers and porters. The last four orders, once in the Church but now abolished, shared some of the functions of the other orders. They were received, not by the imposition of hands, but by the handing over of a symbol of their office. Today there are two ministries, readers and acolytes; but they are *lay* ministries and not orders.[20] St. Thomas was of the opinion that the sacerdotal character was imprinted, when the chalice was handed over to the candidate in the course of the ordination ceremony. Today we associate the impress of the character with the imposition of hands and consecratory prayer.

The bishop alone has the power to confer orders. He cannot lose it, even if he lapses into heresy or schism; but in the latter case he may not exercise the order.

No woman can receive the sacrament of orders validly, because, St. Thomas holds, she is in a state of subjection. Perhaps we can understand St. Thomas' position better by recalling that in most societies, past and present, women did not, and do not, fulfill positions of leadership, whereas priests must fulfill a position of leadership in the Church. Boys and those who lack the use of reason can receive orders validly, if not lawfully, because infused powers, like natural powers, can be granted without an act on the part of the recipient. St. Thomas also lists some of the impediments to ordination that existed in his day, including the status of a slave, homicide, illegitimacy and notable bodily deformity. These impediments did not hinder the valid, but only the lawful reception of orders.

St. Thomas speaks of tonsure, a ceremony that used to be a preamble to the reception of orders and involved the shaving or cutting of the hair. This ceremony is no longer observed in the Roman Church. St. Thomas, with the whole of Catholic tradition, understands the episcopacy to be a spiritual power superior to that of priests; but it is not so much a distinct order as the fullness of the priesthood. The papacy is above the episcopacy; its purpose is to unite the whole Church in its various ministries and offices. In a final remark about orders, St. Thomas sees good reason for the various liturgical vestments worn by the clergy.

Matrimony (Suppl.41-68)

The other sacrament which, along with orders, looks to the good of the community is matrimony.

Jesus affirmed the indissolubility of marriage (Mt 5:31-32; 19:3-9; Lk 16:18). He appealed to Genesis 1:27 and 2:24 as the Biblical basis of his teaching. In Matthew's gospel, Jesus seems to permit divorce for one reason, namely, unlawful sexual activity (Mt 5:32; 19:9). However, the Greek word *porneia* which is translated "unlawful sexual activity" (J.L. McKenzie), means in this case an illicit union of concubinage. Therefore, what Jesus "permits" in Matthew's gospel is not the dissolution of a true marriage, but the dissolution of a union which has only the appearance of a marriage. Paul permits divorce, that is, the dissolution of a true marriage, in the case of a believer, whose unbelieving spouse departs when the partner becomes a Christian (1 Cor 7:12-16).

The fullest treatment of marriage in the New Testament is to be found in 1 Corinthians 7. There Paul writes that marriage is the normal thing and necessary to avoid immorality. Marriage involves a mutual surrender of the rights over one's own body (7:1-11). Still, virginity is better than marriage (7:32-34). In other places, Paul exhorts husbands to love their wives, and wives to be submissive to their husbands (Col 3:18). In Ephesians 5:22-33, Paul repeats the same exhortation; and he compares the union of husband and wife to the union between Christ and his Church.

The Council of Trent had something to say about matrimony (in 1563). Matrimony is a sacrament instituted by Christ, and it confers grace. One may not have several wives at the same time. The Church can establish impediments dissolving marriage. The bond of matrimony cannot be dissolved by heresy, difficult cohabitation, or the voluntary absence of one of the parties. The solemn religious profession of one of the parties dissolves a marriage that has been contracted, but not consummated. Adultery does not dissolve the bond of matrimony. Separation from bed and board is permitted for many reasons. Clerics in sacred orders and religious who have made a solemn profession of chastity cannot contract a valid marriage. The state of virginity excels the married state.[21]

The *Code of Canon Law*, echoing the teaching of the Second

Vatican Council, speaks of marriage as a covenant, by which a man and woman share the whole of life with each other. By its very nature, this covenant looks to the good of the spouses and the procreation and education of children. This covenant between baptized persons has been raised by Christ to the dignity of a sacrament. The essential properties of marriage are unity and indissolubility. Marriage is contracted by the consent of the parties. All persons who are not prohibited by law can contract marriage. A valid marriage between baptized parties is consummated by a conjugal act.[22]

St. Thomas considers marriage under three general headings: as something natural, as a sacrament, and in itself.

Matrimony is something natural in the sense that nature inclines human beings to embrace it freely for the generation and education of children in the mutual support which spouses can give to each other. The majority of men and women are called to matrimony, but it is not the only calling. Some men and women are called to the contemplative life, to which marriage could be an obstacle, as St. Paul notes. The marriage act is not a sin; on the contrary, it is a good act and a meritorious one, because it is directed to the procreation of children and the preservation of the human race.

St. Thomas says that matrimony is a sacrament because it is a remedy against sin offered to human beings under sensible signs. Marriage was instituted for the generation of children even before the fall of the human race, since the begetting of children was necessary to the human race even before sin. Matrimony confers a special sacramental grace which enables the spouses to fulfill their duties to each other and their children. Carnal intercourse is not an integral part of matrimony in the sense that a marriage exists even before it is consummated.

Very quickly then, St. Thomas comes to consider marriage absolutely and in itself. He speaks first of the betrothal. The betrothal or engagement is not a marriage, but a promise of marriage. It is regulated by particular law, ecclesiastical and civil. It is a contract; but it can be dissolved by the mutual consent of the parties and in other ways determined by law.

Matrimony is the union of husband and wife for the purpose of begetting and bringing up children and leading a common marital life. Perhaps, St. Thomas suggests, the word "matrimony" is derived from the Latin words, *mater* and *munus*, which mean "mother" and "duty" respectively, since, he says, the duty of bringing up children chiefly devolves on the women. Peter Lombard defines matrimony as "the marital union of man and woman involving their living together in undivided partnership."[23]

The efficient cause of matrimony is the consent of the parties entering into the matrimonial contract. This consent must be expressed externally by words or at least by unmistakable signs. The consent must be expressed in the present tense and not in the future tense; otherwise, it effects a betrothal and not a marriage. External consent must be accompanied by interior consent; otherwise, there is no marriage. In St. Thomas' day, two persons could contract a valid, although unlawful, marriage without any witnesses. Since the Council of Trent, however, the Church requires the presence of a priest and two other witnesses if Catholics are to contract a valid marriage.

Even if a promise to marry is confirmed by an oath, there is no present marriage; and even if a promise to marry is followed by carnal intercourse, there is no marriage.

A marriage is invalid if it is contracted as the result of force or grave fear arising out of an extrinsic cause.[24] Marriage based upon a condition concerning the future is invalid; but a marriage based upon a condition relating to the past or present is valid or invalid insofar as the condition is verified or not.[25]

So that the matrimonial consent may be valid, it is necessary that the contracting parties know at least that marriage is a permanent union between a man and a woman, which is ordered to the begetting of children by means of some sexual cooperation.[26] The essential end of marriage is the begetting and rearing of children and the avoidance of fornication. The parties may have many other accidental or nonessential ends in view, good and bad. A person who marries for wealth is a married person, notwithstanding his or her reason for taking a spouse.

Marriage has its compensations as well as its burdens; and ever since the time of St. Augustine, theologians have identified the three goods of marriage, which compensate for the trials and difficulties that come with it. These three goods are the child, the mutual fidelity of husband and wife and the sacrament. The child is the fruit of the marital act and the incarnation of the love of the spouses. Mutual fidelity means not only the exclusion of all others from the marital relationship of husband and wife, but also the mutual giving of self, as far as this is humanly possible. The sacramental good has to do with the holiness of the married state, the conferral of grace, and the indissolubility of the marriage bond, which is a symbol of the union between Christ and his Church. Of the three marriage goods or blessings, the sacrament is the most excellent because of its supernatural character. St. Thomas says that the marriage act is not only good but holy, and the goods of matrimony remove it entirely from the category of sin. Therefore, without the marriage blessings or goods, the marriage act could not be justified as a good act, since it entails a temporary loss of reason and temporal trials (1 Cor 7:28). A spouse seeking only pleasure in the marital act would be guilty of a venial sin.

Next, St. Thomas takes up the impediments to marriage. An impediment is any obstacle which hinders the parties from contracting marriage. Impediments arise out of the nature of marriage as a contract and sacrament and out of the desire of the Church to safeguard its essential properties. When St. Thomas wrote, the Church recognized two kinds of impediments, diriment and prohibiting. The former made a true marriage impossible, while the latter did not make a true marriage impossible, but only unlawful.

Still, to some degree, the number and kinds of impediments depend upon the circumstances of time and place; and today the Church recognizes only diriment impediments to marriage.[27]

St. Thomas goes on to examine some of the impediments to marriage in particular. Error concerning the identity of the person one wishes to marry renders a marriage invalid, for one cannot enter upon a free agreement without sufficient knowledge. However, an error concerning the unity, indissolubility, or sacramental dignity of matrimony does not vitiate matrimonial consent, as long as it does not determine the will.[28]

When St. Thomas wrote, slavery was an impediment to marriage, so that a marriage was invalid if a person did not know that his or her partner was a slave. On the other hand, if the person knew about the partner's slavery, the marriage was valid.

Neither persons who are in holy orders nor those who are bound by a public, perpetual vow of chastity in a religious institute can contract a valid marriage.[29] The fact that a man is married, however, does not necessarily bar him from the reception of a sacred order.

Consanguinity or blood relationship is an impediment to marriage. Consanguinity is established by natural descent from a common ancestor. Degrees of consanguinity are distinguished according to lines. The ascending and descending line, as in the case of a mother and son, is the *direct* line. Those who belong to the same ancestral stock but not in a direct line of descent, as in the case of a brother and sister, pertain to the *collateral* lines. By the natural law consanguinity between closely related persons is an impediment to marriage, since inbreeding is opposed to the welfare of the offspring. By her laws the Church fixes the degrees of consanguinity within which marriage is forbidden. According to the present legislation of the Church, marriage is invalid between all ancestors and descendants in the direct line of consanguinity, and up to and including the fourth degree in the collateral line (first cousins).[30]

Affinity is the relationship of a married person with in-laws.

Affinity in the direct line in any degree whatsoever invalidates matrimony,[31] but affinity in the collateral line is no longer an impediment.

No longer is the spiritual relationship contracted by one baptized with his or her sponsor an impediment to marriage; but it was an impediment prior to the present *Code of Canon Law* (1983).

Legal adoption is an invalidating impediment to marriage in the direct line; and in the collateral line those related in the second degree (brothers and sisters) cannot validly marry.[32] It is not seemly for those who live together as family to intermarry.

Impotence is a diriment impediment to matrimony. Impotence is the physical inability on the part of a man or a woman to have intercourse. Of its very nature it renders a marriage impossible. Sterility, on the other hand, neither prohibits nor invalidates marriage.[33]

Insane persons and those who lack sufficient use of reason are incapable of contracting a valid marriage,[34] because they cannot knowingly and freely make a valid contract.

Insufficient age is an impediment to marriage, since a person must have the mental and physical capacity to assume the obligations of the marital covenant. According to Church law, a man cannot enter a valid marriage before he is sixteen years of age, and a woman cannot enter a valid marriage before she is fourteen years of age.[35]

Disparity of worship is a diriment impediment to matrimony.[36] Disparity of worship exists between a person baptized in the Catholic Church and a non-baptized person. It is opposed to peace in the family and the good of the child, since each parent will seek to educate the children in his or her own faith. However, the Church will dispense from this impediment if the Catholic party, with an awareness of the non-Catholic party, promises to have all the children baptized and brought up in the Catholic Church.[37] St. Thomas notes that a marriage between unbaptized persons is a true marriage.

St. Thomas, along with Church law,[38] acknowledges the existence of the Pauline privilege (1 Cor 7:12-16). In virtue of this privilege, a marriage entered by two non-baptized persons is dissolved when one of the parties is baptized and contracts a new marriage, after the non-baptized party refuses to live in peace with the baptized party.

One who murders his or her own spouse or the spouse of another for the purpose of marrying that other person invalidly attempts such a marriage. Moreover, they invalidly attempt marriage between themselves, who murder the spouse of one of them through mutual physical or moral cooperation.[39]

A ratified and consummated marriage can be dissolved only by death.[40] A non-consummated marriage, even between baptized persons, can be dissolved by the Roman Pontiff for a just cause.[41]

Spouses have the duty and the right to live together, unless there is a just reason for separation.[42] Adultery is a reason for severing conjugal life,[43] and so is serious danger to the mental or physical welfare of one spouse or the children.[44] Such separation does not dissolve a marriage; and neither spouse, including the innocent one, is free to marry again. Separated spouses should strive to be reconciled and take up married life together, if and when this becomes possible.

At the death of either spouse the marriage bond ceases to exist for the other. Widowed spouses are free to marry again. A second marriage is a sacrament even as a first.

A husband and wife are mutually bound to pay each other the marriage debt as it is called (1 Cor 7:3-4); that is to say, each is bound to perform the marriage act at the other's request. Husband and wife are equal in paying and demanding the debt. Since marriage involves the duty of paying the debt, neither spouse, without the full consent of the other, is free to make a vow which conflicts with the marriage duty. One is bound to pay the debt to the other at any season or hour.

God permitted a husband to have several wives simultaneously under the Old Testament in order to increase his chosen people. A plurality of wives does not impede the generation and education of children; but it does militate against peace in the family, and it does not reflect the unity of Christ and his Church. According to the present legislation of the Church, a man baptized in the Catholic Church who had several unbaptized wives before he was baptized, can keep one of them as his wife, while dismissing the others. The same is true for a non-baptized woman, who simultaneously has several non-baptized hubands.[45] It is a mortal sin for a man to have intercourse with a woman who is not his wife.

When St. Thomas wrote, a succession of marriages, even lawful ones, prevented a man from receiving holy orders. Such a man had not been the husband of just one wife, as Christ is the husband of the Church, which is the union of one with one. Today this restriction or irregularity, as it is called, does not apply.

By the intention of nature parents have to provide for their children not merely for a time, but throughout their whole life; hence, the natural law requires that a husband and wife live together inseparably forever. Under the Old Law, however, Moses permitted a husband to divorce his wife for various reasons (Dt 24:1-4). Jesus explained this permission by saying that Moses permitted divorce only because of the stubbornness of the people; but in the beginning it was not that way (Mt 19:3-9).

A child born out of wedlock is called illegitimate. An illegitimate child suffers certain disabilities, such as disqualification for certain offices. Both parents of illegitimate children are bound by the natural law to provide for them. Illegitimate children can be legitimized by the subsequent marriage of their parents or through a rescript of the Holy See.[46]

Chapter 22

THE RESURRECTION AND LIFE EVERLASTING (Suppl.69-99)

Four last things await each individual at the end of life on this earth, namely, death, judgment, heaven or hell.

In the Old Testament death was viewed as terminal. The body was placed in the grave and the spirit descended to Sheol, where it was incapable of any vital activity. Sheol did not thank Yahweh, nor did death praise him (Is 38:18). Yahweh no longer remembered those in Sheol and did not care for them (Ps 88:6). In the New Testament, Paul viewed death as the consequence of sin (Rm 5:12-14), but Jesus overcame death (1 Cor 15:26; Rm 14:9). The Christian overcomes death by sharing in Christ's death through baptism (Rm 6:2-11). The Christian will surely die, but faith in Jesus brings him or her back to life (Jn 11:26). The Holy Eucharist is the bread of everlasting life (Jn 6:50).

In a passage, which we have already quoted elsewhere, the Second Vatican Council spoke of death and everlasting life: "Although the mystery of death utterly beggars the imagination, the Church, taught by divine revelation, teaches that man has been created by God in view of a blessed destiny beyond the reach of earthly misery. . . . God has called man and still calls him, so that with his entire being he might be joined to him in sharing forever a divine life free from all corruption. Christ won this victory when he rose to life, for by his death he freed man from death. Hence, to every thoughtful man a solidly established faith provides the answer to his anxiety about the future. At the same time faith gives him the power to be united in Christ with his loved ones who have already been snatched by death. Faith arouses the hope that they have found true life with God."[1]

Judgment is a recurrent subject in both the Old and New Testaments. Perhaps we can summarize the teaching of the New Testament by saying that judgment is both historical and eschatological. Judgment is historical in the sense that a person is effectively judged when he or she accepts or rejects Jesus Christ (Jn 3:18; 5:24). In this case God's judgment takes place in time and history. However, judgment is also eschatological in the sense that it takes place at the end of history and outside of time (2 P 2:6, 9; Rv 14:7; 20:12; etc.). With this judgment God will banish evil finally and completely.

Of course, the Apostles' Creed speaks of the judgment of the living and the dead and of life everlasting. The Second Vatican Council taught that each one of us will have to render an account of his or her own life before the judgment seat of God,[2] and the Lord himself will render to each one according to his or her works.[3]

Prior to the judgment which takes place at the end of time and history, Christians expect the resurrection of the bodies of all the dead. In this case resurrection does not mean restoration to the conditions of the present life, but the conferral of a new and permanent form of life. The Scriptures speak of the resurrection of the dead. There is a reference to the resurrection of the dead in Daniel 12:2 and 2 Maccabees 7:9, 11, 23; 14:46; although in the latter instance it is clearly affirmed only of the righteous. Paul teaches that he who raised up the Lord Jesus will raise us up along with him (2 Cor 4:14). Paul hopes that he may arrive at resurrection from the dead by sharing in Jesus' suffering and death (Ph 3:10). Paul argues that if the dead are not raised to a new life, then Christ was not raised from the dead (1 Cor 15:16).

The Church repeats the teaching of the Scriptures. The Fourth Lateran Council (1215) solemnly taught that the Lord Jesus Christ will come at the end of time to judge the living and the dead. All will rise with their bodies to be rewarded or punished according to their works.[4] The Second Vatican Council looked forward to a new earth and a new heaven and to the moment when the sons and daughters of God will be raised up in Christ.[5]

Those who rise from the dead with their bodies will either be rewarded or punished according to their works. Heaven is the reward of the just. Heaven means the fullness of life after death in close union with God or the possession of eternal life in the world to come. One obtains eternal life by keeping the commandments (Mt 19:16-21; Mk 10:17-19; Lk 18:18-20) and by renouncing all things for Jesus (Mt 19:29; Mk 10:30; Lk 18:30). According to Paul, eternal life is the gift of God (Rm 6:23), and it comes through good works (Rm 2:7) and faith (1 Tm 1:16). Eternal life is initiated even now by union with the death and resurrection of Jesus through baptism (Rm 6:4). This life is a participation of the Christian in the risen life of Jesus, which comes to its fulfillment in the resurrection of the Christian; and it is sustained by the Spirit of him who raised Jesus from the dead (Rm 8:10-11).

While Paul emphasizes the inchoate nature of eternal life here and now, John emphasizes eternal life as an eschatological reality. According to John, those who have done right shall rise to live, but evildoers shall rise to be damned (Jn 5:25-29). The one who feeds on the Eucharistic bread shall live forever (Jn 6:50, 58). Death is not final for those who believe in Jesus (Jn 11:25-26). Eternal life consists in the knowledge of the one true God and Jesus, whom he has sent (Jn 17:3).

One of the Church's most definitive statements about heaven is the constitution of Pope Benedict XII (1336), which begins with the Latin words, *Benedictus Deus*. According to this constitution, the pure souls of the just, who have died, see God intuitively and face to face even before the resurrection of their bodies; and immediately after death the souls of the damned descend into hell, where they are tormented by eternal punishment.[6]

Hell is the punishment of the wicked after death. Hell is often called Gehenna in the New Testament. Originally, the name Gehenna referred to a valley near Jerusalem, which had been the site of human sacrifice. Later, the name was used in extra-Biblical Jewish writings and rabbinical literature to designate a place of fiery punishment after death. In the New Testament, Gehenna is a place where the worm dies not and the fire is never extinguished (Mt 5:22; 18:9; Mk 9:48). It is a pit into which people are cast (Mt 5:29-30; Mk 9:45). It is a place where the wicked are destroyed body and soul (Mt 10:28). Other places in the New Testament, without using the name Gehenna, speak of fire which is eternal (Mt 18:8), a fire prepared for the devil and his angels (Mt 25:41). The final destination of the wicked is a pool of fire (Rv 19:20; 20:9-15). The idea of Gehenna is also supposed in passages which speak of a place of punishment described as a prison and a torture chamber (Mt 5:25-26), a place where the wicked wail and grind their teeth (Mt 8:12; 13:42).

In John's gospel, we read that the wicked are punished by exclusion from the eternal life communicated by the Son (Jn 5:29; 8:24; 12:25). According to Paul, sinners store up retribution for the day of wrath, when the just judgment of God will be revealed (Rm 2:5). Death is the wages of sin (Rm 6:23). Sinners are excluded from the kingdom of God (1 Cor 6:10; Gal 5:19-21). They will suffer the penalty of eternal ruin apart from the presence of the Lord (2 Th 1:19). It is a fearful thing to fall into the hands of the living God (Heb 10:26-31).

Both the Fourth Lateran Council (1215) and the solemn constitution of Benedict XII (1336) taught that souls who die in mortal sin descend into hell, where they are tormented by eternal punishment.[7] Surely, too, the body of Catholic bishops dispersed throughout the world teaches as a matter of faith the eternal punishment of souls, who die unrepentant. God takes human freedom very seriously.

Purgatory is often pictured as a temporary hell, with fire and torments similar to those of the damned. Purgatorial suffering is indeed true suffering, but we know almost nothing about its nature from the fonts of revelation. The souls in purgatory have passed from this life as friends of God, but they are in need of some purification before entering the beatific vision of God. The doctrine of purgatory is vividly suggested in the Old Testament, where the inspired author wrote: "It is a holy and wholesome thought to pray for the dead, that they may be loosed from their sins" (2 M 12:46). The doctrine of purgatory is reflected in the liturgical usage of the early Church, which offered prayers for the dead. The great task of the present life is to conform ourselves to Christ. Men and women experience varying degrees of success in accomplishing this task. Those who have not fully conformed themselves to Christ in the present life are obliged thereto after death. They do so in purgatory.

The constitution of Benedict XII, *Benedictus Deus* (1336), and the Council of Trent (1563) upheld the doctrine of purgatory.[8] The Second Vatican Council encouraged Catholics to cultivate the memory of the dead and offer suffrages for them.[9]

An issue related to purgatory is limbo. We must distinguish the limbo of the Fathers from the limbo of children. The former limbo was the place where the just of the Old Testament awaited the opening of the gates of heaven. It was the "hell" to which our Savior descended after his death on the cross; and it ceased to exist when he ascended into heaven and opened its gates.

The limbo of children refers to the everlasting lot of those who die without being justified by Christ, but also without any personal sin. Such, for example, are the infants who die without baptism. Many theologians believe that such infants are deprived of the vision of God, although they enjoy a "natural" happiness in their special state. In any event, parents should see to it that their children are baptized in accord with the traditional practice of the Church.

After St. Thomas studied the sacraments by which human

beings are liberated from the death of guilt, he took up the resurrection by which they are freed from the death of punishment. There are three subdivisions within the remainder of this chapter dealing with those things which precede, accompany and follow the resurrection of the body.

Before the Resurrection (Suppl.69-74)

We rightly say that the souls of the departed are in heaven, purgatory, limbo and hell; and they are in these places after a manner befitting spiritual substances, a manner that we cannot fully comprehend. As soon as the soul is separated from its body in death, it goes either to its reward or punishment. Heaven, purgatory, limbo and hell are places and states. No soul can ever leave its *state*, but it is possible by divine dispensation for a separated soul to leave its *place* for a time and appear to the living on earth. The limbo of the just is known as the limbo of the Fathers. It is possible that the limbo of the Fathers and the hell of the damned were in the same place; but of course they were not the same state. The Fathers in the limbo of the just suffered no punishment, but they had not yet achieved their end. The limbo of children is the state and place of unbaptized children who have original sin only. The place of the limbo of the Fathers and the limbo of children may have been the same, but it was not the same state. There is no suffering in the limbo of children. The limbo of the Fathers ceased to exist when our Lord ascended into heaven.

A separated soul can no longer exercise its sensitive powers, because it is deprived of its body; however, these powers remain in the soul radically, and they will be exercised when the soul is reunited with its body. Even though the fire of hell is a physical fire, it torments the spiritual soul just as it torments the demons. Some say that the soul actually feels the fire; but St. Thomas holds that the fire has a penal effect by hindering the soul from fulfilling its own will, that is, by hindering it from acting where it will and as it will.

St. Thomas goes on to discuss suffrages for the dead. All the faithful united by charity are members of the one body of Christ; and just as one member of the human body can help another, so one member of the body of Christ can help another. Such help is possible by praying, meriting and satisfying for another. Because of the bond of charity the dead can be assisted by the prayers and good works of the living. Even sinners can assist the souls in purgatory, for example, by having Mass offered for them. As an act of charity, the assistance given to the souls in purgatory avails those who give it too. One cannot help the souls in hell; they are beyond all help. Without any doubt, the suffrages of the living on earth help the souls in purgatory pay their temporal debt. Infants in limbo cannot be helped by those on earth; their state is set. We cannot help those in heaven; they are eternally established in bliss.

The chief means of relieving the souls in purgatory are offering the holy sacrifice of the Mass for their benefit, praying for their release, and giving alms on their behalf, although any good work done out of charity for the dead is profitable to them. The faithful can apply indulgences for the dead by way of suffrage. The burial service, St. Thomas notes, consoles the living and encourages them to pray for the dead. It seems reasonable to suppose that, in view of the intention of the doer, suffrages for one definite person are a help to him or her rather than to one who is perhaps more worthy of help. Suffrages offered for several souls are divided among them.

In heaven, the blessed know all that pertains to them in the beatific vision; and so they know the vows, devotions, and prayers of those who have recourse to their assistance. We ought to call upon the saints in heaven to pray for us, since God is wont to confer his blessings on the lower through the higher. The prayers of the saints in heaven are always heard, for they always pray in complete conformity to the will of God.

When our Lord comes again in glory to judge the living and the dead at the end of time, certain signs will herald his coming (Lk 21:25); but what these signs will be we do not know for certain. Possibly the sun, moon and stars will be darkened for a time immediately preceding the coming of the Judge.

At the end of time there will be a new heaven and a new earth (Rv 21:1); the world will be cleansed of any stain it may have contracted as the result of human sinfulness; and it appears that the cleansing agent will be fire (2 P 3:12). The cleansing fire will be the kind with which we are familiar. This fire will precede the judgment, but it will engulf the wicked after the judgment. The final fire will be an instrument of divine justice. All that is evil and ugly will be cast into hell with the wicked; and all that is beautiful and noble will be taken up to heaven for the glory of the elect.

The Resurrection of the Body (Suppl. 75-86)

Since human beings are composed of body and soul, the ultimate state of human beings must involve the body as well as the soul; hence, the body will rise again from the grave. This is true of all human beings, saint and sinner, without exception. Strictly speaking, this resurrection is miraculous.

Thomas calls the resurrection of Christ the quasi-instrumental cause through which God will raise up our bodies. At the end of time Christ will appear in his glory, and his appearance will be as a trumpet summoning the dead from the grave. In all of God's bodily works, he employs the ministry of angels; and so the angels will gather up the mortal remains of human beings prior to the resurrection; but the actual reunion of soul and body will be the immediate work of God himself.

The resurrection of the body will take place when the heavens come to rest, that is, at the end of the world. The time of our resurrection is hidden from us. Many think, however, that it will take place at night when Christ arose from the dead. The resurrection of the body will take place in an instant and not by degrees.

St. Thomas believes that all will die before they rise again, and this for several reasons, including the fact that all have contracted the stain of original sin for which the penalty is death. All human beings will rise from the dust and ashes to which death and decay (or the final fire) will reduce them.

In the resurrection the soul will be reunited with the same body from which it was separated in death. The selfsame person who dies will rise again; he or she will not be turned into someone else.

The resurrected body will have all that pertains to the integrity of the human body, including hair and nails. Blood will flow, but the risen body will not sweat or urinate, because these processes will be unnecessary. Obviously the risen body will not have all the material or fluid elements which were a part of its makeup at some point in its earthly existence.

Thomas thought that the risen body would have the development of a person thirty years old, the age at which one achieves the perfection of growth before decline sets in. Not all risen bodies will be of the same size; each person's body will be of the size most suitable to him or her. Human beings will continue to be male and female. Resurrected individuals will forego all animal life. Risen bodies will not eat or drink or sleep or beget offspring or feel the pull of fleshly appetites or passions.

After the resurrection, the bodies of the saints will be immune from suffering and substantial change. The bodies of the wicked will endure the pains of hell, but they will not undergo substantial change. The risen bodies of the just will have sensation and movement, because these things pertain to the perfection of the body. All the senses of the blessed will be rewarded, while all the senses of the wicked will be punished.

Among the qualities of the glorified body is subtlety. This means that the glorified body is altogether subject to the glorified soul as its form, from which it derives its specific being. Subtlety does not deprive the glorified body of its dimensions nor of the need to occupy a distinct place from another body. By divine power, however, a glorified body is able to penetrate other non-glorified bodies, as our Lord's body penetrated the room where the disciples were, the doors being shut (Jn 20:19, 26). Two glorified bodies will never be in the same place. The risen body is a true body; it has spiritual qualities; but at the same time it is something that can be touched, as our Lord's risen body could be touched (Lk 24:39).

Another quality of the glorified body is agility, whereby the body is wholly subject to the soul as its mover. The body will move from place to place with the quickness of thought at the command of the will. This movement involves no fatigue and neither will it deprive the just of the beatific vision nor diminish their happiness.

Finally, the glorified body will have a certain luminous quality, which St. Thomas calls clarity. This clarity results from the overflow of the soul's glory into the body. As one glorified soul differs from another by reason of its greater merit, so one glorified body will differ from another in clarity (1 Cor 15:41-42) and reveal the glory of the soul. The clarity of a glorified body is naturally visible to the non-glorified eye of the damned. This clarity will appear or disappear as the soul wills.

The bodies of the wicked will rise in their natural perfection without any defect; but they will lack the qualities of the glorified body. The bodies of the wicked are incorruptible, since their lot is eternal; and they are subject to suffering as the punishment of their sins.

After the Resurrection (Suppl.87-99)

After the resurrection of the body from the grave, all will appear before the judgment seat of Christ, so that each one may receive a recompense, good or bad, according to his or her life in the body (2 Cor 5:10). Each one will remember, as though it were written down in a book, the good or bad he or she has done. Moreover, everyone will be able to know whatever is in another's conscience. In this way, each one will understand the rectitude of the Judge's decision. So often in this life the justice and mercy of God are hidden. Despite the revelation of their sins, the just will suffer no discomfiture, because their courage and repentance will also be revealed.

The final separation of the good from the wicked will take place at the time of the general judgment. Neither will be able to profit any longer from the presence of the other. St. Thomas believes that the general judgment will transpire, not by word of mouth, but mentally. The day of the last judgment is altogether uncertain (1 Th 5:2). Perhaps the nations will be gathered before the Judge in the valley of Jehoshaphat (Jl 4:2).

In virtue of his divine nature, Christ has the authority to judge all creatures by right of creation; but in virtue of his human nature, he has the authority to judge all creatures by right of his redemptive death and resurrection. At the judgment, Christ will appear to all in his glorified humanity (Lk 21:27), so that all may see his exaltation; but the wicked will not have a vision of his divine nature, for this would afford them joy.

What is to be said about the condition of the world after the judgment? The Scriptures speak of new heavens and a new earth (Is 65:17; Rv 21:1). St. Thomas thinks the heavens and the earth will be changed in a marvelous way, not indeed so as to change their species, but so as to add a certain perfection of glory. This change will come about so as to afford the corporeal eye, which is incapable of the beatific vision, a suitable measure of comfort and enjoyment. The motion of the heavenly bodies will cease, but their brightness will be increased. Dumb animals and plants, whose being is totally corruptible, will not remain in this renewal. At least this is St. Thomas' opinion.

Next Thomas considers the state of the blessed after the general judgment. They will have a vision of the divine essence. In support of this position, Thomas appeals to such passages of the New Testament as: "We see now through a glass in a dark manner, but then face to face" (1 Cor 13:12) and "We shall be like him, for we shall see him as he is" (1 Jn 3:2). Since the divine essence is pure act, Thomas argues, it is possible for it to be the form whereby the intellect understands; and this is the beatific vision. Will the saints see God with the eyes of the body? Not directly, St. Thomas answers, because the corporeal eye cannot see what is incorporeal; but indirectly the corporeal eye will see the glory of God in bodies. Even though the saints see God in his essence, they do not see all that God sees in himself.

The happiness of the saints will be greater after the judgment than before, because soul and body will be reunited and the operation of the soul will be more perfect; hence, the soul will be borne towards God with greater intensity. There will be inequalities in heaven: one saint will see God more perfectly than another according to his or her degree of charity. The various degrees of beatitude are called mansions in the gospel of John (14:2).

The blessed in heaven will be aware of the sufferings of the damned, so that they may render more copious thanks to God for their own salvation. The blessed in glory will have no pity on the unhappiness of the damned, because they understand that the state of the damned cannot be altered. The saints will not rejoice in the misery of the damned, but they will rejoice in the implementation of God's justice.

St. Thomas distinguishes between the essential and accidental rewards of the blessed in heaven. These rewards are fittingly called crowns, because in olden days crowns were given to those who emerged victorious in special kinds of conflict. In heaven a person's essential reward consists in the perfect union of the soul with God. Therefore, we may say metaphorically that each of the blessed receives a golden crown, which means union with God for the victory they have won over themselves and the world. Some of the blessed, however, merit certain accidental rewards over and above their essential reward. This accidental reward is a kind of joy in the works the blessed have accomplished, works that have the character of a notable victory in a particularly difficult struggle. This joy is distinct from the joy of being united to God and is called an aureole. St. Thomas believes that three categories of persons merit aureoles: virgins, who triumph over the temptations of the flesh; martyrs, who suffer death for Christ's sake; and teachers and preachers, who drive out error. The aureole, therefore, denotes something added to the golden crown.

What is to be said about the condition of the damned after the judgment? Both the Scriptures and the teaching authority of the Church affirm the existence of hell. Thomas holds that the damned will be tormented not only by fire, but in many other ways and from many other sources. The worm by which the damned are tormented is really remorse of conscience, which is called a worm because it originated from the corruption of sin. The weeping of the damned is not the actual shedding of tears, but a certain commotion and disturbance of the head and eyes. Both light and darkness are to be found in hell, insofar as each contributes to the unhappiness of the damned by revealing ugly objects or concealing pleasant ones. The fire of hell is of the same species as ours. St. Thomas said elsewhere how the souls of the damned are punished by this corporeal fire. He believed that the fire of hell was beneath the earth.

The will of the damned is completely turned away from God. They continue to consent to the malice of their sins, although they grieve for the suffering they experience as the result of their sins. The sight of the happiness of the saints will give the damned great pain. The damned hate God for the punishment he inflicts on them. After judgment day, the damned are beyond the possibility of any further demerit. The knowledge, which the damned had in this life, will be a source of torment to them, for they will remember both the evil they did and the good they lost. Prior to judgment day, the damned will see the blessed in glory and realize what they have forfeited; but after judgment day, they will no longer see the blessed, although the remembrance of them will remain.

The punishment of hell is eternal, because the sinner, by contravening the laws of God, has in effect placed his or her final end in a creature. The sinner has chosen to be separated from God, and his or her will remains firm in that choice, once the time of human probation has been concluded by death. If the punishment of hell were not eternal, a person might well offend God as he or she pleased, confident that some day there would be an end to one's punishment. St. Thomas sees no escape from hell for sinners, whether they be demons or human beings, whether they were Christians or those who performed certain works of mercy in their lifetime.

Finally, in some editions of the *Summa*, one finds appendices treating of limbo and purgatory. This material was compiled by Nicolai from St. Thomas' commentary on the *Sentences*. Limbo is a place of natural happiness, free of the torments of hell, yet without the vision of God. It is the place of infants who die without baptism. Such infants will know perfectly things subject to natural knowledge. They will know too that they have been deprived of the vision of God and the reason for this depravation. However, they will not be grieved by this knowledge, for a wise person does not grieve through being deprived of what is beyond one's power to obtain. Thus a wise person does not grieve for being unable to fly like a bird.

Purgatory is the place where unforgiven venial sins and the unremitted temporal punishment due to sin are purged. Both the pain of loss, that is to say, the delay of the divine vision, and the pain of sense or the punishment by corporeal fire exceed the greatest punishment of this life. The pain of purgatory is voluntary in the sense that the sufferer accepts it to acquire a greater good. Those in purgatory are not tormented by demons. The guilt of venial sin and the debt of punishment are remitted by the fire of purgatory. Not all the souls in purgatory are released at the same speed. Perhaps the place of purgatory is situated near hell, so that it is the same fire which torments the damned in hell and cleanses the just in purgatory.

Footnotes

Introduction

1. *Aeterni Patris* (1879), no. 18.
2. C. 1366. 1
3. *Studiorum Ducem* (1923).
4. *Optatam Totius* (1965), no. 16.
5. *Gravissimum Educationis* (1965), no. 10.
6. *AAS* 71 (1979), 493, no. 7.
7. Cf. J. Schall, S.J. (ed.), *The Whole Truth about Man*, Boston, 1981, St. Paul Editions, 262-280.
8. C. 252. 3.
9. New York, 1938-42, Sheed & Ward, 4 vols.
10. *Cursus theologicus*, Paris, 1931, Desclée & Co., vol. 1, p. 146.
11. *Historia ecclesiastica* 1, 22, c. 39. Quoted by M. Grabmann-J. Zybura, *Introduction to the Theological Summa of St. Thomas*, St. Louis, 1930, B. Herder Book Co., 186-187.

Chapter I

1. While St. Thomas does not draw this conclusion, it seems to follow that, all other things being equal, the professor of theology will occupy the place of honor when students invite him or her and professors of other disciplines to dinner.

Chapter II

1. DS 3004. See Rm 1:20. #113, pp. 40-41, *The Christian Faith*.
2. *Dei Verbum*, no. 6.
3. DS 3001. #327, p. 112, *The Christian Faith*.

Chapter III

1. DS 75. #16, pp. 11-12, *The Christian Faith*.
2. Thomas' treatise on the Trinity is man's supreme attempt to probe the fundamental mystery of the Christian religion. His treatise presupposes a good education in Scholastic philosophy; and, in any event, it is quite difficult to understand. However, a failure to grasp this material will not impair one's understanding or appreciation of the other parts of the *Summa*.

Chapter IV

1. *The City of God* 11, 22.

Chapter V

1. DS 800. #19, p. 14, *The Christian Faith*.
2. *Lumen Gentium*, no. 50.

Chapter VII

1. *Gaudium et Spes* nos. 12-17.

First Part of the Second Part

1. *The Orthodox Faith*, 2, 12.

Chapter IX

1. *The Consolation of Philosophy* 3, 2.
2. *Benedictus Deus* (1336), DS 1000. #2305, pp. 684-85, *The Christian Faith*.

Chapter X

1. *Confessions* 8, 9.

Chapter XII

1. *Ethics* 2, 6.
2. *Sentences* 1. 2. 27. 2-3.
3. *Against Faustus* 22, 27.
4. DS 1679, 1681, 1707. #1625, p. 461; note to #1626, p. 462; #1647, p. 469, *The Christian Faith*.
5. DS 1512-16. #509-513, pp. 138-39, *The Christian Faith*.

Chapter XIII

1. *Dignitatis Humanae* no. 3.
2. *Etymologies* 5, 21.
3. This teaching is derived especially from the decree of the Council of Trent about justification, DS 1520-83. Thomas' influence upon the decree was substantial. See #1924-1983, pp. 555-70, *The Christian Faith*.

Chapter XIV

1. DS 3008. #118, p. 42, *The Christian Faith*.
2. *Dei Verbum* nos. 4-5.
3. It seems though that Thomas' position on the necessity of explicit faith in the mystery of Christ and the Trinity cannot be reconciled with the teaching of the Second Vatican Council. This council foresaw salvation for all those who strive to do God's will, as it is known to them through the dictates of conscience, even though they do not know the gospel of Christ and his Church (*Lumen Gentium* no. 16).

4. St. Thomas justifies religious freedom by the need for civil peace. The Second Vatican Council justifies religious freedom on the basis of the dignity of human beings, who may not be coerced to act against the dictates of conscience (*Dignitatis Humanae* no. 2).
5. The Second Vatican Council explicitly rejects Thomas' opinion in this regard (*ibid.*).
6. *Gaudium et Spes* no. 18.
7. *The City of God* 19, 13.
8. *The City of God* 9, 5.
9. *The Merchant of Venice*, Act 4, Sc. 1.
10. *Gaudium et Spes* nos. 79-82.

Chapter XVI

1. *On Clemency* 2, 4.
2. *Book of Morals* 23, 6.

Chapter XVIII

1. DS 125-126. #7-8, p. 6, *The Christian Faith*
2. DS 250-264. #604-606/12, pp. 148-51.
3. DS 301-302. #614-615, p. 154.
4. DS 556-558. #635-37, pp. 172-3.

Chapter XIX

1. DS 2803. #709, p. 204, *The Christian Faith*.

Chapter XX

1. DS 1601. #1311, p. 371, *The Christian Faith*.
2. DS 1604. #1314, p. 371.
3. DS 1608. #1318, p. 372.
4. DS 1609. #1319, p. 372.
5. DS 1610. #1320, p. 372.
6. DS 1612. #1322, p. 372.
7. DS 1615. #1421, p. 393.
8. DS 1617, #1423, p. 393.
9. DS 1618. #1424, p. 393.
10. DS 1619. #1425, p. 393.
11. DS 1621. #1427, p. 394.
12. DS 1626. #1432, p. 394.
13. *Lumen Gentium* no. 33.
14. *Unitatis Redintegratio* no. 22.
15. *Code of Canon Law* c. 861, 1.
16. The Church recognizes even an *implicit* desire of baptism as salutary. An implicit desire of baptism is included in the determination to do all that is necessary for salvation, even if one is unaware of the obligation to be baptized (DS 3866-3872). See #854-57, pp. 241-42, *The Christian Faith*.

17. DS 1628-1629. #1434-35, p. 395, *The Christian Faith*.
18. *Lumen Gentium* no. 11.
19. *Code of Canon Law* c. 880, 1.
20. *Ibid.*, c. 893, 2.
21. *Ibid.*, c. 882.
22. DS 1651. #1526, p. 419, *The Christian Faith*.
23. DS 1652. #1527, p. 419.
24. DS 1751. #1555, p. 427.
25. DS 1752. #1556, p. 427.
26. DS 1753. #1557, p. 428.
27. *Gaudium et Spes* no. 38.
28. *Presbyterorum Ordinis* no. 6.
29. *Ibid.*, no. 5.
30. *Unitatis Redintegratio* no. 2.
31. *Code of Canon Law* c. 230, 3.
32. Vatican Council II, *Sacrosanctum Concilium* no. 47.

Chapter XXI

1. DS 1701. #1641, p. 468, *The Christian Faith*.
2. DS 1702. #1642, p. 468.
3. DS 1703. #1643, p. 468.
4. DS 1704. #1644, p. 468.
5. DS 1707. #1647, p. 469.
6. DS 1709. #1649, p. 469.
7. DS 1710. #1650, pp. 469-70.
8. DS 1712. #1652, p. 470.
9. *Lumen Gentium* no. 11.
10. *Letter* 130.
11. *On Psalm 21*.
12. *Code of Canon Law* c. 1331.
13. *Ibid.*, cc. 992-997.
14. *Ibid.*, cc. 998.
15. DS 1716. #1656, p. 471, *The Christian Faith*.
16. *Lumen Gentium* no. 11.
17. DS 1771-1778. #1714-1721, pp. 498-99, *The Christian Faith*.
18. *Code of Canon Law* cc. 1008-1009.
19. *Sentences* 4, 53.
20. *Minsteria Quaedam AAS* (1972) 529-534.
21. DS 1801-1812. #1808-19, pp. 529-30, *The Christian Faith*.
22. *Code of Canon Law*, cc. 1055-1061.
23. *Sentences* 4, 27.
24. *Code of Canon Law* c. 1103.
25. *Ibid.*, c. 1102.
26. *Ibid.*, c. 1096.
27. *Ibid.*, cc. 1073-1094.
28. *Ibid.*, c. 1099.
29. *Ibid.*, cc. 1087-1088.
30. *Ibid.*, c. 1091.

31. *Ibid.*, c. 1092.
32. *Ibid.*, c. 1094.
33. *Ibid.*, c. 1084.
34. *Ibid.*, c. 1095.
35. *Ibid.*, c. 1083.
36. *Ibid.*, c. 1086.
37. *Ibid.*, c. 1125.
38. *Ibid.*, c. 1143.
39. *Ibid.*, c. 1090.
40. *Ibid.*, c. 1141.
41. *Ibid.*, c. 1142.
42. *Ibid.*, c. 1151.
43. *Ibid.*, c. 1152.
44. *Ibid.*, c. 1153.
45. *Ibid.*, c. 1148, 1.
46. *Ibid.*, c. 1139.

Chapter XXII

1. *Gaudium et Spes* no. 18.
2. *Ibid.*, no. 17.
3. *Ibid.*, no. 45.
4. DS 801. #20, p. 15, *The Christian Faith*.
5. *Gaudium et Spes* no. 39; *Lumen Gentium* no. 51.
6. DS 1000-10002. #2305-07, pp. 684-85, *The Christian Faith*.
7. DS 801, 10002. #20, p. 15; #2307, p. 685.
8. DS 1000, 1820. #2305, pp. 684-85; #2310, p. 687.
9. *Lumen Gentium* no. 49.

BIBLIOGRAPHY

Editions of the *Summa Theologiae* (among many others):

Sancti Thomae Aquinatis, *Opera Omnia*, Rome, 1888-1906, Ex typographia Polyglotta S.C. De Propaganda Fide, tom.4-12 (Latin). With the commentary of Cajetan.

S. Thomae De Aquino, *Summa Theologiae*, cura et studio Instituti Studiorum Medievalium Ottaviensis, Ottawa, 1941, 5 vol. (Latin).

St. Thomas Aquinas, *Summa Theologica*, Blackfriars, New York, 1964- , McGraw-Hill Book Co. (Latin text and English translation).

St. Thomas Aquinas, *Summa Theologica*, New York, 1947-48, Benziger Brothers, Inc., 3 vol. (English). Transl. by Fathers of the English Dominican Province. With commentary.

Saint Thomas Aquinas, *Summa Theologica*, Westminster, Md., 1981, Christian Classics, 5 vol. (English). A reprint of the Benziger edition of 1948.

Secondary works:

M.D. Chenu, O.P., *Toward Understanding Saint Thomas*, Chicago, 1964, H. Regnery Co. Transl. by A.-M. Landry and D. Hughes.

G.K. Chesterton, *St. Thomas Aquinas*, New York, 1933, Sheed & Ward.

F.C. Copleston, S.J., *A History of Philosophy*, Westminster, Md., 1950, The Newman Press, vol. II.

__________, *Aquinas*, Baltimore, 1955, Penguin Books.

M.C. D'Arcy, S.J., *Thomas Aquinas*, Westminster, Md., 1944, The Newman Bookshop.

W. Farrell, O.P., *A Companion to the Summa*, New York, 1939-42, Sheed & Ward, 4 vol.

W. Farrell and M. Healy, *My Way of Life*, Brooklyn, 1952, Confraternity of the Precious Blood.

E. Gilson, *The Philosophy of St. Thomas Aquinas*, Cambridge, 1924, W. Heffer & Sons, Ltd. Transl. by E. Bullough.

__________, *The Spirit of Thomism*, New York, 1964, P.J. Kenedy & Sons.

P.J. Glenn, *A Tour of the Summa*, Rockford, 1978, Tan Books and Publishers, Inc.

M. Grabmann, *Thomas Aquinas*, New York, 1928, Longmans, Green. Transl. by V. Michel.

__________, *Introduction to the Theological Summa of St. Thomas*, St. Louis, 1930, Herder Book Co. Ed. by J.S. Zybura.

A. Kenny, *Aquinas: A Collection of Critical Essays*, Notre Dame, Ind., 1976, Univ. of Notre Dame Press.

J. Maritain, *St. Thomas Aquinas*, New York, 1958, Meridian Books, Inc. Transl. by J.W. Evans and P. O'Reilly.

R. McKeon, *The Basic Works of Aristotle*, New York, 1941, Random House.

New Catholic Encyclopedia, New York, 1967, McGraw-Hill Book Co.

J. Pieper, *Guide to Thomas Aquinas*, 1962, Pantheon Books. Transl. by R. and C. Winston.

———, *The Four Cardinal Virtues*, New York, 1965, Harcourt, Brace & World, Inc.

Supplementary References:

J. Coriden, T. Green and D. Heintschel, eds., *The Code of Canon Law: A Text and Commentary*, New Jersey, 1984, Paulist Press.

R. Deferrari, *A Latin-English Dictionary of St. Thomas Aquinas*, Boston, 1960, Daughters of St. Paul.

J. Neuner, S.J. and J. Dupuis, S.J., eds., *The Christian Faith in the Doctrinal Documents of the Catholic Church*, revised edition, New York, 1982, Alba House. (This is an updated version of Denzinger-Schönmetzer plus other more recent documents including the latest encyclicals of Pope John Paul II.)

Also by EDWARD J. GRATSCH

PRINCIPLES OF CATHOLIC THEOLOGY: A Synthesis of Dogma and Morals

"This book treats with clarity, that is, in simple unadorned English, and with authority, that is, with no mincing of words, the principal teaching of traditional dogmatic and moral theology in interpreting the sources of Revelation, i.e., Sacred Scripture and the Magisterium of the Church." *Philip F. Mulhern, O.P.*

"This synthesis of Catholic dogmatic and moral theology will be a valuable aid to priests and other teachers of religion. They will find in this volume an overview and systematic presentation of the whole range of Catholic theology." *Liguorian*

410 pages **$10.95**

WHERE PETER IS: A Survey of Ecclesiology

"This book gives a panorama of Catholic ecclesiology from the origin of the Church in the New Testament through the patristic, medieval and post-reformation periods, to the post-Vatican II era. It quite successfully places in historical setting the development of ecclesiology. Since the book mentions many names and significant trends and movements, it provides a very good handbook for quick references to elements of history about ecclesiology." *Sisters Today*

283 pages **$5.95**